INDIA AND AUSTRALIA IN INDO PACIFIC

DYNAMICS OF DEFENCE, DIPLOMACY AND DIASPORA

DR TEJINDER HUNDAL

Notion Press

No. 8, 3rd Cross Street
CIT Colony, Mylapore
Chennai, Tamil Nadu – 600004

First Published by Notion Press 2021
Copyright © Dr Tejinder Hundal 2021
All Rights Reserved.

ISBN 978-1-63806-629-3

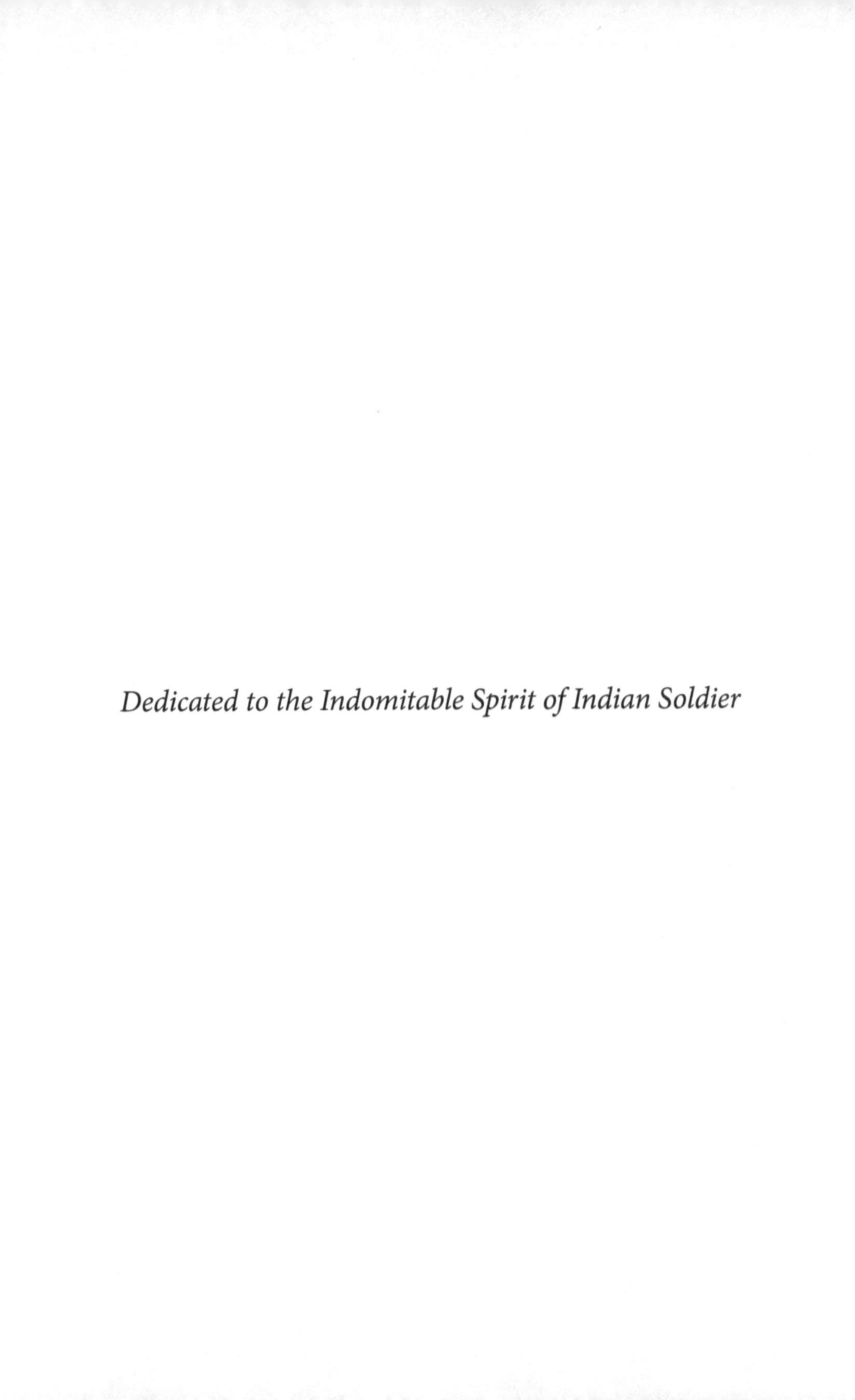

Dedicated to the Indomitable Spirit of Indian Soldier

FOREWORD

The geopolitical developments in the Indo-Pacific have brought India and Australia at the centre stage of a new strategic paradigm. Overcoming the minor irritants of the past, the two countries today are well poised to play a significant role in the balance of power in the Indo-Pacific. The most critical and impelling factor in the bilateral and multi-lateral relations has been the strategic imperative of balancing a hegemonic and belligerent China. Bilaterally, the relations between the two countries have been elevated to the level of comprehensive strategic partnership. After a hiatus of more than one decade, Australia has joined India led Malabar naval exercises. India and Australia are the founding members of Quadrilateral Security Agreement. QUAD is gaining traction with the prospects of enhancing width and depth of its expected mandate, role and possibility of incorporating other countries that have high stakes in the peace and development of the Indo-Pacific region. The two countries are bound to play a significant role towards an open, peaceful and inclusive Indo-Pacific region.

Recently, India-Australia ties are on an upward trajectory. The surge in improved diplomatic relations is manifesting in visits of heads of state, official engagements and the spate of agreements signed between the two countries. The number of international students from India and the corresponding increase in the Indian diaspora in Australia are providing crucial fillip to the people to people relations between both the countries. Complementarities in trade between India and Australia have also been instrumental in boosting economic relations in a win win paradigm. The upswing in the bilateral relations is backed by robust progress in the arena of Defence, Diplomacy and Diaspora.

It is in the aforesaid backdrop that Dr Tejinder Hundal has skillfully dissected the dynamics of Defence, Diplomacy and Diaspora in the Indo-

Australia comprehensive strategic relationship. His scholarly work is easy to read and grasp. The book encapsulates a seamless narrative that is supported by exhaustive references. The author has succinctly captured the ebb, flow and nuances of bilateral relations and clearly mapped emerging challenges and opportunities. He has displayed masterly skill in dilating the elements of Defence, Diplomacy and Diaspora in an inter-related manner. On the whole, the book presents a very authoritative and plausible account of the historical background, the present state of bilateral relations and its future potential.

This book is a must read for researchers, academicians and practitioners of strategic studies and international relations in both India and Australia. More significantly, the book will provide policy-makers well-researched inputs for formulation of a policy framework for strengthening the India Australia bilateral relations in a wider strategic framework. I take this opportunity to wish Dr Tejinder Hundal all the best for this endeavor. I am sanguine that his scholarly work will serve the purpose for which he undertook this important research work.

Jaihind

Major General BK Sharma, AVSM, SM and Bar (Retd)
Director, United Services Institute of India
New Delhi
Mar 2021

PREFACE

For a considerable period of time since the independence of India, both India and Australia have viewed each other through respective prisms of self interest, as a result of which the economic, strategic and people to people relations between the two countries have been held hostage to the their world view of self interests. Both the countries in the past have deliberately downplayed and in some cases have largely been unaware of the potential of bilateral relationship with each other. Though the relationship has witnessed several false starts, but the contemporary congruence between strategic and economic interests of both countries has never been so aligned to mutual understanding.

The rise and traction of the geo political construct of Indo Pacific along with the growing realisation of the mutual complementarities and similarities between each other on the aspects of freedom and openness of sea lanes of communication, rules based international order and opposition to arbitrariness in the handling of international affairs has brought both countries closer and supportive of each other. The up gradation of existing strategic partnership to the levels of Comprehensive Strategic Partnership in 2020 coupled with increased diplomatic and defence cooperation in multilaterals, minilaterals and bilateral forums has propelled the bilateral relationship to the newer levels. This increased level of cooperation and strategic alignment would not have been made possible without the explicit and intimate diplomatic and defence engagements.

Diaspora plays an important and critical role in the cementing of people to people relationships. The Indian diaspora in Australia aided and assisted by increased partnerships in knowledge economy and transnational education is likely to become largest diaspora in Australia by 2031. The migration of skilled professionals from India to Australia is increasingly manifesting in the concept of 'Brain Circulation' rather the 'Brain Drain' or 'Brain Gain'. If harnessed in a scientific and deliberate manner, this 'Brain Circulation' has massive potential to facilitate the 'Brain Gain' in India through innovation, investment, and business expansion. This diaspora is playing an important role in the increased people to people contacts between both the countries and is facilitating the bilateral relationship. The opportunities and strategies of diaspora and alumni engagement have accordingly been modified and have seen a due inclusion, import and emphasis in the contemporary government policies.

This book is an attempt to unravel the strategic congruence between India and Australia through the spectrum of Defence, Diaspora and Diplomacy. The dynamics of Defence, Diaspora and Diplomacy in the geostrategic construct of Indo Pacific are getting India and Australia together. The book attempts to argue that the relationship between India and Australia is much more than the contemporary alignment of strategic interests. The dynamics of people to people contacts through knowledge partnerships and higher education avenues for Indian students in Australia, though having been researched, documented and deliberated independently by various researchers in the past; I have tried to articulate the aspect that transnational education and knowledge partnerships are indeed a key to the bilateral relationship. The book is based on the core argument that the India Australia relationship is not anymore being held hostage to the historical prejudices and due to the current calibrations in the dynamics of defence, diaspora and diplomacy in the region, the relationship is bound to grow and has a great potential and significance for the region as a whole.

In order to bring an historical perspective into the narrative, the first chapter of the book deals with the instrumentality of a range of factors to include differing perceptions on 'Core Interests'. The chapter deals with the differing perceptions and policies of both countries on a wide range of issues, as followed by both the nations over a period of time. The relationship has survived a period of spurts and indifference, thereby making consistency, a biggest casualty in the journey. It will be seen that both India and Australia have tried to preserve and protect their respective 'Core Interests', and as a result the policies and perceptions about each other have largely been at tangent only and in no way have contributed to the cause of mutual relationship.

In the second chapter, an attempt has been made to deconstruct the notion of Indo Pacific from the perspective of India and Australia. Due to the emerging dynamics of the collapse of the Cold War coupled with a severe financial crisis, India was nudged to Look East in the early nineties. Nearly two and half decades later, the emerging traction of the concept of Indo Pacific is facilitating Acting East by India. Australia also realizing the reality of the concept of the emerging geostrategic construct and a massive economic and military cooperation potential of India has started to look and act west towards the Indian Ocean, an area which has been relatively neglected by the country. The emerging diplomatic and defence compulsions of the region have catalysed India and Australia to propel their relationship from multilaterals to minilaterals and further to bilateral dynamics.

The third chapter of the book is devoted to the increasing frequency and dimensions of transnational education and knowledge partnerships between India and Australia. The outflow of Indian students to Australia for higher education has increased exponentially. The universities in Australia are forging individual knowledge partnerships with institutes of higher learning in India. These individual partnerships are supported by knowledge partnership agreements and Memorandums of Understanding at apex levels. The quantum and diversity of research collaboration between higher education institutes of both the countries has been a witness to an upswing, both quantitatively and qualitatively. This chapter underscores the significance of knowledge partnerships and transnational education in promoting the bilateral relationship between India and Australia.

Contribution of Indian diaspora to the Australian society has been widely acknowledged and recognised. The pathway to migration offered by higher education opportunities in Australia has facilitated the growth of Indian diaspora in the country. The fourth chapter in the book deals with the role of diaspora in promoting the bilateral relationship between the two countries. The dynamics of diaspora involvement and intervention in the soft power aspect of the foreign policy has yielded encouraging results in emerging contexts. The bilateral relationship between India and Australia has witnessed immense benefits from the Indian diaspora in Australia and has huge residual potential in furthering the bilateral relationship.

As we sign off a decade of cooperation and mutual understanding, and enter into a new decade, a plethora of opportunities await the bilateral relationship to grow and sustain itself. A large number of initiatives have been taken by both the countries in the fields of Defence, Diplomacy and Diaspora, which have the potential to make the relationship work. The upcoming decade is the time for these initiatives to materialize and provide the relationship a long lasting and truly symbiotic value. The last chapter of the book attempts to prognosticate the relationship and endeavours to provide certain recommendations for this bilateral relationship to nurture and grow. A quantum leap is being witnessed in the bilateral relationship between India and Australia and the world in general and the immediate regions in particular are witnessing the upliftment of the relationship to newer and higher levels. There was so much happening on the daily basis in this relationship that I really found it difficult to overcome the temptation to include more rather than freeze the manuscript and forward it to the publisher.

The quest and sojourn for researching and writing of this book has been long and arduous. Like the bilateral relationship between India and Australia, this journey has also witnessed its ups and downs. I take this opportunity to acknowledge the support and motivation provided by my better half Neelam Hundal, the shining light of inspiration behind this endeavour. The understanding and help rendered by my sons, Karanbir Hundal and Jaibir Hundal has been instrumental in perfect culmination of this sojourn. I would also like to express my sincere thanks and gratitude to Notion Press for the guidance and assistance provided in shaping the effort and initiative into a book.

Dr Tejinder Hundal
Mar 2021

ABBREVIATIONS AND TERMS

Abbreviation	Terminology
AEP	Act East Policy
ADMM	ASEAN Defence Ministers' Meeting
ARF	ASEAN Regional Forum
TAC	ASEAN Treaty of Amity and Cooperation
APEC	Asia Pacific Economic Cooperation
ASEAN	Association of South East Asian Nations
AusIMM	Australasian Institute of Mining and Metallurgy
AIBC	Australia India Business Council
AIB-X	Australia India Business Exchange
AIEC	Australia India Education Council
AII	Australia India Institute
AILD	Australia India Leadership Dialogue
AISRF	Australia India Strategic Research Fund
AIYD	Australia India Youth Dialogue
ANCP	Australia NGO Cooperation Programme
ABS	Australian Bureau of Statistics
ACOLA	Australian Council of Learned Academics
ADF	Australian Defence Forces
AEI	Australian Education International
AQF	Australian Qualifications Framework
AVID	Australian Volunteers for International Development
BIT	Bilateral Investment Treaty
BCM	Billion Cubic Metres
BWC	Biological Weapons Conventions
CBG	Carrier Battle Group
CIAS	Centre for India Australia Studies
CBW	Chemical and Biological Weapons
CWC	Chemical Weapons Convention

Abbreviation	Terminology
ChAFTA	China Australia Free Trade Agreement
CASS	Chinese Academy of Social Sciences
CHOGM	Commonwealth Head of Governments Meeting
CAGR	Compound Annual Growth Rate
CECA	Comprehensive Economic Cooperation Agreement
CSP	Comprehensive Security Partnership
CII	Confederation of Indian Industry
DFCCIL	Dedicated Freight Corridor Corporation of India Limited
DRDO	Defence Research and Development Organisation
DSTO	Defence Science and Technological Organisation
DWP	Defence White Paper
DBT	Department of Bio Technology
DETYA	Department of Education Training and Youth Affairs
DAP	Direct Aid Programme
DGMS	Directorate General of Mines Safety
EAS	East Asia Summit
EAEG	East Asian Economic Group
EIC	East India Company
ELICOS	English Language Intensive Courses for Overseas Students
EAMF	Expanded ASEAN Maritime Forum
FDI	Foreign Direct Investment
FTA	Free Trade Agreement
GIAN	Global Initiative of Academic Networks
GDP	Gross Domestic Product
HELE	High Efficiency Low Emission
HSBC	Hong kong and Shanghai Banking Corporation
HADR	Humanitarian Assistance and Disaster Relief
ICAR	Indian Council of Agricultural Research
IIT	Indian Institute of Technology
IONS	Indian Ocean Naval Symposium
IOR	Indian Ocean Region
IOR -ARC	Indian Ocean Region- Association for Regional Cooperation
IORA	Indian Ocean Rim Association
ISM	Indian School of Mines
IPOI	Indo Pacific Oceans Initiative
ICT	Information and Communication Technology
IT	Information Technology
IoE	Institute of Eminence

Abbreviation	Terminology
IAEA	International Atomic Energy Agency
iCEM	International Centre for Excellence in Mining Automation
IMF	International Monetary Fund
LNG	Liquefied Natural Gas
LEP	Look East Policy
MAHE	Manipal Academy of Higher Education
MIPP	Melbourne India Postgraduate Programme
MoU	Memorandum of Understanding
Mtoe	Millions of Tonnes of Oil Equivalent
MEA	Ministry of External Affairs
MTCR	Missile Technology Control Regime
MECR	Multilateral Export Control Regime
MLSA	Mutual Logistics Supply Agreement
NSDC	National Skill Development Corporation
NOM	Net Overseas Migration
NCP	New Colombo Plan
NEP	New Education Policy
NFSC	New Framework for Security Cooperation
NGN	New Generation Networks
NSW	New South Wales
NAM	Non Aligned Movement
NGO	Non Governmental Organisation
NPT	Non Proliferation Treaty
NRE	Non Renewable Energy
NTS	Non Traditional Security
NATO	North Atlantic Treaty Organisation
NSG	Nuclear Suppliers Group
OMARA	Office of Migration Agents Registration Authority
JGU	OP Jindal Global University
OSC	Overseas Student Charge
PAF	Pakistan Air Force
PASSEX	Passage Exercise
PLAN	People's Liberation Army Navy
QSD	Quadrilateral Security Dialogue
RDA	Racial Discrimination Act
RCEP	Regional Comprehensive Economic Partnership
RBI	Reserve Bank of India
SIMTAR	Safety in Mines, Testing and Research Station

Abbreviation	Terminology
SPARC	Scheme for Promotion of Academics and Research
STEM	Science Technology Engineering and Mathematics
SLOC	Sea Lanes of Communication
SEATO	South East Asian Treaty Organisation
SOP	Standard Operating Procedure
SCRI	Supply Chain Resilience Initiative
TVET	Technical Vocational Education and Training
TSS	Temporary Skill Shortage
UNCLOS	United Nations Convention on the Law of the Sea
UNSC	United Nations Security Council
UGC	University Grants Commission
UNSW	University of New South Wales
VAJRA	Visiting Advanced Joint Research Faculty Scheme
WSU	Western Sydney University
WHA	World Health Assembly
WHO	World Health Organisation

CONTENTS

Introduction *21*

1. India & Australia Relationship: Unraveling the Narrative 27

2. Indo Pacific: Converging Defence & Diplomatic Compulsions 53

3. Transnational Education & Knowledge Partnerships:
    A Symbiotic Thread 101

4. Diaspora & Trade: Defining the Dependency 131

5. Looking Ahead: Prognosis of Relationship 165

Reference *175*
Index *201*

LIST OF FIGURES

Fig 1:   Increasing importance of India & Indo Pacific in Australian Strategic Discourse. 60

Fig 2:   Views about China as a Security Threat or an Economic Partner . . . 77

Fig 3:   Surge in the Bilateral Visits 86

Fig 4:   Three Stage Process 104

Fig 5:   Percentage of Indian Students to Overall International Students Enrolment (1995 to 2002). 106

Fig 6:   Percentage of Indian Students to Overall International Students Enrolment (2002 to 2013). 107

Fig 7:   Percentage of Indian Students to Overall International Students Enrolment (2014 to 2020). 108

Fig 8:   Change in Preferences of Indian Students: 2000 to 2017. 111

Fig 9:   Rise in the numbers of Indian Students in Australia. 112

Fig 10: Commencements by Indian Students in Different Sectors: 2017 to 2020 113

Fig 11: Commencement of Indian Students by Sector: 2005 & 2009 114

Fig 12: Number of Projects Approved Under AISRF 118

Fig 13: Type of Activities Carried out under AISRF 119

Fig 14: Dimensions of Approved Projects with Australia 120

Fig 15: Role of AIYD in Promoting Bilateral Relationship: Results of Survey 123

Fig 16: Net Overseas Migration to Australia – 1971-72 to 2018-19 135

Fig 17: Percentage of Australian Population Born in India. 136

Fig 18: Primary 457 Visa Grants by Year: Top Three Countries 137

Fig 19: Percentage of Net Overseas Migration to Overall Migration: India and China 140

Fig 20: Percentage of India born Population in Australia in Census Years . 140

Fig 21: Religious Diversity of Indian Migrants (In Percentages) 144

Fig 22: Real GDP Growth and Net Overseas Migration - Australia 147

Fig 23: Visa Type by Country of Birth: Permanent Migrants 148

Fig 24: Percentage of Labour Force (Skilled) to Total Population of
Skilled: India & China 149
Fig 25: Percentage Proficiency in spoken English/language by Country
of birth, Permanent Migrants 149
Fig 26: Time Series Migrant Remittance Inflows: India (US $ million) . . . 151
Fig 27: Bilateral Remittances Flows from Australia ($ Billion) 151
Fig 28: Grant of Tourist Visas to Indians 158
Fig 29: Pattern (2003-2019) of FDI from India to
Australia (US $ Billions) 162
Fig 30: Pattern (2003-2019) of FDI from Australia to
India (US $ Billions) 163

LIST OF TABLES

Table 1: Major Defence Exercises Between India and Australia 98

Table 2: Importance of the Knowledge & Awareness of the Host
Country as an Influencing Factor in Motivating Student
Destination Choice 109

Table 3: Perspectives of Education Agents 110

Table 4: Temporary visas selected categories, 2015-16 to 2018-19 115

Table 5: AIEC: 2019 Grant Round Outcomes. 122

Table 6: Significance of Migration from India: 2015 to 2019 141

Table 7: Hofstede Insights: India and Australia 143

Table 8: Top Ten Professions for Skilled Migration (India): 2015-2018 . . 145

Table 9: Proportion of Total Income of Indian Migrants by Visa
Stream and Type of Income 150

Table 10: Proportion of Income by Top Five Countries of Birth 2016-17. . . 150

Table 11: Temporary Visa for Foreign/Defence Students: Australia 166

INTRODUCTION

"India-Australia relations are wide-ranging and deep. And this depth comes from our shared values, shared interests, shared geography and shared objectives. We have immense possibilities to make our friendship stronger. There are challenges on how to translate this potential into reality so that links between citizens, businesses, academics, researchers, etc. of both countries become stronger; how our relationship can be a factor of stability for our region and for the world?"[1]

Geographically Indian and Pacific Oceans have long been considered as a single entity, but it is in recent times that these two oceans have started being considered together in strategic parlance as well, thereby facilitating coining of a new terminology of Indo Pacific. Historically, Asia has always been seen from a unified perspective. "Both Alfred Thayer Mahan and Halford Mackinder, had observed Asia as an integrated region."[2] In fact, Mahan and Mackinder alone cannot be singled out for this perspective, but a range of European and Asian geo strategists, from the German Karl Haushofer (who in the 1920s saw the Indo-Pacific as imperial Japan's to conquer) to India's K. M. Panikkar have held out the view of Asia as an integrated geostrategic space. The recent traction of the term Indo Pacific therefore can be ascribed to the increasing recognition and acceptance of the accelerating economic and security connections between the Western Pacific and the Indian Ocean and the resultant single strategic system.

The basis of coining the origins of this new Indo-Pacific terminology though has been primarily credited to the economic imperatives and necessities, however the consequences of this convergence are immensely strategic and the management of the implications correspondingly complex. This new integrated space cannot be treated as an ordinary geographic region but happens to be a super-region in which the sub-regions cannot be neglected. The region is a super flux of a number of countries/regions, thereby necessitating requirement of bilateral/trilateral/multilateral initiatives pegged at various levels to ensure effective cooperation to address its security and other corresponding and complex issues.

As the region takes shape, bilateral relations between different states of the region also undergo rapid transformations. The associated economic and strategic implications of the new construct nudge the countries of the region to look at each other from different perspectives. The genesis of a bilateral relationship between two states in the contemporary world owes its genesis to different perspectives of each state, thereby providing a dominant significance to the respective 'Core Interests' of each. A strong and sustaining bilateral relationship does not develop at the spur of the moment, but takes decades to flourish. "Good bilateral relations do not develop overnight. They require genuine, sustained efforts often over years, putting in place the building blocks that nurture the future diplomacy, and, consequently, the quality of the relationship."[3] With growth of the relationship, the Congruence of 'Core Interests' of the involved states starts materializing and over a period of time this alignment and congruence starts providing a strong foundation to the bilateral relationship between the states.

The arrival of the terminology of Indo Pacific has provided crucial impetus to the bilateral relationship between India and Australia. The relationship between India and Australia can be considered as very unique and singular in all the aspects of bilateralism. Both the countries have been off from each other's horizon for a long period of time and had rarely considered each other from a strategic partner point of view. Though off and on in the past some attempts were made by both of them to work out a relationship but the relationship did not sustain itself. These short term relationships were not based on strong foundations and as a result the relationship has suffered from several false starts in the past. The occasional warmth in their relationship in the past has always been overwhelmed by their differing perspectives on a variety of issues, leading to cold shouldering of the relationship by the various governments in the past. A host of commonalities existing in the fields of curry, cricket and commonwealth, though have played their respective roles in improving the bilateral relationship, the relations between the two nations had stagnated over a period of time. Notwithstanding the differing perceptions, the underlying understanding of mutual complementarities, on the other hand have continued to provide occasional spurts to the relationship. Therefore, the alternate cycles of warmth and coldness in the bilateral relationship between India and Australia have been more of a norm rather than an exception and have largely been taken for granted.

Though both the countries share a language, a colonial heritage, Westminster political institutions, and a democratic tradition, in practice these links have rarely brought them together in strategic terms, at least until recent years. India and Australia's relationship in 1947 can be termed as cordial, being former British dominions, but with the rapid advent of cold war in Asia, these countries found themselves on opposite sides of political and security divide. Both the countries have avoided each other for a substantial period of time so much so that "India was neither conscious of being neglected by Australia, nor particularly interested in upgrading the relationship."[4] Australia on its part was also tied up in the dynamics of Asia Pacific and Indian Ocean was completely neglected by the strategic planners of the time. The arrival of the terminology of Indo Pacific has improved upon the existing Asia Pacific and has distinctly brought centrality of India into the forefront. "Whereas at geographic level, it attempts to bring in the Indian Ocean while at the state level it brings in India."[5] Australia has gradually and officially accepted the importance of Indo Pacific and India in the emerging strategic scenario. The region therefore has accordingly being provided adequate importance by the government of the day in Australia. "Indo Pacific is the region spanning the Indian Ocean through to the western Pacific Ocean. Indo-Pacific emphasises the growing significance of this geographic corridor and of India".[6]

The role played by the renewed absorption and wider acceptability of the terminology of Indo Pacific has been very significant in getting India and Australia to come together. With Indo Pacific region finding traction in the geo polity of the region, Australia and India's spheres of strategic interest are now converging and their strategic interests are coming into much greater alignment, as both are stake holders in the emerging region of Indo Pacific. "Trade routes…are drawing links again between the Indian and Pacific Oceans. That is one reason why today it makes more sense to think of the Indo Pacific, rather than East Asia or even the Asia Pacific, as the crucible of Australian security. This broader definition returns India to Asia's strategic matrix. It connects the Indian and Pacific Oceans, thereby underlining the crucial role that the maritime environment is likely to play in our future strategic and defence planning…The Indo Pacific represents the centre of gravity of Australia's economic and strategic interests. It includes our top nine trading partners. It embraces our key strategic ally, the US, as well as our largest trading partner, China. It reinforces India's role as a strategic partner for Australia and it brings in the big Asian economies of Japan, Korea, Indonesia and Vietnam as well as the diplomatic and trade weight of ASEAN."[7]

Apart from the factor of Indo Pacific, which is facilitating congruence of strategic interests between the two countries, a set of another three very significant factors of Defence, Diplomacy and Diaspora are also fueling the bilateral relationship. The complex interplay between these three aspects has ensured that the bilateral relationship continues to stay in an overdrive. The up gradation of bilateral relationship to a Comprehensive Strategic Partnership is an indicator of the level of mutual understanding at the diplomatic and political levels. The number of bilateral visits, both political and diplomatic are providing an increased strategic connect between the two countries. An active cooperation in a large number of multilateral, minilateral and bilateral forums are facilitating an exponential increment in the mutual understanding of interests and concerns. This has been made possible though a concerted diplomatic drive and has provided an envious hue to the bilateral relationship.

The historical baggage carried by both the countries, in terms of alliances and non alliances have restricted Australia and India to forge a strong defence relationship for quite some time in the past. The understanding facilitated by diplomatic initiatives has also propelled the bilateral defence relationship to graduate from nontraditional to traditional security domains. The bilateral defence relationship had commenced from cooperation in the nontraditional security arenas to include cyber, terrorism and other related issues. The dynamism provided to the relationship by the increased political and diplomatic connect at the apex levels, culminating in the signing of the Comprehensive Security Partnership in 2020 have resulted in the exponential increment in the bilateral and plurilateral defence engagements between both the countries. Australia's participation in the recently held Malabar series of defence exercises in a multilateral setting after a period of thirteen years has a tremendous potential for bilateral defence cooperation in the multilateral settings. Coupled with the signing of a Mutual Logistics Support Agreement, the bilateral defence relationship and the engagements in the field are going to be an important and significant aspect of the relationship.

The bilateral relationship between India and Australia is also unique and singular in the aspect that the increased defence and diplomatic cooperation is supplemented by a strong and prosperous Indian diaspora in Australia. India's bilateral relationship with no other country in the world is based on the three pillars of Defence, Diplomacy and Diaspora. The opportunities provided by the world class Australian universities to the international students from India have resulted in the Indian diaspora to be on the verge of becoming the largest diaspora in Australia. The concept of brain drain having been substituted by brain circulation, the collateral advantages of migration of students, academics, researchers and professionals are not only restricted to Australia but the benefits are also being accrued by the Indian society. The Australian alumni in India and Indian diaspora in Australia are the two very critical denominators which are facilitating the bilateral relationship between India and Australia to achieve the escape velocity of the historical baggage, carried by both countries.

The diaspora and alumni driven business and trade relationship is an important part of the bilateral relations between India and Australia. Though the specifics of Free Trade Agreement between India and Australia and India's concerns on Regional Comprehensive Economic Partnership have not been ironed out and assuaged, the momentum and depth provided to the relationship by the defence, diplomacy and diaspora engagement strategies has ensured the trade relationship to prosper. The opportunities offered by the trade relationship in energy and resources sector are immense and can provide a quantum boost to the relationship. First time perhaps in the history of bilateral relationship between any two countries, both Australia and India have come out with a specific road map for engagement strategies with each other. Leaving aside the implementation part of these strategies, the formulation and release of these strategies in itself is an admission of the gravity and seriousness with which the bilateral relationship is being nurtured for future by both the countries. The mutual interests and the shared concerns however, are very likely to promote and drive an active implementation of these strategies by the concerned departments in both the governments. Just as past of the bilateral relationship between India and Australia is marked with trust deficit and defined by a host of critical differences over issues of 'Core Interests', the future of the relationship can be prophesized to be very promising for both the countries. Both India and Australia are central to the emerging strategic landscape and geopolitical connotations of Indo Pacific and the existing and futuristic contours of their bilateral relationship will augur very well for the region.

CHAPTER 1

INDIA & AUSTRALIA RELATIONSHIP: UNRAVELING THE NARRATIVE

"Both the countries are historical and vibrant democracies, both the nations have an envious set up of political and civil liberties, and both share their respective ideals about greater economic interdependence and political stability in Asia and around, yet so far they have been unable to achieve a quantum leap in the relationship."[8]

It has been scientifically proven that until about 160 million years ago, India and Australia, the two major Indian Ocean littoral states of contemporary times had been part of the same landmass, known as Gondwana super. This land mass, at that point of time in its wider variant, also used to encompass Africa and Antarctica besides India and Australia. It is also believed that these components, over a period of time separated from each other, and later drifted away to their present geographical locations. As a result of the depreciation of sea level between them, the massive sea bed transformed into a land bridge, which has since facilitated migration of flora and fauna and ancient people to each other, which albeit in a different context and purpose, in fact is continuing till date.

Experts have also hinted at the strong possibility of historical linkages between indigenous people in southern India and those in Australia. However, despite lack of evidence of blood group compatibility between these two groups, certain ethno linguistic evidences and the microliths pointing to the prehistoric links between these indigenous people cannot be discarded altogether.[9] The latest studies on the subject have also genetically corroborated these thoughts and have concluded that people indeed migrated from India to Australia as early as 4300 years back carrying with them stone tools and later blended into the Australian society. Carrying on these similarities further, in spite of being geographically and spatially dislocated, the dominant weather pattern in India and Australia, possess distinct commonalities to include similar rainfall matrix, similarities in terms of tropical, sub tropical and temperate climatic conditions along with the aridity and drought templates.

When Britain colonized the present day territories of both countries, it reignited the lost human contact between the two countries and further rekindled and strengthened the similarity index between India and Australia. It is a commonly known fact that, the continuation of these historical linkages further facilitated the strengthening of relations, as both the territories adopted commonalities of English jurisprudence, English language and British Commonwealth. East India Company (EIC) facilitated India to become an important trade partner with Australia, primarily supplying food and provisions to the colony. England transformed into an interface to further the interactions between India and Australia and helped both countries to know more about each other. These three way linkages between India, Australia and England have also been acknowledged by the historians of the times. "Australia seemed to be a satellite of India as well as a colony of England." [10] The mutual connect with Britain though facilitated a lot of commonalities and similarities between India and Australia, but these similarities and commonalities were not robust and durable enough to sustain the relationship.

The relationship as such based on mutual trade and political connect with Britain lost its steam as soon as the decline of the British Empire commenced. This chapter as the primary foundation block of the book, attempts to reconstruct the separate and distinct narratives, which crept into the matrix of the bilateral relationship between India and Australia. The current complementarities in the relationship between the two countries have developed after decades of indifference. This indifference started creeping into the relationship initially itself and manifested itself fully after the independence of India. The underlying subtle but certain differences about the intention and resistance to colonization in respect to both these countries have been important factors in the subsequent historical narration of bilateral matrix. The colonization of Australia by Britain was apparently not accompanied by the initiatives for institutionalized inclusion processes of indigenous people in the governance and sub governance structures. The arrival of British in Australia was with an explicit and declared intention to colonize and use Australia as a penal colony. The initial arrival of the British in India however, begun with a primary intention of trade, which gradually transformed into governance and finally colonization. The British competition with the French in the sphere of trade facilitated the British EIC to establish itself strongly into the governance processes in India. As the British intention was to develop Australia into a penal colony, accordingly permanent settlements for the convicts and the British citizens were planned. In the entire process the local population was considered an obstacle and was treated as such. In contrast, as the process of colonialism in India was driven by trade considerations and was planned as a gradual process, the involvement of the local populace was imperative and was accordingly considered and catered by the colonial masters.

Though both India and Australia resisted the colonial administration of British, the asymmetry in the resistance being offered was quite spectacular in terms of scale, timing and organization to the resistance. As the arrival of British in Australia was sudden, with the clear and defined aim of colonization, the indigenous people were taken in for a surprise and the resistance was immediate and violent in some cases. In India, however things were in different perspective from the very beginning. The British had been present and trading in India for quite long and the resentment towards the British presence and exploitation took time to manifest. Over a period of time, Indians were used to the British presence in the country and it dictated their responses towards colonization. As a result, resistance to colonial rule in India was not very immediate and took time to get organized.

Accordingly, after the independence, the effects of colonialism along with the manifestations of exploitation and brutality have been a major influence in the shaping of India's foreign policy. As a result of the brutal and bitter experiences of exploitation during the period of colonialism, India took it upon herself to oppose colonialism in all its forms. In a further opposition to the colonialism, India also framed anti-colonialism, racial equality and Non Alignment as bulwarks of her foreign policy. With India espousing the cause of colonies for independence, the independence of increasing number of colonies was a cause of concern for Australia. The emerging nationalism in Asia, accompanied by a rapid rise of former colonies getting independence in the post World War II scenario created serious apprehensions for Australia. It was considered that the decolonization of colonies in Asia was exposing Australian federation to severe perils which might endanger the very existence of the federation. "Decolonization in Australia's region also challenged the tenets of faith; such as racial homogeneity, protection from Asia, and regional

European influence, which had circulated in Australia from the time of federation."[11]

With her experiences of having suffered the effects of colonialism very intimately and her belief in the tenets of the Non Aligned Movement (NAM), India was continuing to root for independence of greater number of colonies. It was a firm belief of India that the flawed policies of colonialism had arrested the growth of the Indian sub continent; while at the same time had facilitated a huge quantum of economic progress for the 'Colonial Masters'. India was of the opinion that colonialism can benefit only the imperial countries, while India as a former colony has suffered tremendous difficulties and serious setbacks due to the colonialism, "all the problems that had accumulated during the period of our arrested growth in the past…"[12] Australia on the other hand was very comfortable with the notion of colonialism. For her, the process had rendered tremendous advantages to the betterment of economic cooperation between the colonies and the masters. From time to time it was justified that colonialism being practiced by several of its allies of time, was responsible for lifting up people from the clutches of poverty. The increased frequency with which freedom was being granted by the Britain to the erstwhile colonies was also not very much liked by Australia. "People who keep on saying that colonialism is bad should look at the history of the old African colonies before either the British, or even the Germans, went to Africa. They were witchcraft-ridden countries and the people lived under terrible conditions. Whenever anyone criticizes colonialism he needs to be careful what he says. There are examples in which the British erred in the face of pressure by granting self-government too soon."[13]

Australia continued to oppose the anti colonial rhetoric being spear headed by India. The Australian government of the day was against any demands for decolonization and strongly condemned any demands for this. This stand of the Australian government was reiterated very frequently by the government of the time. "Not only did the Australians oppose the anti-colonial demands… they were the most rigid in their opposition. Only a handful of the colonial old-guards such as South Africa, Belgium and Portugal showed greater hostility to decolonization."[14] These opposing positions on the issue of colonialism significantly impacted the bilateral relationship between India and Australia, in the initial years of independence of India and laid a very strong and stable foundation for facilitating the further divergence in the relationship.

Australia of today is home to a large Indian Diaspora which has been instrumental in providing substantial leverage to the bilateral relations, but the situation was not always like this. Initial arrival and settlement of migrants from Indian subcontinent in Australia was not a very smooth and cordial arrangement. The available records suggest that the first group of Indians, which arrived in Australia in the years 1800-1816, were sent as convict labourers by the British colonial authorities. In order to explore the feasibility of importing labour from other countries, in 1837, a select committee of Legislative Council in Australia had tentatively recommended the trial importation of 300-500 hill tribesmen from India to test their suitability for pastoral work. Therefore, during the first half of the 19th century, most of the Indians who arrived in Australia were recruited as labourers by the colonial Government.

As the settlers from India of the time, started arriving in the colony and economic conditions of the time being what they were, the recruitment and import of indentured labour was not favoured by the original settlers. There were apprehensions about the loss of employment for the people of other nations, primarily Europeans, if the plan for import of indented labour from India was implemented. The government of the time had tried to quell these apprehensions and justified the planned import of indentured labour. "The employment of coolies as shepherds would not interfere with the Europeans engaged in other branches of industry, such Europeans being generally averse to pastoral pursuits, while the coolies have been found well adapted for that employment, and have exhibited a remarkable example of honesty, sobriety and thrift."[15]

Due to this import a large number of Indians, especially Sikhs and Muslims from Northern Indian state of Punjab, settled on the northern coast of New South Wales (NSW) as agricultural labourers, hawkers or traders. Several Indians from the Punjab and North West Frontier Province ran the famous "Camel Trains", as primary means of transport into the interiors of Australia, prior to the development of the road and rail networks and were collectively known as Afghans, abbreviated by Australians to 'Ghans'. In an apparent tribute to these Indians, an experiential train 'The Ghan', an abbreviated version of 'The Afghan Express', still runs between Adelaide and Darwin in Australia.

Though the import of indentured labour was happening in the colony for specified purposes, the immigration policies of Australia at that time were also heavily tilted in favour of United Kingdom and had resulted in more than half of immigrants being from United Kingdom. This tilt towards the British has also been officially acknowledged and recognised. "Far from the British flow falling away, I am happy to be able to report to honorable members my belief that interest has never been keener in the United Kingdom, despite the prosperous and full employment situation there. We are getting a continuing flow, on the scale that we desire, of immigrants from that country. If our resources were greater, we would be able to cope with a bigger British intake, and would be glad to do so. But within the programme we have decided upon, we are getting the numbers of British migrants that we are seeking."[16]

This apparent favoritism towards the British on the other hand was also a cause of concern for the people from India who were already in Australia or were in the process of relocation. As the population from the UK was being re-located to Australia, the beliefs, attitudes, prejudices and colonial experience were also simultaneously taking roots in the new colony and the aversion and the deep rooted antipathy of already settled Europeans in Australia to the efforts of immigration of Indians was equally evident in the apprehensions of the Colonial Office. "To expedite augmentation of wealth in New South Wales by introducing the black race there from India would, in my mind, be one of the most unreasonable preferences of the present to the future, which it would be possible to make. There is not on the globe, a social interest more momentous, if we look forward for five or six generations, than that of reserving the continent of New Holland as a place where the English race shall be spread from sea to sea unmixed with any lower caste. As we now regret the folly of our ancestors in colonizing North America from Africa, so should our posterity have to censure us if we should colonize Australia from India?"[17]

Australian attitude towards the immigration of Indian laborers in Australia was more based on the aspects of necessity and the indentured labour was considered a desirable and necessary arrangement of exploiting the economic opportunities of the 'Tropical North' but at the same time the Indian labour was unacceptable as permanent settlers for the obvious economic, political, racial and social reasons. "I would direct the attention of people who think in that way to the fact that the British Government today admit the power of this Commonwealth and of the people of Australia to differentiate between Indian British subjects and white British subjects, because they themselves differentiate between them. The British Government does not think of putting the Hindoo or any other native of India upon the same plane as the people of the United Kingdom. The natives of India are British subjects and subjects only, whilst the people of the United Kingdom are citizens as well, and British subjects in Australia are citizens also."[18]

Australia being located near the Asia and having seen Japanese aggression closely during the World War II was principally against any large scale organised immigration from Asia. "What we mean, in the view of all Australia at the present time, is that we will prevent any large infiltration of alien elements into the component parts of our national life, and that we will preserve pure for all time the British element with which we started. There are two modes by which this population may become infiltrated by alien elements, and one is almost as dangerous as the other. No matter what one's opinion may be on this subject, either in general or in detail, we all agree that there is an inherent power in the Government to keep out hordes of undesirable citizens." [19]

In continuation of these existing and rapidly developing prejudices and as an off shoot of Immigration Restriction Act of 1901, Australia had slowly but steadily started implementing 'White Australia Policy'. This was primarily aimed to severely restrict non-European immigration to Australia. From India's perspective, the 'White Australian Policy' was a major factor in undermining the relationship between the two countries than any other issue, whereas from an Australian perspective the 'Policy of Exclusion' was considered essential for the very existence of the colony and the policy was justified by Australia on several occasions. "The racial and economic barriers between us and them are insuperable. We cannot marry their women nor they ours without producing a race of half-castes at which both races would spit contempt. Nor can we permit them to labour alongside us without destroying that high standard of living which is an integral part of our national life.[20]

Australia's leaders after the Second World War had either held the contradictions of the White Australia policy in check, or ignored them, as they simultaneously embraced the multilateralism of the United Nations and sought to maintain their exclusive immigration policy. [21] As far as Indian sensibilities were concerned, the practical dimensions of the policy were very offensive and discriminatory and no amount of justification could have lessened the underlying vitriolic attitudes. General Cariappa, the then Indian High Commissioner to Australia and New Zealand was appalled to observe that citizens from former enemy countries, particularly Germany and Italy, were welcomed into Australia, while the immigration of Indians was being restricted on racially discriminatory terms and conditions. "Australia's immigration policy had more to do with skin colour than character and might result in turning millions in India and Pakistan away from the commonwealth and towards communism."[22]

The Australian government from time to time defended its immigration policy and said that every state should be its own judge of the composition of its nationhood, and must consequently be granted the right to restrict or control immigration. "But the whole point that I make is that, while I believe that our immigration policy is both wise and just, is based not upon any foolish -notion of racial superiority, but upon a proper desire to preserve a homogeneous population and so avert the troubles that have bedeviled some other countries, it is a domestic policy. And the right to determine our domestic policy is part of our sovereignty as a member of the Commonwealth."[23]

These discriminatory policies of immigration obviated people to people relationships between India and Australia and as a result the bilateral relationship was also adversely affected. The thorn in Australia's side instances (Commonwealth and White Australia Policy) was India, with Jawaharlal Nehru the undisputed leader of the non-aligned movement then gathering momentum in Asia and Africa and leader of a nation with particular reason to feel affronted by the White Australia policy.[24] Stewart Wigmore, the then Australian High Commissioner to India, had written back to Department of External Affairs, Government of Australia way back in 1945 about the resentment in India due to the White Australian Policy. "I have been told by a highly placed Indian intellectual that "Australia is one of the most hated countries in India" primarily because of the White Australia policy."[25] During this period Australia identified itself as white and India continued to be most vocal proponent and espouser for the dismantling of the White Australia policy. Meg Gurry, an authority on the history of bilateral relations between the two countries during the period has argued that 'neglect' best characterised Australia's relationship to India in the second half of the twentieth century.[26]

Due to the international pressures and internal demands, some policy changes were introduced by Australia in 1966, which were initiated to allow increased levels of immigration from non Europeans. Surrendering to the immense international opposition, Australia started dismantling the provisions of the policy by early sixties of the last century, with the final remnants of the policy having been discontinued by 1973. The policy changes and the corresponding elimination of immigration restrictions from Asia have resulted in the establishment of Indian diaspora as one of the largest Diasporas in

Australia. These people to people contacts are playing a very significant role in the bilateral relationship between India and Australia as shall be seen in the subsequent chapter of the book.

Both India and Australia also happen to be one of the earliest members of the British Commonwealth. In spite of being important members of the grouping, the bilateral relationship between both the countries has also been devoid of any mutual bonhomie. These mutual differences of interests and concerns had started to manifest immediately after the independence of India. On the eve of independence and as a sovereign nation, the onus of joining the Commonwealth was on India. India, on its part had refrained from applying the idea of Non Alignment for the membership of Commonwealth and had decided to continue to be a member of British Commonwealth even after independence. The then Indian Prime Minister had vehemently defended the decision to stay in the Commonwealth. "So far as the Republic of India is concerned, her constitution and her working are concerned, she has nothing to do with any external authority, with any King, and none of her subjects owe any allegiance to the King or any other external authority. That Republic may however agree to associate itself with certain other countries that happen to be monarchies or whatever they choose to be. This Declaration therefore states that this new Republic of India, completely sovereign and owing no allegiance to the King, as the other Commonwealth countries do owe, will nevertheless be a full member of this Commonwealth. We join the Commonwealth obviously because we think it is beneficial to us and to certain causes in the world that we wish to advance."[27] Citing the welfare of entire mankind, the Australian polity of the time greeted the decision of India to stay in Commonwealth and was of the view that, "the complete severing of links which join the British and Indian peoples would be greatly prejudicial to them both and to all mankind and that dominion status was independence with something added and not independence with something taken away."[28] It was believed by Australia that India would continue to participate in all the activities of empire as hither to fore and will defend the interests of empire, as has been a practice. India was considered as a fulcrum for the existence of the British Empire in the region and an empire without India was definitely not envisaged by Australia. "Without India the British Empire could not exist. The possession of India is the inalienable badge of sovereignty in the eastern hemisphere."[29]

Till 1948, no other member of commonwealth had explored the possibility of dual relationship within the Commonwealth i.e. membership without allegiance to Crown. India, on the other hand, after independence, had started the process to become a Republic, an idea which was anathema to the very core of Commonwealth, "It must be remembered that the Commonwealth is not a super state in any sense of the term. We have agreed to consider the king as the symbolic head of this free association. But the king has no function attached to that status in the commonwealth. As far as the constitution of India is concerned, the King has no place and we shall owe no allegiance to him."[30] In order to, cater for Indian aspirations for a Republic, a special Commonwealth Prime Minister's conference was held in April 1949, the decision of which permitted India to stay in Commonwealth as a Republic. "The Government of India have informed the other Governments of the Commonwealth of the intention of the Indian people that under the new constitution which is about to be adopted India shall become a sovereign independent republic. The Government of India have however declared and affirmed India's desire to continue her full membership of the Commonwealth of Nations and her acceptance of The King as the symbol of the free association of its independent member nations and as such the Head of the Commonwealth."[31]

It has been observed that overbearing and overwhelming allegiance to British Commonwealth of the then Australia was responsible for creating impediments for India to retain the membership of commonwealth with certain amendments, which were considered very vital for the commonwealth by Australia. "Allegiance to the Crown will remain, intangible, not susceptible of legal definition, the most profound of all the unifying influences for the Crown dominions."[32] Within Australian polity of the time there were differences over the configuration of the new commonwealth. While H. V. Evatt, Labor's minister for external affairs argued for the continuance of the Royal Prerogative, Menzies, leader of the Liberal Party took a narrower view, proposing an exclusive inner circle of old 'white dominions', or a 'Crown Commonwealth'.[33]The decision of India to withdraw its allegiance to the crown was not taken positively by Australia and it was termed as amounting to reducing the Crown only to a symbol, a reality which was not acceptable to Australia in any case. "While I regret that the decision of India to become a Republic, rendered necessary the calling of the conference to discuss her future relationships with Australia and the other Dominions whose allegiance to the Crown remains unchanged, I feel that in all the circumstances the agreement reached is in the best interests of the British Commonwealth. [34] Australia was also of the view that the decision by India to move away from the sovereign has considerably damaged the family relationship under the Crown. India, on its part had her own reasons to continue to be in Commonwealth, yet retaining its separate and distinct identity. The then Defence Minister of India had summated this dilemma. "We were not tied to the commonwealth in the same way, in the same sense, that Australia was and is; yet we took the initiative after we became a Republic, after we had established ourselves as an independent nation. So that is not the tie, it is more rational pragmatic and sensible factors."[35]

The principles of racial equality are deeply enshrined in the constitutions of both India and Australia. Both being members of the British Commonwealth provided reasonable assurances to the rest of the world that these two countries stand for the principles of racial equality. The open apartheid policy practiced by South Africa of the time was another source of conflict between India and Australia. India, as a young member of the grouping was totally against the policy of racial prejudices being practiced by the government of South Africa. Indian concerns, naturally apt were against the treatment of Africans and Indians in South Africa. "The question of the people of Indian descent in South Africa has really merged into bigger questions where not only Indians are affected but the whole African population along with… any other people who happen to go to South Africa and who do not belong to the European or American countries."[36] Sharpeville incident represented a turning point in the history of apartheid in the history of South Africa, when 69 people were killed[37] by the South African Police on 21 March 1960, in an attempt to quell a demonstration against the 'Pass Laws'. India joined the African States in calling for Security Council discussion of apartheid after the Sharpeville massacre and co-sponsored the General Assembly resolution, urging all States to impose sanctions against South Africa and establishing the Special Committee against Apartheid. In the specialized agencies of the United Nations, the Movement of Non-Aligned Countries and the Commonwealth, as well as in numerous other organizations and forums, India was active in calling for the isolation of the apartheid regime and support for the liberation struggle.[38]

Australia on the other hand was against the issue being raised in the commonwealth. "But Sharpeville had brought up into the public mind the whole problems of apartheid, or separate development of separate races within the one country. In the result, apartheid, which has been the accepted policy of South African Governments for many years and has never previously been brought up at a Prime Ministers' Conference, flared into the news and into debate?"[39] Australia had termed the issue as a domestic problem for the Union of South Africa and not suitable for discussion or debate in the meetings of the Commonwealth. "We re-affirmed our practice that the domestic policies of member nations are not matters for debate or decision by the Conference. But the point to be made is that the Prime Ministers' Conference is not a quasi-judicial body. Nor is it a Committee of the United Nations. Nor is it under some duty to discipline its own members into obedience to the Charter of the United Nation"[40]

Australia's continued the unabashed support for the racial policies of South Africa and so continued the increasing diversion between principled stand of India and Australia against racial prejudices. Australian Prime Minister deplored the overwhelming consensus built against South Africa in the Prime Minister's conference as part of meeting of British Commonwealth "Well, I think this fixes it, one, two, three, four, five people got up and made it completely clear that they wouldn't have this, that they didn't want South Africa in, and that every convenient opportunity, or inconvenient opportunity, would be taken to attack her."[41] In an indication of an open support for racially inspired policies of South Africa, the Australian Prime Minister also attempted to defend the speech of Dr Verwoerd, the Prime Minister of South Africa. "This he did with a great deal of competence and some effectiveness and… made a certain number of digs at aspects of internal policies in Ghana, Nigeria, Malaya, Ceylon and India."[42] As a result of the discussions at the Prime Minister's meeting, South Africa had decided to withdraw her application for continuation in the Commonwealth. This decision of South Africa to withdraw from the Commonwealth was welcomed by India. In the words of the then Indian Prime Minister, it "has strengthened the Commonwealth" and the historic nature of the Commonwealth decision, reaffirmed and reiterated the Indian stance on the issue of apartheid. "This very tenuous and vague association has developed certain basic formulae… one of them is equal treatment of races, equal opportunities, no racial suppression and certainly no segregation."[43] Australia on the other hand lamented the forced decision of South Africa to leave the Commonwealth and its Prime Minister in his address to the Australian Parliament was very critical of the turn of the events. "Under inexorable pressure, South Africa is out of the Commonwealth. It is not the Verwoerd Government that is out. It is the Union of South Africa; the nation evolved by the great liberal statesmanship of 1909; the nation of Botha and Smuts;... the nation... which recently voted to remain within the direct allegiance to the Throne. I hope I may look to my fellow members of this Parliament to share in my sorrow at these unhappy circumstances."[44]

This period of indifference between India and Australia was also characterized by the freedom of a large number of colonies. The social and economic conditions of these colonies were indeed dreadful. In order to kick start the economies of these erstwhile colonies, there was a race for provisioning of aid to these countries by the relatively developed nations. But more often than not, the provisioning of aid was related to the ideological leanings and affiliations of these countries. India and Australia in the initial years of Indian independence had also differed on the involvement of political considerations in the provisioning of aid. Following India's lead, which as a Republic had sought and obtained the membership of British Commonwealth, a large number of these newly independent countries had sought the membership of the Commonwealth in the middle of the last century. Australia, as a strong ally of the British till end of World War realized the growing might of the US and the declining power of the British and coupled with this, the danger of spread of communism was found to be clear and present by the then Australian polity. The main consideration of the Australian polity of the time therefore was to control the spread of communism. "The 'White Australia' policy- as it is generally called - is an integral part of the national life of the Australian people, and although the subject of much hostile criticism, the geographical, racial, and economic circumstances of the Commonwealth amply justify it. The "White Australia Policy" policy is a gesture of defence, not of defiance. We do not regard Asiatics as inferiors, but as different from ourselves, believing that the ideals, traditions, and standards of living in the East are so incompatible with our own that we could never live with them as fellow-citizens. We could not assimilate Asiatics without radically changing our racial, social and economic character."[45]

The Colombo Plan, an initiative for the provisioning of aid in terms of economic assistance to the poorer members of the Commonwealth, particularly in Asia, which was subsequently extended to non-member countries also, had come into being in January 1950, at the meeting of the Foreign Ministers of Commonwealth countries held at Ceylon (Sri Lanka). This aid plan proved to be another area where both India and Australia were not able to resolve their mutual differences. Australia was of the view that economic aid was an imperative if the rapid rise of communism has to be stopped. India though supported the notion that improvement of living standards of downtrodden was an essential prerequisite to counter the spread of communism, but was averse to link the provisioning of aid with any political or strategic considerations. "Mutual action by British Commonwealth countries to build up Asian living standards will be suggested by the External Affairs Minister (Mr Spender), to the Ceylon conference. The aim is to remove conditions under which Communism, viewed by Mr Spender as a threat to Australia's national existence, has a breeding ground in Asia. The Government's view is that Communism cannot be fought purely by force, but must also be combated on the economic level."[46] Australia however was convinced that linking of economic assistance with the allied ideological leanings will provide greater dividends. "The assistance can help the countries of South East Asia to develop their own democratic institutions and their own economies and thus protect them against those opportunists and subversive elements which take advantage of changing political situations and low living standards."[47]

Under the aegis of the Colombo Plan, another issue of concern and mutual distrust between India and Australia was the amount of aid difference being given to India and Pakistan, in spite of there being a huge differential in the population as well the size of the two countries. There appeared to be an apparent disparity in the quantum of aid being disbursed to the two countries. "With a fraction of India's population, Pakistan received more aid from Australia (as at 1957) under the Colombo Plan than India did. Casey informed Parliament in April 1957 that Colombo Plan aid to India amounted to $ 6,700,000 with a further $ 4,160,000 pledged. For Pakistan, the comparable figures he tabled were $ 6,800,000 and $ 5,000,000 pledged a difference in Pakistan's favor of nearly $1,000,000."[48] India continued to object to the support being provided by Australia to Pakistan. The Australian involvement in the India Pakistan bilateral matrix is being discussed in the later part of the chapter. The popular perception in India of the Colombo Plan therefore, revolved around the notion that the programme predominantly aimed to serve Australia's interests as a subset of the broader US strategic aims in South and South East Asia rather than representing a genuine aid initiative for the alleviation of India's poverty and the raising of living standards. As a result the initiative was largely inconsequential for the improvement of the relations between the two countries and furthered the acrimonious exchange of statements which definitely did not help to raise the relationship bar between the two nations.

This existing divergence in the relationship was further deepened and crystallized by the Suez Canal crisis and the crisis invariably mirrored in the bilateral relationship between India and Australia in the same proportion if not more. The Suez canal was opened up for operations in 1869 and was being operated by the Universal Company of the Suez Maritime Canal, an Egyptian chartered company, with the area surrounding the canal being retained as sovereign Egyptian territory. The only land-bridge between Africa and Asia, its strategic importance was not lost on strategic planners. When the United Kingdom invaded and occupied Egypt in 1882, the control, operations and finances of the canal came under her jurisdiction. The 1888, Convention of Constantinople had declared the canal as a neutral zone, under the British protection. The huge and untapped economic potential of the Middle East coupled with its vast oil reserves, and increasing geo strategic importance of Suez Canal, was not lost to the Britain and Britain initiated steps to consolidate and strengthen its position in the region. Perturbed by these designs, the then Egyptian government in 1951 had unilaterally abrogated the Anglo-Egyptian Treaty of 1936, the terms of which had granted Britain a lease on the Suez base for 20 more years. Banking upon the huge presence of British troops in the country and citing historical treaty rights, Britain refused to withdraw from Suez. As a last straw to the culmination of events, President Nasser of Egypt nationalized the Suez Canal on 26 Jul 1956. He announced that the Nationalization Law had been published, that all assets of the Suez Canal Company had been frozen, and that stockholders would be paid the price of their shares according to the day's closing price on the Paris Stock Exchange.[49]

The British government decided in favor of military intervention against Egypt to avoid the complete collapse of British prestige and interests in the region and the British actions were strongly supported by Australia, being the closest ally of the British. "It's apparently not fashionable to talk of prestige, yet the fact remains that peace in the world and the whole authority of the Charter of the United Nations alike require that the British Commonwealth and in particular its greatest and most experienced member, the United Kingdom, should retain power, prestige and moral influence."[50] The twenty two nation London conference, which was held to defuse the crisis, chose Australia to chair a committee representing western interests in resolving the crisis through a proposal. Australia, on the other hand continued to support the option of military intervention in the crisis by an Anglo French alliance. The negotiations led by Australia however failed as the then US President ruled out any military intervention to resolve the crisis. "It is all very well for people to denounce the idea of force, but in a negotiation of this kind, it is good sense to keep the other man guessing."[51] Australia, in spite of a strong opposition at home continued to support the British policies of a military intervention. "An open canal is essential to the British prosperity; a closed canal could mean mass unemployment in Great Britain, a financial collapse there, a grievous blow at the central power of our Commonwealth."[52]

The unilateral decision of the Egyptian government to nationalize the canal though was responsible for the precipitation of the crisis; India supported the decision of Egypt. "The Egyptian nationalization decision was precipitated by the Aswan Dam decision of the United States government in which the United Kingdom government later joined. More than the decision, the way it was done, hurt Egypt's pride and self respect and disregarded a people's sentiments."[53] India condemned the Anglo-French plan of invasion in the strongest terms possible. "The French and the United Kingdom Governments reacted to the Egyptian announcement quickly, sharply and with vehemence. The military and naval movements ordered by French and the United Kingdom governments and some military measures in Egypt have aggravated the situation."[54] India and Egypt were on very friendly terms with each other and the aggravation of security situation in the region was of great concern to India. "India is passionately interested in averting a conflict. She is in friendly relations with Egypt, and associated with her in the acceptance of the Bandung Declarations and the Five Principles."[55] The unilateral aggression being planned by the western alliance was not approved by India. "I cannot think of a grosser case of naked aggression than what England and France are attempting to do."[56]

The expansionist and imperialistic mind set of the British was considered responsible by India for the crisis. The crisis had threatened interests of India in the region and there was a need to resolve the crisis at the earliest. Indian Prime Minister Nehru while responding to the crisis in an address to the lower house of the Indian Parliament in September 1956 had justified the need for the negotiations. "At the conference held in London we pleaded… for steps to be taken to bring about negotiations, and certain broad proposals were laid out by us."[57] The proposals forwarded by India were dismissed by Australia by citing the reasoning that the proposed solutions were providing too much to Egypt. The proposals are "pious talk about peace... would give Nasser practically everything and which no self-respecting British Government could accept."[58]

India's neutral stance in the crisis and demand for an early resolution of the crisis was very well taken by the international community. But, the crisis left an indelible impression on the already wedged relations between India and Australia, though none of the country was a direct stakeholder in the crisis. Indian attitude to the Australian perspective on the crisis is best summed by Indian Foreign Affairs Minister, VK Krishna Menon in his statement. "British public opinion, Commonwealth public opinion, was almost entirely against the invasion... I say "almost" because Australian governmental opinion was an exception."[59]

The very fact that most of the Australian politicians and bureaucrats have had served in the colonial India as part of the British government, the possessive mind set imbibed during the colonial times, also sustained in the subsequent relationship between India and Australia. A considerable number of Australia's diplomats, moulded as such in British traditions, were disposed towards adopting a British approach in dealing with the sub-continent in general. The partition of India into dominions in 1947 had a major effect on the geo strategic dynamics of the region. When a large number of mercenaries duly supported by the nascent Pakistan army raided Kashmir and occupied large swathes of territory in 1947-48, Justice Owen Dixon from Australia was appointed by the United Nations Security Council (UNSC) as a mediator to resolve the issue. India, on its part had hoped that a neutral stance will be adopted by the mediator and the case will be adjudged in a pure objective manner. The intricacy and complicity of Pakistan with the whole invasion plan for Kashmir, however was overlooked by Australia, an aspect which severely perturbed Indian sensibilities. "As the party in possession of the larger and the more desirable part of Kashmir, India has had more to gain than Pakistan by the postponement of a formal settlement."[60] Australian polity of the time also had tried to link the under development of India with the arms race in which India was engaged with Pakistan. The compulsions of India in lifting of millions of its citizens from the clutches of poverty and hunger after centuries of colonialism and simultaneously dealing with misadventures of Pakistan were not sympathetically considered by Australia. "In spite of the depression and squalor and misery of the underfed people in India, this country is spending a large proportion of its income on defence because it cannot come to terms with Pakistan about Kashmir."[61]

India, while strongly reacting to the Australian comments, did not agree to the aspersions of Australia on the issue. "While that [Pakistan's occupation] continues, we are asked repeatedly by some Western powers to make it up with Pakistan, to agree to what Pakistan says, or to agree to a plebiscite."[62] The communications from Australian diplomats of the time to Canberra are also highly suggestive of Australia's open bias towards Pakistan. "Based on Australian diplomatic communications, the discussion to this stage would suggest that a less belligerent India, prepared to seek democratic approaches to the conflict, was given relatively less recognition by Australia's diplomats in their on-the-ground assessments of the Kashmir question."[63]Australia's insensitivity to Indian concerns on the Kashmir issue, whether by default or design played a dominant role in the discordant relationship and coupled with the repeated statements by the Australian polity, underscored its interest in Pakistan and no deliberate attempt was made to address the concerns of India on the issue.

In another issue of dissonance, the membership of South East Asian Treaty Organisation (SEATO) by Pakistan had brought super power rivalry at India's door steps, much against her consternation and with the type of the independent foreign policy being followed by her; India was not very comfortable by the turn of the events. "The main object of the Manila Treaty is to divide Asia, is to encourage dissensions among the Asiatic Powers. It is a direct reply to the recent upsurge of Asian nationalism. It is merely an eye-wash to attract the Asiatic nations to come into the grip of Manila Treaty."[64] The objections of India to the provisions of the treaty related to the resurgence of colonialism in the region and the tendency of certain countries to use the treaty for the vested interests. "These treaties, especially the South East Asia Treaty, take the shape of certain colonial powers, not colonial in themselves but interested in colonialism and certain associated countries trying to decide or control the fate of this great area of South-East Asia."[65]

Australia on the other hand was too much pre occupied with the looming threats of communism and with the very premise of the treaty being based upon the concept of provisioning of military enhancement of the member nations, both for individual as well as collective security, her stand was in direct contrast with the declared position of India on the subject. "It is of immense importance to us that the free countries of South-East Asia should not fall one by one to Communist aggression. Security in the area must, therefore, be a collective concept. We believe that participation in regional arrangements for collective defence is the most effective method of securing the safety of Australia and the other countries who are parties to these arrangements. Such participation also provides the best means of coordinating our defence policy and planning with that of our allies. We cannot stand alone; and therefore we stand in good company in SEATO, ANZUS and in ANZAM."[66]

The provisions of collective and individual security in the treaty were very likely to be misutilised by Pakistan and would have provided an undue strategic advantage to it. India was very apprehensive of this particular aspect of the treaty as it had the potential to tilt the conventional balance in the favour of Pakistan. "Instead of going out, Pakistan has entrenched itself. In the name, perhaps, of fighting communism, Pakistan has got enormous aid from the U.S.A.; and it may be getting from the Baghdad Pact or SEATO. I should like our friends concerned to realize how by some of their policies of military alliances and military aid they have added, to the burdens of India a feeling of insecurity."[67]

Australia's membership of SEATO and its resultant commitment to the cause of the pact did not at all help the cause of relationship with India. Australia on its part had justified the provisions of treaty and had attempted to delink the pact from the security concerns of India. "The association of the massive power of the United States with the regional arrangements I have referred to, and her assurances of support in the event of Communist aggression, are vital factors in maintaining security in this part of the world. "Means of continuous and effective self help and mutual aid will maintain and develop their individual and collective capacity to resist armed attack and not one of us can avoid the Treaty obligations by making our performance dependent upon the action of any other Party."[68] Australia of the time had her own compulsions for the treaty like SEATO and did not want the provisions of the treaty to be diluted for anyone. The defence and security of Australia was connected with the treaty. "The truth is that SEATO is a military organization created for the defence of Australia. Is only Russia to be allowed to have agreements, such as the Warsaw pact? A weakening of the SEATO pact would mean a weakening of the defence of Australia."[69]

India was against any type of interference in its internal affairs by another country or a group of countries. India had drawn attention of the world towards the SEATO's stated objective of defence against outside aggression and internal subversion. "The declared purpose of the South East Asia Treaty is to increase the defensive strength of the parties to the treaty against aggression from outside and against internal subversion. How the question of Kashmir could come within the scope of the SEATO Council is not clear to us. Its reference to Kashmir could only mean that a military alliance is backing one country, namely, Pakistan, in its disputes with India. For any organisation to in this way to the detriment of a country, which is friendly to the individual countries comprised in the organisation, would, at any time be considered an impropriety."[70] The apparent closeness and convergence of interests between India with the erstwhile USSR bloc was also a cause of concern between India and Australian polity of the time. The drift of the relationship between Australia and India was complete as is evident from a communication from the Australian High Commissioner in New Delhi to the Australian Department of External Affairs. "One factor which has strengthened the USSR in India has been its support for India over Kashmir, in contrast with the American and particularly the British position, which was generally regarded here as pro-Pakistan."[71]

Apart from the military aid to Pakistan provisioned under the SEATO and other US led blocks, Australia in April 1990 concluded a bilateral contract with Pakistan to supply spares of Mirage aircraft, the mainstay of Pakistan Air Force (PAF). This was a time when the relationship between India and Pakistan was at its lowest ebb. The Kashmir issue was flaring up, raising concerns about the possibility of another war between the two neighbours. The US, one of the staunchest allies of Pakistan of the time, taking due notice of Pakistan's complicity in the internal disturbances in Kashmir and the resultant flare up between India and Pakistan had also invoked a Presidential amendment to halt the supply of military hardware to Pakistan.

Australia on the other hand decided to continue with the proposed supply of military hardware to Pakistan. The proposed sale of 50 Mirage III aircraft, including spares and stores, for $36-million as against the asking price of $100 million, to Pakistan was opposed by India. "There is near unanimous acknowledgment that the timing has been poor or unfortunate. Further, that the sale does not send a message of restraint to Pakistan is also widely shared. What has, however, received insufficient attention is that the sale does not accord well with Australia's recently reiterated policy of promoting peace and stability in the region. It is also not conducive to healthy development of bilateral relations, which were gaining in content since Prime Minister Hawke's visit to India in February 1989."[72]

In spite of a strong opposition from India, the sale went ahead and was supplemented with an explicit advice to India to exercise restraint and caution. In fact, the Senate committee of Australian Parliament advised India to diffuse the concerns of Pakistan and had pointed that India has to work towards defusing the concerns of Pakistan. As per Australia, India needed to undertake proactive measures for the promotion of peace and reducing the arms race between it and Pakistan. Robert Ray, the then Australian Defence Minister, had strongly defended the sale despite questions about possible efforts by Pakistan to use the planes to deliver nuclear weapons. The sale of the fighters to Pakistan, much against the protests by India was flagged widely. "The most notable of these was the sale of 50 Mirage fighters to Pakistan in 1990, which raised two important issues. One, that had foreign policy considerations been given more weight, the almost derisory sum of money involved ($36 million) would surely not have been enough to win the argument in favour of the sale. The other was the Defence Department 's interpretation of the concepts of 'major military significance' and 'regions of instability."[73]The emergence of a controversial evidence that ex-RAAF Mirages were used by Pakistan to test its nascent cruise missiles, which were capable of carrying a nuclear payload, further distanced India and Australia from each other. The details of the missile test were published in an internet blog for the Lowy Institute for International Policy, The Interpreter, "There's a good chance that an aircraft sold by Australia is being used by Pakistan to improve and enlarge its nuclear arsenal."[74]

Among a host of issues responsible for divergences in India - Australia relations, nuclear issues also hold a definite and credible stake. These issues proved to be a pinnacle of the divergence between India and Australia. Retrospectively it will not be wrong to say that the divergences in the nuclear arena proved to be the highest point of differential between the two countries. The relationship between India and Australia touched its lowest ebb due to the differences between the two countries on the nuclear issues. The bilateral relationship worsened to such an extent that it couldn't have gone further down than this. The only way out for the relationship was to get better and better it did.

The provisions of Nuclear Non Proliferation Treaty (NPT) were signed by Australia in 1973 and she has been one of the most active proponents of the causes of the treaty. Australia has held the belief that the NPT provides the best instrument to prevent the further spread of nuclear weapons in the international system.[75] The ratification of the NPT, potential uranium 'boom', and aboriginal land rights had converged from 1972 onward to stimulate public debate on whether or not Australia should export uranium, and if so, on what basis?[76] In order to provide a justification for the decision making, Australian government had established a "Ranger Uranium Environmental Inquiry" in 1975 to find out environmental impact of proposals forwarded by the Australian Atomic Energy Commission and the mining and milling of uranium at the Ranger site. The report was supposed to give recommendations with respect to the three major elements of the uranium issue; the implications of the mining and export of uranium for the existing non-proliferation regime, the potential contribution of nuclear energy to world energy security and the economic potentialities of uranium mining.[77] Australia saw "nuclear weapons as a stabilizing force in international relations, provided they are wielded by systemic powers, that is, by those 'responsible' great powers, which shape the structure of the international system and have an interest in maintaining a stable global order."[78]

India, on the other hand as part of its Non Aligned Policy, was strongly in the favour of nuclear disarmament. India was the first country which had called for an end to all nuclear testing way back in 1954. Though India had reviewed her nuclear programme post 1962 war with China and Chinese embarkation on nuclear weaponisation programme in 1964, she continued to defend her goal of nuclear disarmament. Even after the conduct of nuclear test in 1974, in 1978 India had proposed negotiations for an international convention that would limit the threat of use of nuclear weapons. India from time to time has made public her serious reservations on the discriminatory nature of NPT and as a result has not signed the treaty till date citing the discriminatory provisions of the treaty. In 1998 at the third Special Session on Disarmament (SSOD III), the then Indian Prime Minister Rajiv Gandhi deliberated upon "a world free of nuclear weapons" and presented the Rajiv Gandhi Action Plan seeking a "binding commitment by all nations to eliminate nuclear weapons in stages, by the year 2010."[79]

India and Australia's bilateral relations suffered a severe setback when India conducted a series of nuclear tests in May 1998. Australia had serious observations to these nuclear tests and the conduct of these tests was going to shake the foundations of a nascent and a fragile relationship between the two countries. "We deplore and condemn absolutely what India has done. It is an irresponsible genuflection to transient domestic political popularity. And what the Indian Government has done is to play fast and loose with international safety and security in the interests of a short-term domestic political game. India's behaviour, of course, has gravely compromised her previous claims to exercise the role of an international moral policeman."[80] Australia, in a strong retaliation to Indian nuclear tests suspended all official visits, bilateral defence links and non-humanitarian aid to India. Australia strongly criticized Indian action and justified the NPT as the strongest bulwark against the nuclearisation of the world. "This morning at the meeting of the National Security Committee, the Government has decided to take a number of further steps to reinforce the point that India's behaviour is unacceptable to the international community and of necessity to Australia. The Government will suspend defence contacts with India and that will mean that our defence attaché will be withdrawn from New Delhi. We've also decided to go a step further and to suspend all non-humanitarian aid to India. An outrageous step perpetrated by India and NPT continues to remain the world's best defence against the spread of nuclear weapons."[81]

The growing strategic importance of India and the consequent massive potential of demographic and democratic profile, made US realize the importance of India in the region, which in 2005 decided to strengthen its bilateral relationship with India. As part of the process to normalise India's participation in international nuclear cooperation, the US undertook to seek an exemption from the NSG's comprehensive safeguards requirement, so as to allow nuclear supply to India and resulted in the conclusion of the US–India Nuclear Cooperation agreement of March 2006. Australian government though sticking to its stand of "No Nuclear Cooperation without NPT" was broadly in line with the logic provided by the US about the US-India Nuclear Cooperation. All these musings facilitated a slight change in the Australian mindset about India, "Even though, for once, the Indians struck a very sensitive Australian nerve, non-proliferation, the simple fact is that Australia stands to gain more from India than vice versa. So, having mounted our high horse, we must now look for a way to climb down in a reasonably face-saving manner. One popular solution to this sort of dilemma is to 'quarantine' the problem area in the relationship, to set it apart somehow so that both sides can get on with developing the rest of the relationship to their mutual advantage."[82]

Indo-US Nuclear Cooperation was followed by the Nuclear Suppliers Group (NSG) waiver to India in 2008 and India-specific safeguards by IAEA. This opened a new door for India in the nuclear commercial market dominated by the 48 member NSG that control around 80 per cent of world's uranium reserves. "Australia's decision to supply or not to supply uranium to India will have little material implications on India's access to uranium so long as India is granted access to the world market. Since Australia continues to sell in that market, it is not wise now on Australia's part both economically and diplomatically to deny uranium to India."[83] The leader of the Labour Party, Prime Minister Julia Gillard, in December 2011 at Australian Labour Party (ALP) National Conference succeeded in obtaining her party's vote to reverse the policy on the sale of uranium to India, though by a slim majority: 208 in favour and 185 against.[84]

After the independence of India and the general decline of British power, deep rooted compulsions of both India and Australia prevented development of close partnerships with each other. India opted for a policy of Non Alignment and resisted the temptations of aligning with the two predominant blocks of the time. Australia on its part also reconciled to the loss of global reach post World War II by the Britain and chose to align its security and economic interests with the emerging power of the US. Thus both India and Australia terminated their common connection with the Britain in the near immediate succession. The bilateral defence and strategic partnerships and alliance policy being followed by Australia with the particular reference to the US and independent foreign policy being pursued by India were mutually contradictory. Australia was too far from India and correspondingly the bilateral relationship did not get the due attention and significance. This indifference of each towards the other, developed over a period of time, has been so distinct and marked that, Standing Committee on Foreign Affairs of Australian Senate in 1990 had dismissed the probability of any relationship between the two countries, "Australia's areas of direct military interest, while encompassing the more proximate eastern part of the Indian Ocean do not overlap the areas in which India could be expected to exert strategic influence or maintain an effective maritime presence. India's military power is unlikely to have much effect outside the South Asian region."[85]

The involvement of extra regional powers in the region was diametrically opposed to the considered Indian stance on the neutrality and non involvement in the bloc politics. India, on its part, being busy with the nation building after independence and coupled with the non aligned foreign policy firmly in place, did not think of Australia as a friend let alone as strategic partner. The British decision to withdraw from its bases east of Suez, forced Australian polity to shift to the US based alliances in the region, but fell well short of a concrete Indian Ocean Region engagement policy. On the other hand, the initiatives and activities followed by India as part of her Look East Policy (LEP) reached out to the countries of South East Asia but also fell well short of Australia, leaving both countries estranged and unknown to each other.

Though both India and Australia have been dominant regional powers, operating in the Indian and Pacific oceans respectively, the realisation of their mutual interests being interwoven and intertwined have only been facilitated by the recent rise of the geographical construct of Indo Pacific. The construct initially associated with marine sciences, graduated to the economic parlance and off late has achieved geo political significance. The rise and realisation of the significance of the construct has made India and Australia to come together. The major contribution of the construct to the relationship has been that both countries have started seeing each other as a security and strategic partner. The India Australian bilateral relationship, held hostage to a large number of issues has turned a corner and the geo political construct of Indo Pacific has started providing the necessary traction to the relationship.

CHAPTER 2

INDO PACIFIC: CONVERGING DEFENCE & DIPLOMATIC COMPULSIONS

"Spanning the Indian Ocean through to the western Pacific Ocean, Indo-Pacific emphasises the growing significance of this geographic corridor and of India."[86]

Indian Ocean Region (IOR) has historically been considered as the cradle of maritime civilization. The region has been instrumental in facilitating the maritime highway, linking numerous cultures and civilizations which took birth and flourished along this region. The zone has been acting as a modicum for movement of men and material since times immemorial, having raised and flourished a large number of civilisations, a great number of them having been obliterated over a period of time. The domination of Asian landmass by the Persians, Greeks, Romans in the medieval period and Dutch, French, Portuguese and English in the modern period has also been made possible only through their forays into this ocean.

Not just identical in the names, India and Indian Ocean have been central to each other's existence since times immemorial. This regional centrality of India in IOR has been stressed upon by many thinkers and writers in the Indian history, which actually has manifested and can be seen in reality. "The vital feature which differentiates the Indian Ocean from the Atlantic or the Pacific is the sub-continent of India, which juts out far into the sea for a thousand miles. It is the geographical position of India that changes the character of the Indian Ocean."[87] The Ocean has always stayed in prominent public consciousness and has continued to demonstrate its strategic significance for India. Post independence, India was not able to assume its rightful place in the region primarily due to inward looking policies of Non Alignment and also up to some extent due to relatively unrealized security and economic potential of the country. Historically also, India has been considered more of a continental power, with strategic and security interests having been concentrated in its North and West. Past seventy years history of independent India has been witness to this continental mindset of India.

But, the significance of having occupied a central and important position in the Indian Ocean region has always been lurking in the backdrop of Indian strategic interests and has exerted a very important and profound influence on security and defence related issues of Indian subcontinent. "The IOR is vital to India's security and prosperity. As a maritime nation historically and by virtue of its geo-physical configuration and geopolitical circumstances, India is dependent on the oceans surrounding it."[88] The strategic and economic import of the geographic centrality of the Indian peninsula, in the Indian Ocean has raised awareness and the need to physically dominate the entire northern Indian Ocean. "While to other countries the Indian Ocean is only one of the important oceanic areas, to India it is a vital sea. Her lifelines are concentrated in that area, her freedom is dependent on the freedom of that water surface. No industrial development, no commercial growth, no stable political structure is possible for her unless her shores are protected."[89]

The slow but steady evolution and implementation of maritime strategy by India has ensured that Indian Ocean has retained its pivotal position in facilitating the expansion and extension of India's strategic influence in the region. The geographical centrality of the country has offered India a natural role of a great power in the region. With the centrality of India in the Indian Ocean having been re-established, it is evident that all events occurring within this geographical space affect her strategic and economic interests. As an extension of strategic importance of region for her, India is currently also acting as a security provider to, and even a security guarantor of, several smaller islands in the region.[90] Interests and concerns of India are not restricted to one sub region only, but spans various sub regions of IOR, thereby entitling her a very unique and singular position in the geopolitics of IOR. "India and the Indian Ocean are inseparable. In the midst of the third largest ocean in the world, India's location is in many ways her destiny. That is not just a statement regarding a fact of geography but of deeper civilizational, historical, cultural, economic and political linkages that have been forged between India and the Ocean that bears its name. Apart from the Monsoon, the India-link, in its broadest sense, is the single common thread that is visible in the Indian Ocean region."[91]

As part of the same region of larger Indian Ocean, India and Southeast Asia share a vibrant and historic past. Land and maritime connectivity between these two regions is of historical significance and has led to extensive influence of Indian culture in the region. "These relations were affected by India's turbulent history of invasions and the advent of British colonizers, but until then the interface was entirely peaceful and willingly accepted and adapted by Southeast Asia."[92] After independence, as India toyed with the idea and policy of Non Alignment, it was gradually realized that the initiative was not fitting in the overall scheme of things for effecting regional security architecture, as most of the countries were already aligned with some or the other bloc, in the form of security treaties and organisations. This fixation with the idea of non alignment, though principally evolved with good underlying intentions ensured that during the entire period of Cold War, India's foreign policy was de-coupled from South East Asia, lest she be alleged for taking sides in an intensely divided region. In keeping with the stated policy of Non Alignment, India's political emphasis therefore metamorphosed into multilateral arrangements. "But the obsession with the multilateral initiatives inevitably diluted the inheritance from British Raj, which was at the heart of the imperial defense system in the entire Indian Ocean littoral."[93] When at the termination of Cold War, India began to reorient its foreign policy in tandem with the changed world order, the realisation of age old notion of 'extended neighborhood' in Asia and Indian Ocean region was imperative. With strong historical, cultural and religious affinities already in place, the strategic planners of the time found this to be an ideal opportunity for transforming Indian foreign policy.

In this series of transformations, the first regional initiative was towards Southeast Asia, and was called the 'Look East' policy. The implementation of this policy allowed India to be a part of the region's new economic up-gradation and at the same time conceded it to mend the disturbed relations of cold war era with the neighborhood. As on date India's Look East policy (LEP) has become a cornerstone and a deeply entrenched component of its external relations. Its engagement with South East Asia offered India, a model for sustained globalization at a time when apprehensions were being raised on the viability of the economic reforms in the country. "I must pay tribute to our East and Southeast Asian neighbours for shaping our own thinking on globalisation and the means to deal with it ... in 1992 our Government launched India's "Look East" policy. This was not merely an external economic policy; it was also a strategic shift in India's vision of the world and India's place in the evolving global economy. Most of all it was about reaching out to our civilisational Asian neighbours."[94]

The second phase of the policy, an up-gradation of the existing policy, was aptly named as Act East Policy (AEP). While in the first phase of the LEP, the emphasis was on political, diplomatic and people to people relationships, improved connectivity and enhanced trade, the second phase revolved around strengthening of economic relations, defence and security cooperation besides strengthening relationships in other areas.[95] As part of AEP, India has endeavored to step up its engagements with the region and beyond even in the aspects which till recently were considered as sacrosanct as far as bilateral relations were considered. This was a paradigm shift in the foreign policy engagements of India which has facilitated India to regain and reclaim its rightful place in the region.

In the earlier nineties, though, India's LEP enlarged its strategic focus from its own immediate neighbourhood to embrace and encompass East and Southeast Asia, Japan and even South Korea, but had stopped tantalizingly short of South Pacific region as historically, these South Pacific island states have not featured in Indian foreign policy discourse and sporadic and erratic interaction was limited to the major South Pacific powers of Australia and New Zealand.[96] In its reinvigorated avatar of LEP, India has endeavored to amend this flaw and in Phase II of this policy, the AEP; it has actively sought to engage with the South Pacific region in general and Australia in particular. Invocation of India's AEP has imparted necessary impetus and greater dynamism in its relations with countries to its east. It is a significant initiative, which is contributing towards development of mutual contacts and greater understanding of each other in the region. The policy has definitely provided great dividends and greater relevance to India in the global geostrategic space in general and IOR in particular. As a result, India's political, strategic, security, economic, commercial, cultural and people-to-people relations with Pacific countries have expanded, thereby providing India with an opportunity to play its rightful role in the emerging construct of Indo Pacific.

This emerging geo strategic construct of Indo Pacific has been accepted as a distinct bio geographic region in marine science for long and possesses a distinguished standing in the marine and biological studies. Earliest recordable reference to the term, in the context other than marine or biological sciences, can be attributed to the Singapore-based Australian journalist and analyst Michael Richardson who in 2005 had related East Asian Summit (EAS) with the Indo Pacific. "The nascent East Asia Summit could be the emerging capstone for an Indo-Pacific order."[97] Though the basis of coining the origins of this new Indo-Pacific terminology has primarily been related to the economic imperatives and necessities only, however, the consequences of this convergence have immense strategic implications and the management of these implications is correspondingly very complex. In geopolitics, the term is relatively recent phenomenon and the traction gathered in security and geo political realms has also been not very old. The term 'Indo-Pacific' broadly refers to the Indian Ocean and Pacific Oceans and specifically alludes to the mixed and intertwined waters of the East Indian Ocean and Western Pacific Ocean with the South China Sea as an intervening stretch. The increased strategic significance of the region has also yielded an increase in the literature on the subject. An article in the Australian Defence Forces Journal alluded to the emerging concept by defining the limits of the region. "Indo-Pacific is the entire area of the combined Indian and Pacific Oceans and their littoral nation states."[98]

The existing centrality of India in the IOR has rendered India, a quantum push in the emerging realms of Indo Pacific, making her a strategic centre of gravity. This has correspondingly brought with it associated ramifications for India's regional security as well as for India's strategic relationships, both bilateral and multilateral within the region. The strategic calculations, permutations and combinations are manifesting themselves like never before in the region and India finds herself at the cusps of massive geo strategic realignments, ranging from multilaterals to minilateral and bilateral associations. This centrality of India in the affairs of the region; be it existing IOR or emerging Indo Pacific was never lost to her leaders. India's first Prime Minister Jawaharlal Nehru indeed had some realistic premonitions about the emerging concept. "The Pacific is likely to take the place of the Atlantic in the future as a nerve centre of the world. Though not directly a Pacific state, India will inevitably exercise an important influence there. India will also develop as the centre of economic and political activity in the Indian Ocean area, in South-East Asia and right up to the Middle East. Her position gives an economic and strategic importance in a part of the world, which is going to develop rapidly in the future."[99]

As observed in the first chapter, both India and Australia have operated in largely separate strategic spheres for the greater part of their independent history. India has largely been preoccupied with in its immediate neighbourhood, while Australia had always considered Asia Pacific as its backyard and area of immediate concern. Australia was satisfied with its strategic gaze being confined towards its north and maximum till Southeast Asia, with the Indian Ocean having been restricted to a large and unknown black spot in distant horizon. The strategic alliances with the US have taken care of Australia's security issues in the region and IOR was not considered strategically important. This imbalance in the strategic priorities of Australia, with over emphasis on an outside power and a total neglect of resident powers was also questioned by the strategic community of the country. Writing in 1949, J. Gentilli had raised questions about Australia's connections with Pacific. "Australia must therefore realize that 300,000,000 Indians now constitute the nuclei of future political and economic developments in the Indian Ocean. Australia is nearer to them than to anyone else, and no one else is likely to intervene between her and her neighbours. Australia's geopolitical situation is at the crossroads of the Indian and Pacific Oceans, but with a crowded part of the Indian Ocean and an empty part of the Pacific Ocean close at hand, is it possible to ignore the crowds and to turn to an empty space?"[100]

In the contemporary times, the enthusiasm about India's phenomenal rise, both as an economic and military power, coupled with the firming up of the concept of Indo Pacific has found resonance and traction in Australia. The centrality of India in the IOR and now Indo Pacific has also been duly acknowledged. Identifying India as a key country, the report of the Senate Foreign Affairs, Defence and Trade References Committee Report of Australian Parliament, endorsed the centrality of India in the region. "On regional basis, the countries of the Indian Ocean region can be understood to include established and readily understood sub-regions (for example the Gulf countries), geographic areas (African countries are often referred to collectively as simply Africa) or key countries (for example India). There can be little doubt that Australia should be giving greater attention to the Indian Ocean."[101] On the other side, the economic and military rise along with the necessary changes in the foreign policy is catering for confidence for India to take additional responsibilities in Indian Ocean security and also a greater interest in erstwhile Asia Pacific and contemporary Indo Pacific order. Post Cold War realities have also forced Australia to concentrate on the region and evolve new bilateral and multilateral engagements in the region. "Asia that Australia needs to engage, economically, societally and strategically, is no longer limited to the Southeast Asia, Japan, and Korea of the 1970s, 80s and 90s, or the China of the 90s and early 2000s; it is also South Asia but especially India, now a major trading partner, substantial investor, growing military power and diplomatic player, the source of one of our largest skilled migrant communities, and a major relationship with vast potential for further growth."[102]

The recognition that, beyond bilateral trade as a driver of stability, some independent Australian thinking on Indian Ocean policy is desirable, has led to a progressive shift in the geostrategic orientation and alignment priorities for Australian strategists and polity. Strategic discussions apart, importance of a region/country for another country can be ascertained from institutionalization of these discourses. Formal Defence White Papers (DWP) released by Australia provides an insight into the growing importance of region for Australia. An analysis of all the DWPs released by Australia, since 1976 reveals an increased frequency of India and Indo Pacific in the discussions about defence of Australia. Starting 1976, as the time has progressed other White Papers with some focus on the Indian Ocean followed, and the intervening and subsequent years also witnessed the baton of policy discussions being picked up by scholars and strategists in the lead -up to the formation of the IOR -ARC in 1997, adding depth to iterations of Australia's "look West" policies.[103] India/Indian Ocean were mentioned three times in Australian Government DWP of 1976, whereas the same is mentioned 51 times in DWP of 2016, thereby hinting at the growing importance, both economic and strategic for Australia. As India and Australia started to move beyond zero in the 21st century, Australian strategic consideration of India rose dramatically, especially as the Australian Defence Department embraced the concept of the Indo-Pacific instead of the Asia Pacific.

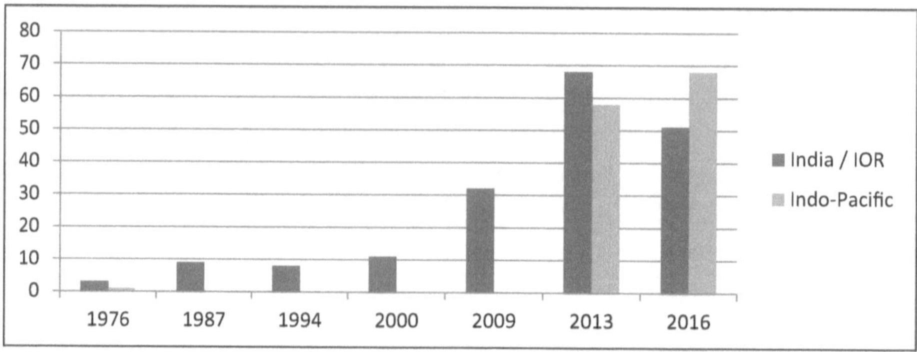

Fig 1: Increasing importance of India & Indo Pacific in Australian Strategic Discourse

As the importance of the emerging region of Indo Pacific increases, there is a corresponding increase in the realization of the potential of India as a strong mutual partner. "The shift of power to the Indo-Pacific is leading to increased growth, wealth and prosperity among regional states. By 2050, almost half of the world's economic output is expected to come from the Indo Pacific, and this region will be home to four of the world's top ten economies. Australia's top five trade partners are all in the Indo-Pacific, and approximately 98% of our international trade by volume travels by sea and more than half of that through the South China Sea."[104]

The Defence Strategic update 2020, released by the Department of Defence, Government of Australia has highlighted the success of bilateral defence cooperation between India and Australia in minilateral and multilateral settings, a crucial aspect of the relationship which has been discussed slightly later in the chapter. As a follow-up to the 2016 Defence White Paper, the update has attributed the transformation of Australian Defence Force (ADF) into a more capable, agile and potent force, to the uninterrupted focus on strengthened international engagement, particularly with the United States, Japan, India and Association of South East Asian Nations (ASEAN).[105] The contours of emerging strategic rapprochement between India and the United States has also facilitated broad alignment of Indian policies with those of the US allies and as the US rebalances towards East Asia, Australia as an important US strategic partner has found it to be playing an active security role in the emerging construct of Indo Pacific. "Australia's immediate region is also the area in which we should be most capable of military cooperation with the United States. Australia is a staunch and active ally of the United States, which continues to underwrite the security and stability of the Indo-Pacific. We will continue working with the United States to build defence cooperation in the region to meet security challenges - such as the ongoing threat from terrorism - and to build common approaches to ensure stability in our region. It also includes responding to natural disasters. Should circumstances require it; this is also the region in which Australia needs to be capable of leading military operations."[106] India, therefore has attained a very central and crucial role in the Australian calculations of the strategic matrix in the broader sense of Indian Ocean, Southeast Asia and the Pacific and in particular Indo Pacific. "India's rise as a world power is at the forefront of Australia's foreign and strategic policy, as is the need to preserve maritime security in the Indian Ocean. India and Australia, with the two most significant and advanced navies of the Indian Ocean rim countries, are natural security partners in the Indo-Pacific region".[107]

Both India and Australia have made considerable efforts to develop a comprehensive strategic relationship between the two nations. This rapid and exponential increase in the engagements at political and diplomatic levels has also facilitated a full spectrum utilization of Military Diplomacy by India. Coupled with this the mercurial economic prowess of India and the evolution of 'Asianist' orientation of Australia, the strategic perceptions and dynamics of both the nations are rising to new and hither to fore new levels.[108] The strategic interests of both the countries in the traditional military domain are aligning and are getting increasingly and 'essentially congruent' with a significant scope for bilateral security cooperation, leading to the Comprehensive Security Partnership declaration of 2020. India also sees massive latent potential for a maritime security partnership between India and Australia that spans the entire Indo-Pacific. Keeping their respective strategic autonomies yet cooperating within the framework of established minilateral and multilateral institutions, the bilateral relationship between India and Australia is singular and unique. These sentiments were echoed by the Indian Prime Minister during his address to the Australian Parliament. "India and Australia can play their part in the region by expanding our security cooperation and deepening our international partnerships in the region. We do not have to rely on borrowed architecture of the past, we should collaborate more on maintaining maritime security. We should work together on the seas and collaborate in international forums. We should coordinate more closely in EAS, G20 and Indian Ocean Region

Association."[109] India has closely co-operated with Australia in numerous multilateral matrices which has assisted both countries in furthering their bilateral relationship. The trend of multilateral relationship transforming into a number of minilaterals, which has further strengthened the bilateral relationship, has been an exclusive characteristic of this relationship. The initiation of LEP by India and its transformation into AEP has facilitated India's entry into the multilateral organisations of the region, in which Australia was already playing a major role.

India correctly identified Southeast Asia as a cornerstone of its foreign policy when it started looking outwards, for economic reasons initially, with security and strategic reasons getting enmeshed into the policy subsequently. The ASEAN was a natural stepping stone for India to reach out to its civilisational neighbours. "I must pay tribute to our East and Southeast Asian neighbours for shaping our own thinking on globalisation and the means to deal with it ... in 1992 our Government launched India's 'Look East' policy. This was not merely an external economic policy; it was also a strategic shift in India's vision of the world and India's place in the evolving global economy. Most of all it was about reaching out to our civilisational Asian neighbours."[110]

Bilateralism in Multilateral Settings

Southeast Asia has also been a primary strategic and economic focus for Australia for many decades and the possibility of the Southeast Asian archipelago being used as likely route by extra-regional powers to pose a serious security threat to Australia, has been considered by policy planners in the country. In the aftermath of World War II, Australia made 'Forward Defence Concept' as a cornerstone of its security policy in Southeast Asia.[111] When in 1967, the foreign ministers of five Southeast nations of Indonesia, Malaysia, the Philippines, Singapore and Thailand signed the Bangkok Declaration for the formation of ASEAN, Australia also realized the importance and significance of shifting the focus inwards to the regional cooperation and became the first formal dialogue partner of ASEAN in 1974. ASEAN has provided Australia rich dividends in economy and security calculations. "It has helped transform a region that was full of strategic tensions and problems into the peaceful and prosperous region it is today."[112]

Both India and Australia being dialogue partners of this important forum in the region, have closely cooperated along with 10 nation ASEAN bloc on various issues of mutual concerns, rule based conventions and nontraditional security threats, which has transformed their bilateral relationship to the newer levels. "As they grow and take on new roles, it is inevitable that China, India and Japan will all loom larger on each other's radar screens. And since East Asian integration will be loosely multi polar, the jostling between New Delhi, Beijing and Tokyo that will certainly ensue must be squarely confronted and cannot be wished away. However, competition need not lead to conflict, if it can be managed within an agreed framework. This, for example, was the original, and remains the essential, raison d'être of ASEAN."[113] Though this aspect has now been relegated to history, but even in the contemporary times the importance of ASEAN for both India and Australia has not compressed, but on the contrary has expanded. Australia is a steadfast supporter of ASEAN's central role in facilitating regional security dialogue and cooperation and plays an active role in the ASEAN Defence Ministers' Meeting Plus to drive practical defence cooperation between regional countries.[114]

ASEAN is also live to the growing geo strategic reality of Indo Pacific and has accordingly made some adjustments in its outlook towards the region. In order to reinforce ASEAN-centered regional architecture, the grouping has come up with the ASEAN Outlook on the Indo-Pacific. ASEAN Outlook on the Indo-Pacific involves the further strengthening and optimization of ASEAN-led mechanisms, including the East Asia Summit, the ASEAN Regional Forum, the ASEAN Defence Ministers Meeting Plus, the Expanded ASEAN Maritime Forum (EAMF) and others such as the relevant ASEAN plus one mechanism.[115] ASEAN holds tremendous economic and strategic significance for India. Outreach of India to Australia has been made possible only through the South-east Asia in which ASEAN has acted as a spring board. It is therefore natural for India to consider ASEAN as such. "South East is our neighbour by land and sea. With each Southeast Asian country, we have growing political, economic and defence ties. With ASEAN, from dialogue partners, we have become strategic partners over the course of 25 years. We pursue our relations through annual summits and 30 dialogue mechanisms, but even more through a shared vision for the region, and the comfort and familiarity of our old links."[116]

Like ASEAN, ASEAN Regional Forum (ARF) is another forum, where bilateral relationship between India and Australia is playing an important role. As a result of deliberations in the ASEAN Post Ministerial Conference between the Foreign Ministers of ASEAN and its full dialogue partners, the ARF came into being in 1993. Complementing the various bilateral alliances and dialogues, ARF is a key forum for security dialogue in Asia and "provides a setting in which members can discuss current regional security issues and develop cooperative measures to enhance peace and security in the region."[117] As per mandated charter, the forum supplants three stage processes, to facilitate its mandated task of tackling security related issues; confidence building measures, development of preventive diplomacy and elaboration of approaches to conflicts.

The importance of platform of multilateral organizations cannot be negated as besides having advantages at their respective levels they also facilitate cementing of bonds at the bilateral levels. India and Australia have maintained an excellent track record of coordination and cooperation in multilateral mechanism of ARF. Continuous and fruitful interaction at the multilateral level has supported the efforts to foster the spirit of cooperation, so essential at the bilateral level. The ARF has been instrumental in providing a forum for constructive dialogue on political and security cooperation between the two countries while operating in a multilateral setting. The structured mechanism mandated for the functioning of ARF has provided an ideal opportunity for both countries to enhance their bilateral cooperation. The three tiered process of ARF machinations to include Track I, Track I ½ (involving scholars and officials from member states acting in their respective personal capacities) and Track-II (platform for academics, scholars, researchers to interact in their private capacities) has facilitated the bilateral partnership.

East Asia Summit (EAS) is another very significant forum, participation in which has propelled the bilateral relationship between India and Australia to a higher and mutually exclusive pedestal. EAS owes its origins to the East Asian Economic Group (EAEG), an idea propounded by the then Malaysian Prime Minister Mohammad Mahathir in December 1990. The proposal did not receive the unanimous support, primarily on "fears that the proposal would exacerbate trade friction with the US, their largest single market."[118] The currency crisis of 1997 facilitated the revival of the concept and two separate groups were formulated by Asia Pacific Economic Forum (APEC) to recommend measures to revive the economy of the region, by institutionalization of East Asian Cooperation and the setting up of an East Asian Forum.

Due to a strong opposition by Malaysia and on the grounds of it not being part of Asia, Australia was not initially included in the membership of the forum. "There may be a time perhaps when Australia is so identified with Asia that we have to accept it as an east-Asian nation, but at the moment, Australia forms a continent on its own: the continent of Australasia, so obviously it is not of East Asia."[119] Australia, taking strong umbrage on the Malaysian stand on the Australian membership, reiterated that Australia had never claimed to be part of Asia. "We've never said we're going to be a part of Asia, but we're linked with Asia as never before, both economically and security wise."[120] India, on its part has been a strong proponent of Asian unity and cooperation and has advocated the concept of Asian solidarity to facilitate and raise the consciousness about Asia and forge regional unity and solidarity. The rich historical legacy for Asian integration possessed by India was subsumed by the imperatives of cold war and inward looking off shoots of NAM. During the deliberations for expansion of EAS, China favoured restricting the membership of EAS, maximum up to ASEAN plus Three, whereas countries like Singapore, Indonesia and Japan had insisted further expansion of the group to include India and Australia. As a result the proposed membership expansion was made contingent upon proposed member's accretion to ASEAN Treaty of Amity and Cooperation (TAC). "It further legislated that prospective member must have substantive relationship with ASEAN and must be in possession of the status of ASEAN dialogue partner".[121]

The TAC in Southeast Asia, first signed on 24 February 1976 by the members of ASEAN, traced its origins to the Bandung Conference of 1955. Since the proposed treaty was broadly aligned to the concept of non-interference; a bed rock of Indian foreign policy, India, therefore did not have any reservations in signing the accession and the treaty was signed by India on 08 October 2003. Australia, on the other hand was not in favour of this 'norm setting' as it challenged Australia in terms of its alliance responsibilities towards the United States. "First of all, in its [the TAC's] preamble it talks about the Bandung principles. Australia has never been a supporter of the Bandung principles in the sense that we are not a member of the non-aligned movement, we never have been and under this government we will not be."[122] Though later on Australia acceded to the treaty and became member of the extended EAS, but subject to the conditions that its "signing the Treaty of Amity and Cooperation would not affect its 'existing security arrangements', Australia's obligations and rights under the UN Charter and Australia's relations with the countries other than members of ASEAN."[123]

The growing convergence between India and Australia in the Southeast Asian region and the subsequent amalgamation of Indian and Pacific Oceans into Indo Pacific has also facilitated both the countries to work in parallel terms, if not necessarily together to promote the development of open, inclusive and balanced regional groupings in East Asia and also to secure their respective national core interests. The leaders of both the countries, over a period of time have reiterated their commitment to working together to strengthen the East Asia Summit (EAS), the premier regional forum for leader-led strategic dialogue and addressing strategic, political and economic issues. During the state visit of the Australian Prime Minister to India in 2017, both countries reaffirmed that building cooperative maritime partnerships should be a priority area for EAS engagement.[124] Both India and Australia have been cooperating on the issues of protection of marine resources, prevention of environmental degradation and tapping the potential of the blue economy, under the EAS framework.

India has organized a series of conferences on Maritime Security and Cooperation, with the first one being held at New Delhi in 2015. As part of joint commitment towards maritime security and safety and Indo Pacific Oceans Initiative (IPOI), India and Australia, organised the Fourth EAS Conference on Maritime Security Cooperation in February 2020 in Chennai. "The IPOI is an inclusive and open initiative, seeking to better manage, conserve, sustain and secure the maritime domain. It does not envisage creating a new institutional framework and will rely on ASEAN led EAS framework, though not necessarily limited to it."[125] The emerging geostrategic concept of Indo-Pacific therefore has particular significance for India's and Australia's potential role in Southeast Asia and hints at broad convergence of interests between these two nations in the region. As part of IPOI both India and Australia are collaborating in all the seven mandated pillars of the initiative and have planned to host a conference on combating Marine Pollution & Marine Plastic Debris which will bring together many countries of the region next year.[126] By joining together in Southeast Asia, India and Australia are definitely poised for a greater role in the new Indo Pacific region in which both of them have shared economic, geo strategic and geo political interests. India and Australia have been cooperating very closely on the sidelines of another multilateral initiative of ASEAN Defence Ministers' Meeting (ADMM-Plus). This multilateral was launched in October 2010 and comprises of the Defence Ministers of 10 ASEAN member states and Dialogue Partners. The new entity of ADMM - Plus has extended the geographical reach of ASEAN based defence meetings to the Indo-Pacific and has incorporated India, Australia among other nations, with an explicit aim "to create a forum for 'transnational security challenges that are beyond the scope of any country to handle alone."[127]

The bilateral relationship between India and Australia has received a boost, some credit of which can be accredited to Non Traditional Security (NTS) issues as both the nations being members of ADMM Plus, have used NTS issues as leverage to push for actionable regional security cooperation. "Australia is a steadfast supporter of ASEAN's central role in facilitating regional security dialogue and cooperation and plays an active role in the ASEAN Defence Ministers' Meeting Plus to drive practical defence cooperation between regional countries."[128] The mutual complementarities of engagements between both the countries at multilateral and bilateral levels have been propagated by India from time to time. ADMM Plus initiative is offering a unique opportunity to India and Australia to engage with each other at a multilateral level while at the same time retaining the initiative of strategic autonomy. At the sidelines of the initiative both India and Australia are engaging each other in active cooperation in the fields of both traditional and nontraditional security aspects. "While it takes part in exercises conducted by the ADMM- Plus, it also maintains and emphasizes its bilateral relationships with all the ASEAN countries."[129]

With the current state of India and Australia's independent relationship with China, it is apparent that geostrategic alignment between India and Australia is going to stay and develop further. With common and shared concerns in the region ADMM-Plus initiative offers a unique opportunity to both the countries to forge a strong and stable strategic partnership. India and Australia have stood for the cause of rule based order in the international commons and have reiterated their stand against the unilateral attempts to alter the status quo. "Some countries will continue to pursue their strategic interests through a combination of coercive activities, including espionage, interference and economic levers. Tensions over territorial claims and the establishment of new military facilities are rising and are involving the use of military or Para-military forces more frequently than in the past, including coercive Para-military activities in the South China Sea."[130] Though the active defence engagements is not a new phenomenon for Australia as in the past it has undertaken such initiatives with a number of countries. India, on the other hand has realized the importance of bilateral defence engagements as a hedging strategy against the geopolitical and geostrategic stratagems of China. "As we enhance mutual trust and confidence, exercising self-restraint in the conduct of activities and avoiding actions that may further complicate the situation, will go a long way in bringing sustained peace to the region. Threats to the rules-based order, maritime security, cyber -related crimes and terrorism…remain the challenges that we need to address as a forum."[131]

India and Australia are among the pioneers of the multilateral grouping of Indian Ocean Region Association for Regional Cooperation (IOR -ARC), the precursor of Indian Ocean Rim Association (IORA) which was established in 1995 in Mauritius. The initiative supposedly owes its origin to the fact that three key obstacles to regional cooperation had been removed or were in the process of change; "the Cold War, India's closed economy and South Africa's emergence as a democratic state."[132] Though in the initial stages the grouping was considered as a parallel if not substitute for Asia Pacific Economic Forum (APEC). However, these assumptions were not able to hold ground as there were considerable developmental differences among Indian Ocean states and regional cooperation was not acceptable to a majority of them due to a host of differences. "Within a couple of years, it had become clear that the IOR-ARC's approach to trade liberalisation had failed and Australia, India, and other key members lost interest."[133] This is also one of the examples of frequent on and off relationship of cooperation between India and Australia.

As the strategic interests of both the nations to include, Non-traditional as well as traditional security issues started getting converged in the new maritime construct of Indo Pacific, the increased cooperation between both the countries also started being witnessed. In 2011, India and Australia were instrumental in bringing maritime security related issues onto the IOR -ARC's agenda, by forming a working group on maritime security. India hosted an inaugural Indian Ocean Dialogue in November 2013, which was very successful in discussing and devising ways for IOR-ARC member states to more effectively cooperate on maritime security issues. At the 13th meeting of the forum at Perth, the name of the association was changed from IOR-ARC to IORA (Indian Ocean Rim Association). "We welcome the adoption of IORA as the new name for our organisation known formerly as the Indian Ocean Rim Association for Regional Cooperation (IOR-ARC).

This as an important step signifying our renewed resolve to strengthen our Association and its work."[134] The significance of the working relationship in IOR-ARC has also percolated to the realms of bilateral relationship as shall be seen in the subsequent part of this chapter. During the visit of the then Australian Prime Minister, Julia Gillard to India in 2012, both the countries had resolved to upgrade the relationship. "India and Australia, as Chair and Vice Chair respectively of the Indian Ocean Rim Association for Regional Cooperation, will work closely to strengthen the Association, the apex pan-Indian Ocean multilateral forum, through concrete steps."[135] With the concomitant policies of sharing a vision of a free, open, inclusive and rule-based Indo Pacific region to support the freedom of navigation, both countries stand for adherence of all nations to international law including the United Nations Convention on the Law of the Sea (UNCLOS) and peaceful resolution of disputes rather than through unilateral or coercive actions. As part of Comprehensive Security Partnership 2020, both countries have reiterated their commitment to support a strong and resilient regional architecture, with ASEAN at its centre.[136]

The common concerns of both the countries have also found resonance in the Indian Ocean Naval Symposium (IONS). The symposium was established in 2008 under the sponsorship of the Indian Navy. "India remains committed to an Indian Ocean region that is stable and peaceful. We would like to cooperate with all like-minded countries so as to ensure the freedom of the seas for all nations and to deepen trade and economic linkages between the Indian Ocean rim countries."[137] The forum primarily involves biennial meeting of Naval Chiefs of member nations with the objective of encouraging an exchange of perspectives on a relatively informal basis. Among the Indian Ocean littorals, with over 150 plus vessels and counting, the Indian Navy has assumed a leading and performing role with a number of initiatives aimed at regional security and cooperation in related fields in the multilateral forum. Australia on the other hand is an important Pacific Ocean power and is building its combat capabilities to include new submarines, air defence destroyers, fighter jets, and long range maritime patrol aircraft, etc. The rise of the geo political construct of Indo Pacific is boosting the defence cooperation between the two countries. Forums like IONS are facilitating the growth in activities that address the range of maritime security challenges, a common concern for both the countries. The two countries have the potential to cooperate on a number of important issues in the sidelines of this forum. "I find IONS to be a uniquely consultative and cooperative initiative … IONS is a robust sign of a paradigm shift from competitive security to cooperative security within the maritime domain."[138]

The 2014 Perth Communiqué also mentioned about the encouragement to a potential dialogue between IORA and IONS. "We are committed to working collaboratively with the Indian Ocean Naval Symposium and other relevant organisations to address shared maritime and security challenges that threaten sea lines of communication and transportation in the Indian Ocean, notably piracy and terrorism."[139] Both India and Australia can further build upon this initiative and identify areas of mutual concern, where domain specialization of both the countries in respective fields can be exploited in furtherance of the mandate of IORA and IONS in the region. In order to realize the vision of the Comprehensive Security Partnership 2020, both the nations can nurture regional platforms such as Indian Ocean Naval Symposium (IONS) to take forward the dialogue on Indian Ocean and maritime security, with the IONS having the potential to serve as a broader platform discussing security cooperation in the Indo Pacific.

Nuclear, Chemical and Biological Domains: Mutually Converging Stands

As discussed in the first chapter of the book, apparent dichotomous stands of both India and Australia on the contentious issue of nuclear tests was responsible for holding the bilateral relationship hostage to mutual distrust for quite some time. For a reasonable period of time, both the countries held on to their respective beliefs of nuclear issues. Though the relationship on the aspect normalized after the decision of Australia to supply Uranium to India, the bilateral relationship is further facilitating India's entry to the exclusive club of Nuclear Suppliers Group (NSG). The group was created in 1974, with the basic idea to avoid misuse of nuclear technology transfer for peaceful purposes. In order to ensure that such transfers would not be diverted to an unsafeguarded nuclear fuel cycle or nuclear explosive activities, the NSG Guidelines were published in 1978 by the International Atomic Energy Agency (IAEA). In the 2001, plenary session of NSG, some suggested guidelines were evolved for admitting new members like India to the organisation. "Membership of NPT is only a guideline, a consideration, and not a mandatory requirement while deciding on a country's application."[140]

India has reached out to almost all of the 48 members of the NSG for pushing India's bid for inclusion as the member, but since all decisions at NSG are taken by consensus, any country can place an objection, which in India's case is being spearheaded by China. "There is broad consensus for Indian membership in Missile Technology Control Regime (MTCR), but regrettably no consensus yet."[141] China is continuing to insist that all countries who have not signed Non Proliferation Treaty (NPT) should be treated together and no special waiver to be granted to India. "Actually, the proliferation carried out by Pakistan was done by Abdul Qadeer Khan, Pakistan's chief nuclear scientist, and was not an official policy of the Pakistani government. Khan was punished by the government afterward with several years of house arrest. If the NPT and the NSG can give India an exemption, it should apply to Pakistan as well."[142]

It is here, where India's and Australia's interests are converging and hold the potential for further improvement. Australian concerns on India's non NPT compliant status have been addressed prior to the signing of India Australia Civil Nuclear Cooperation. India and Australia can work more closely on the issues on nuclear proliferation and seek comprehensive Cooperation. "Prime Minister Narendra Modi thanked Turnbull for Australia's proactive support to India's membership of the elite nuclear trading club. Prime Minister Turnbull assured that Australia will continue to support India's inclusion in the NSG."[143] The Comprehensive Security Partnership 2020 signed between India and Australia also commits Australia's support to India's bid for membership in NSG. "Both sides reiterated their support for continued bilateral civil nuclear cooperation and their commitment to further strengthen global non-proliferation. Australia expressed its strong support for India's membership of the NSG."[144]

Just as NSG primarily deals with the control of nuclear related issues, Australia Group, an informal arrangement aims to allow exporting or transshipping countries to minimise the risk of assisting chemical and biological weapon (CBW) proliferation. All states participating in the Australia Group are parties to the Chemical Weapons Convention (CWC) and the Biological Weapons Convention (BWC). In 2018, India was accorded the membership of the group. "The Australia Group decided to admit India as its 43rd participant. India would like to thank each of the participants. Its entry would be mutually beneficial."[145] Membership of the Australia Group will not only further authenticate India's principled nonproliferation policy on the chemical weapons, but also enhance India's participation in the global non-proliferation drive.

Wassenaar Arrangement on the other hand is a Multilateral Export Control Regime (MECR) for conventional arms and dual-use goods and technologies and is one of the world's four major export control regimes, the other three being the Nuclear Suppliers Group, the Missile Technology Control Regime (MTCR) and the Australia Group. It was established to contribute to regional and international security and stability by promoting transparency and greater responsibility in transfers of conventional arms and dual-use goods and technologies, thus preventing destabilizing accumulations. Given India and Australia's emerging congruence on multitude of security related issues and Australia's conviction of India's non proliferation record despite being a non NPT signatory, India was accepted as 42nd member of this agreement in December 2018.

China Factor in the India and Australia Bilateral Matrix

The increasing assertiveness of China beyond her traditional areas of dominance has been the primary deduction for the rise of 'Indo-Pacific' as a meta geographical term. As China emerged out of the shadows of its '100 Years of Humiliation',[146] and embraced economic development based on free market system, it started exploring vistas out of its traditional areas of interest. With her moving out of its comfort zone, China started to realize the importance of securing of Sea Lines of Communication (SLOC). China initially looked at Asia Pacific to secure its interests and was wary of other major powers trying to gain foot hold in the region. "Relevant major powers are increasing their strategic investment. Some countries have strengthened Asia-Pacific military alliances, expanded military presence in the region, and frequently make the situation there tenser. On the issues concerning China's territorial sovereignty and maritime rights and interests, some neighboring countries are taking actions that complicate or exacerbate the situation."[147] The first 'Annual Report on the Development of the Indian Ocean Region'; published by think-tank, the Chinese Academy of Social Sciences (CASS), mentioned that while India has put forward its own 'Look East' policy, and the US has implemented its 'pivot' or 'rebalancing' strategy towards Asia, China 'has no Indian Ocean strategy'. The report further mentioned that the, "Profound changes are taking shape in the Asia-Pacific strategic landscape.

The United States is reinforcing its regional military alliances, and increasing its involvement in regional security affairs."[148] With the concept of Indo Pacific taking definite shape and India attempting to undertake a paradigm shift in the strategic outlook from an inward continental orientation to an outward maritime orientation, China's ambition of dominating SLOC in the IOR were threatened. As India takes center stage in the proceedings of the Indo Pacific, the resolution of 'Malacca Dilemma' seems farfetched. "This establishes a Chinese national interest in the Indo-Pacific region that draws it into a necessary relationship with other major nations, such as India and the US, and ASEAN nations."[149] The individual bilateral relationships between India-China and Australia-China are independent of India-Australia bilateral relationship. But as the contemporary alignment of interests, primarily strategic unfolds between India and Australia, it is somehow coincident that the bilateral relationship of both countries with China is witnessing a severe strain.

India and China have a long history of border disputes, which to the best efforts of India has still not been resolved by China. As the Chinese perception of undefined border has been dynamic and has not followed a laid down pattern, in spite of institutionalization of dispute resolution mechanisms at the highest possible levels, the border has been left undemarcated and prone to errors of judgment at tactical levels, which more often than not starts taking strategic overtones. This varying perception of LAC accompanied by frequent Chinese aggression has resulted in the 1962 Indo China war and military stand-offs, which have increased off late, more recently in 2013, 2014, 2017 and recently in 2020. India, for most part of her independent history was confined to the continental orientation, a legacy which can be ascribed to different reasons, and was relatively oblivious to the maritime orientation and domination. The rise of the construct of Indo Pacific has underscored the centrality of India in the region, which besides facilitating maritime domination of the region by India also exacerbates the Chinese Malacca Dilemma. There is a striking synchronization in the timings of India's increased maritime orientation and Chinese aggression along land borders. The increased Chinese aggression along undefined borders can also be explained by the likely Chinese motive to restrict India to continental prepotency only and obviate any attempts by India to reclaim its centrality in the Indo Pacific. Frequent incursions by China along the largely undefined borders have the potential to divert India's attention and resources back to the continental mindset and deflect her from the aim of dominating the proceedings in the Indo Pacific and play a bigger role in the region.

The continued concerns about Chinese influence in the immediate neighbourhood of India have also been a cause of concern for India. Under the guise of the Belt and Road Initiative, the investment of greater Chinese economic resources in Sri Lanka, the Maldives, Myanmar, and Nepal as well as military resources in Pakistan and Bangladesh, has fuelled Indian unease, as has the development of a permanent Chinese military presence in the Indian Ocean.[150] India has been wary of increasing Chinese influence in the region, with Indian strategists and commentators from time to time having flagged the issue. "China is shaping the maritime battlefield in the region. It is making friends in the right places. If you don't have the capability to operate in these waters, for a length of time, then you need friends who will support your cause, when the time comes, so definitely China is doing that, as there are Pakistan, Bangladesh, Myanmar and Sri Lanka and on below Africa. So it is a known fact that we are ringed by states which may have a favorable disposition towards China."[151] On the other hand bilateral trade relationship between India and China has also become under strain due to huge quantum of trade surplus in favour of China. In addition, Chinese blatant violation of laid down norms in global governance, aggressive and dominant strategic behaviour, increasing minilateral diplomacy by India and suppression of human rights in Hong Kong and mainland China are some of the other factors which are putting India China relationship under strain.

As far as Australia is concerned, after the establishment of diplomatic relations between Australia and the People's Republic of China in 1972, the China-Australia relationship has developed into one of Australia's most significant trade partnerships and China has grown to be one of the Australia's largest trade partners. Both the countries had concluded China Australia Free Trade Agreement (ChAFTA) in 2014. "Upon enactment more than 85 per cent of the value of Australia's exports to China will be duty free. This number will rise to 95 per cent upon the completion of progressively introduced tariff elimination."[152] China has been able to corner a sizeable chunk of Australian exports and the Chinese growth has driven Australian prosperity and the growth of Chinese diaspora in Australia has been phenomenal. China has also invested heavily in Australian economy. "China is our ninth largest foreign investor, with 2.0 per cent of the total. However, the levels of Hong Kong (SAR of China) and Chinese investment in Australia have grown significantly over the past decade." [153] Trade appreciations apart, historically relations Australia and China have suffered from security related apprehensions. "Australian fears for its own safety have been, since 1949, related primarily to the Chinese People's Republic. Here was the communist monolith in its Asian manifestation, an almost limitless pool of humanity for an army of liberation or a flood of migration, an inscrutable source of oriental cunning or of terrorist subversion."[154]

As far as regional security architecture is concerned, the US has been a traditional strategic ally of Australia. The statement of former Australian Prime Minister John Howard that, "turning our face to the East does not mean turning our back on the West"[155] has often been quoted and the predicament of choosing between the US and China is not a recent phenomenon. "The geographic proximity to the fast-growing markets of East Asia determines that economically Australia cannot turn away from Asia. But on the levels of political and social ideologies and culture the Australian Coalition government puts the emphasis on the conformity with Europe and America. In this context, in making judgments on regional security and in assessing the potential threats in the region, there would be greater common ground between Australia and America to make Canberra a firm cornerstone in the South Pacific for the US security strategy and arrangements."[156]

This dilemma of the Australian polity in balancing between China and the US was further exemplified in 1997, when the Australian White Paper on Foreign Affairs and Trade, claimed that the United States would remain over the next fifteen years "the world's single most powerful country" and "continue to be an indispensable element in any configuration for peace, security and economic growth in the world."[157] China has been wary of the US involvement in the existing and proposed security architectures in the region and from time to time has advised Australia to reduce dependence on the US in the region. "From the white paper we can see that Australia tends to depend excessively on the US in terms of its national security, exaggerate the contribution of the American military presence in the West Pacific, and give approval to the intensified US-Japan defence alliance. This reveals the focus of its foreign policies: facing Asia in terms of trade and economy, and relying on the US in terms of security."[158]

In an apparent message that China's long held aspiration to project military power beyond the South China Sea was rapidly becoming a strategic reality, in January 2014; a flotilla of three Chinese warships had arrived unannounced on Australia's northern doorstep. "The unexpected arrival in Australia's northern approaches of two Chinese destroyers and an advanced 20,000 ton amphibious ship capable of carrying hundreds of PLA-N marines startled Australian planners."[159] With Australia continuing to be a closest strategic ally of the US in the region, it is apprehensive of unfolding of the US and China rivalry in the region. "Strategic competition, primarily between the United States and China, will be the principal driver of strategic dynamics in our region. This competition is playing out across the Indo-Pacific and increasingly in our immediate region: the area ranging from the north-eastern Indian Ocean through maritime and mainland South East Asia to Papua New Guinea and the South West Pacific."[160] This acceptance of a likelihood of a futuristic strategic competition, the early signs of which are manifesting in the region, is putting the Australia and China relationship under a severe strain.

The relationship between Australia and China in recent times has also been marred by Chinese investments in information and communication infrastructure in Australia. Australia was really concerned over China's 2017 national intelligence law, the provisions of which dictate the overriding powers of intelligence services of China. The law prescribes that "any organisation or citizen shall support, assist, and cooperate with state intelligence work."[161] Apprehensive about the provisions of the law, Australia banned the Chinese-owned tech giant Huawei from taking part in the rollout of 5G mobile infrastructure over national security concerns.[162] The relationship has been further exacerbated by Australia's insistence on independent inquiry, outside the aegis of World Health Organisation (WHO) into the origins of COVID-19, pandemic which has outraged the world economy and has heralded an unprecedented health emergency on to the world. China on its part reacted strongly to the proposal and Chinese embassy in Australia decried the move for an independent inquiry by World Health Assembly (WHA). "To claim the WHA's resolution a vindication of Australia's call is nothing but a joke."[163]

The perception of China in Australia has also suffered a serious downturn. The results of the Lowy Institute polls 2020 have further substantiated the dipping in the trust and warmth towards China, which has reached recorded lows in the history of polls. In further retaliation, China issued an advisory against travel to Australia by her citizens due to the racist attacks and has imposed tariffs totaling 80.5 per cent on barley imports from Australia. China also began a trade probe into Australian wine and suspended import permits for four large beef processing plants.[164] Australia on its part, in addition to tightening political financing from foreign sources, has responded with changes in its security strategy, and a major foreign policy push in the South Pacific, Southeast Asia, and with Japan, India, and the United States.[165]

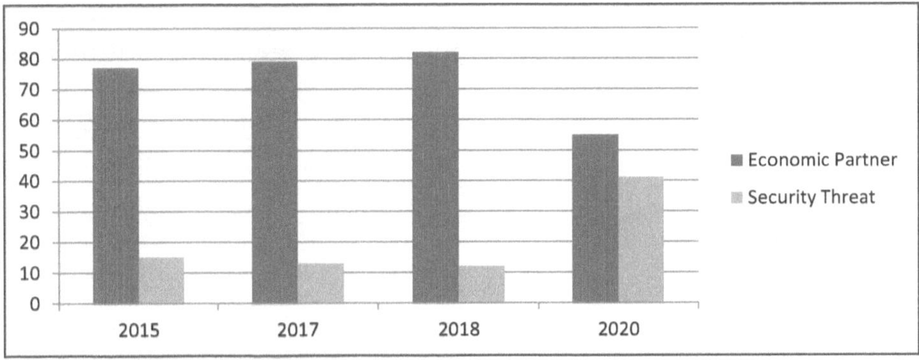

Fig 2: Views about China as a Security Threat or an Economic Partner[166]

Both India and Australia have a unique role to play in the Indo-Pacific strategic game and are diversifying and deepening their strategic, societal and economic relations. Both the countries have repeatedly expressed concerns about China's centralised decision-making, state-led economic policies, territorial revisionism, and erosion of norms, as well as its overall security posture in the Indo–Pacific.[167]

Multilaterals to Minilaterals

An overview of cooperation between India and Australia in the multilateral settings will reveal that both the countries have an exemplary record of mutual understanding and shared concerns in the region. But the very unwieldy nature of the multilaterals does not provide the required flexibility and adaptability to adjust to the mutual concerns. The overwhelming domination of China in these institutions is another deterrent for India and Australia to evolve a consensus along with other likeminded countries. Due to the unabated

Chinese attempts to undermine the consensus in multilateral set ups in the region, to include ASEAN, EAS and others, India and Australia have opted for minilaterals with other compatible nations in the region, the results of which have been very encouraging. Indian Ocean Region in its latest avatar of Indo Pacific has seen Multilateralism hitting a serious downward spiral. The increasing inability of existing multilaterals to address regional conflicting claims of respective members has raised doubts on the effectiveness of these multilateral platforms. The apparent decline of multilateralism has resulted in the rise of minilateral platforms in the region and it is increasingly being accepted that these minilateral initiatives, with their narrower and exclusive membership, have the potential ability to be more effective than their multilateral cousins.

The minilateralism is generally taken as synonymous with exclusion, just as multilateralism is taken as synonymous with inclusion. The contemporary Indo Pacific is witnessing an increasing challenge to the existing multilateral architecture in the region due to a resurgent and arbitrary China, the growing Sino-U.S. rivalry for regional leadership, the Indo - China rivalry and an apparent dismissal of multilateral arrangements by some states. In these types of scenarios, it is assumed that minilateralism could prove more effective than multilateralism in responding to specific contemporary issues and facilitate regional cooperation. Minilateralism under the present and existing circumstances in the region can act as building blocks of multilateralism, by supplementing the inadequacies of existing multilateral agreements. They also facilitate simpler coalition building, a favoured diplomatic strategy of 'middle powers' which must use collective approaches to promote their interests.[168] All the enthusiasm for minilaterals apart, a word of caution for overdependence on these initiatives would also be in order. As these minilaterals are primarily based on the premise of exclusion as against inclusion, it has been suggested that the architecture of these proposed minilaterals should be strong and based on mutual guarantees so as to obviate any chance of capitulation by any member. "There is deep skepticism about whether these partnerships will last in the face of the China challenge, whether one of the partners strikes a deal with China on the side-lines separately or succumbs to Chinese pressure. The question is how can trust or confidence in such trilateral partnerships be built?"[169]

With existing multilateral agreements having failed to ensure the rule of law in the commons and the arbitrariness unleashed by some of the members, both India and Australia seems to have developed a tacit understanding of evolving the existing multilateral arrangements. "India and Australia are two countries with shared interests and shared values. We both value multilateral institutions and recognise the need to reform and renovate them."[170] As a result, in the contemporary context, India and Australia are evolving their bilateral relationship through a series of minilateral arrangements. Based on participation of likeminded governments, committed to a common cause and yet allowing a certain degree of flexibility to the participants, the diplomacy of minilateralism has started facilitating the different aspects of India Australia bilateral relationship. The region's 'thickening architecture'[171] jointly represented by India and Australia has facilitated bilateral dynamics to levels never believed to be achievable earlier.

India –Australia- Japan

The trilateral of India, Australia and Japan has been an active proponent of the Indo-Pacific concept for regionalism in Asia. All three stand for common commitment to 'free, open, inclusive and rules-based principles' for regional governance. The initiative was launched by the three countries during the first incarnation of Indo Pacific and was intended to support and demonstrate a public commitment to international law, global norms and the established regional order. "A focus on defence and diplomacy is an opportunity to enhance relations, demonstrate a commitment to regional security and strengthen the security foundation on top of which diplomatic relations can deepen."[172]

In the contemporary context where rules based multilateralism is experiencing severe strain, manifestation of a certain degree of coordination amongst the trilateral can be observed. Given their relative weight of the group in the Indo Pacific, it has been argued that this trilateral can potentially function as an effective coalition for advancing these interests in key regional fora.[173] This initiative is being projected as a coalition of like-minded democracies that stands for the established regional order and against unilateral attempts to change the status quo by force. "Cultivating forward-leaning trilateral cooperation would encourage behaviour that deepening trilateral engagement also gives us an opportunity to demonstrate the independence of our foreign policy and strategic decision-making, confounding those critics who allege that our capacity to act is compromised by our alliance with the US."[174]

The three countries are also working on a novel initiative of Supply Chain Resilience Initiative (SCRI), which has been proclaimed to facilitate reduction on the supply chain dependency on China. SCRI is a direct response to individual companies and economies concerned about Chinese political behaviour and the disruption that could lead to the supply chain. The initiative, first proposed by Japan with India and Australia as partners, has the potential to gain traction in the region as other countries of the region are also equally affected by the probability of disruption of supply chain by the unilateral and arbitrary actions of China. The initiative aims to identify sectors where shifting of existing supply chains from China is feasible. Automobiles, tourism, pharmaceuticals, textiles and garments, IT and financial services, marine products and skill development are some of the sectors where the initiative can contribute substantially towards the cementing of the trilateral partnership.

India - Australia - France

The minilateral involving India-Australia and France has come into existence due to a long and intense track 1.5 and track II dialogue held between the representatives of three countries. The origin of the initiative can be traced to coming together of Carnegie India, Foundation for Strategic Research of France and the National Security College of the Australian National University in 2018, with a primary aim of studying feasibility of areas of cooperation between the three countries. Thereafter, French President Emmanuel Macron during his visit to Australia spoke of "the Paris-Delhi-Canberra axis that should be strengthened as an established regional structure, reflecting an Indo-Pacific geo-strategic reality in the making."[175] As a follow up of these preliminary discussions and in a first initiative of its kind, India, Australia and France organized a trilateral meet through video conference on 09 September 2020. An analysis of the statements released by the three countries separately post the meeting underscore the congruence of strategic interests and common concerns of the three countries in the Indo Pacific. While Ministry of External Affairs (MEA) of India highlighted the success of first such trilateral meet, the comments of Australia mirrored the sentiments expressed by India. "The outcome oriented meeting was held with the objective of building on the strong bilateral relations that the three countries share with each other and synergising their respective strengths to ensure a peaceful, secure, prosperous and rules-based Indo-Pacific Region. The three sides agreed to hold the dialogue on an annual basis."[176] Based on the transcendence of the bilateral relations amongst themselves, India, Australia and France have underscored the importance of guaranteeing peace, security and adherence to international law in the Indo-Pacific. "India, Australia and France are three countries with increasingly aligning strategic interests in the Indo-Pacific, accompanied by complementary research strengths and resources that can support implementation of a strategic vision. These include securing a sustainable future through addressing global challenges while ensuring regional security."[177]

The significance of the trilateral gets further augmented due to the fact that increasing involvement of India in these types minilateral engagements is a reflection of her growing accommodative stance towards engaging with other countries in the concerns which till now were not being discussed openly. While not naming China openly, all three countries reiterated their respective stands toward rule based governance in the commons. These tendencies were apparent in the follow up statements released post the meeting. The meeting "helped underscore the goal of guaranteeing peace, security and adherence to international law in the Indo-Pacific by drawing on the excellence of bilateral relations between France, India and Australia."[178]

India -Australia- Indonesia

With the gradual relocation of geo-political weight towards Indo Pacific, there is an apparent sense of urgency amongst the countries of the region, to caliber their stance towards shifting geopolitical goalposts. The world order is increasingly getting wary of Chinese assertiveness and coupled with the relative lack of confidence in the US leadership, the frame work of cooperation between countries with converging interests is making a sensible strategy in diplomacy. In the East Asia Summit held at Bangkok in November 2019, the Indian Prime Minister proposed to launch a maritime security pillar, IPOI in conjunction with Australia and Indonesia. "It should be a space in which freedom of navigation, over-flight, and sustainable development, protection of the ecology especially the marine environment, and an open, free, fair and mutually-beneficial trade and investment system are guaranteed to all."[179] There are lot of commonalities and similarities between the three countries, which can supplement their individual efforts in the region. It has also been envisioned that the strategic triangularity between India, Indonesia and

Australia is going to be a gradual process based on a convergence of interests (all three are geostrategic anchors of the Indo-Pacific), some shared values (all three are pluralist democracies) and similar power structures (all three are middle-powers seeking to stem the tide of great power politics).[180]

Among themselves, India, Australia and Indonesia strategically anchor the Indo Pacific in the middle, northwest, and southeast, making it imperative that the long-term strategic stability of the Indo-Pacific depends to a significant degree on these three countries and how they interact with one another. Therefore in a sense, these three countries share "the responsibility to look after the single strategic ecosystem" of the Indo-Pacific.[181] The strategic cooperation between these three countries can emanate from existing bilateral understanding for example between India Australia and Australia Indonesia and once established can facilitate greater bilateral understanding between India and Indonesia. Till that time all three countries can exploit the issue based consensus amongst themselves and forge a strong trilateral. "Cooperation between the three countries should be issue-based … based on a positive construct like the fact that they are democracies and maritime neighbours."[182] The very economic and military might of these three countries in the region has a potential to transform their trilateral alliance into an alliance of great strategic import.

Quadrilateral Security Dialogue

In the aftermath of Tsunami in December 2004, the US, Japan, Australia and India had established an informal assemblage, 'Tsunami Core Group' to facilitate coordination of relief activities.[183] The quantum and scope of relief activities coordinated by the group were exemplary and the contribution by India in terms of efforts and resources were noticed by the world. Taking this idea further, the first phase of the formal initiative was launched by the then Prime Minister of Japan, Shinjo Abe in 2007. "Australia, India, Japan, and the United States, drew these nations towards an alliance, against the normative uncertainties posed to the regional order by China's rise."[184] The year 2007 also witnessed annual India-US Malabar naval exercise, which was transformed into large-scale multilateral exercises in the Bay of Bengal involving three Carrier Battle Groups (CBGs) and other ships from the United States, India, Japan, Australia and Singapore. During his visit to India in August 2007, the Japanese Prime Minister in an address to Indian parliament spoke of a 'broader Asia' partnership of democracies and suggested that the India-Japan partnership would "evolve into an immense network spanning the entirety of the Pacific Ocean, incorporating the US and Australia."[185] All these developments were not taken lightly by China and reactions from Chinese official and semi-official sources to the Quadrilateral initiative and naval exercises in 2007 led to the criticism that the initiatives resurrected 'a cold-war mentality' and marked "the formation of a small NATO to resist China."[186] When questioned about the Abe-Bush-Howard meeting, China had maintained that discussions between the three allies should be 'more transparent.'[187] The then Chinese President Hu Jintao is known to have pointedly asked Indian Prime Minister 'clarification' on India's position in a face to face meeting with the Indian Prime Minister.[188] The newly elected government in Australia also did not want to annoy its largest trade partner and publicly withdrew from the initiative and took pains to emphasize that while it valued stronger economic, cultural and political ties with India, "We do not wish to have a formal quadrilateral strategic dialogue in defence and security matters."[189] The idea of a 'Quad Initiative' thus was shelved by the proponents in the same haste as it was propounded.

The challenge to the established rules and multilateral establishments in the region by a resurgent China had led to collapse of the initiative in 2007 and the same reason is now leading to the revival of initiative. The challenge to the regional order by China's growing assertiveness and economic relationships are getting India, Australia, Japan and the US together. Australia has increasingly been concerned about Chinese investments in critical infrastructure to include nascent 5G telecommunications, serious allegations of Chinese influence in Australian politics, and Chinese military activity in Australia's near neighbourhood.[190] India is also concerned by increasing Chinese assertiveness in the longstanding India–China boundary dispute, which has started manifesting in military stand-offs in a series of predictable certainty, with a bloody clash between the two armies leading to the death of 20 Indian soldiers and an unspecified number of Chinese casualties, being the latest one. China's all pervasive influence in the immediate neighbourhood, to include Nepal, Bangladesh, Sri Lanka and Myanmar apart from Pakistan is likely to result in serious security implications for India.

As a follow up to the inaugural Quad Foreign Ministers' Meeting on 26 September 2019 in New York, a meeting of Senior officials from Australia's Department of Foreign Affairs and Trade was conducted with the representatives from the foreign ministries of India, Japan and the United States in Bangkok on 04 November 2019 for 'Quad' consultations on the Indo-Pacific.[191] The meeting of quad and participation of Australia in Malabar Exercise in 2020 is a strong indication of the increasing strategic cooperation between India and Australia and is in sync with the declaration of Comprehensive Security Partnership 2020. Reflecting popular public opinion against increasing assertiveness of China and threat to the rule based international order, coupled with an increased confidence in India, a massive 88 percent of Australian population surveyed for Lowy Institute Polls 2020, supported the formation of a minilateral between the likeminded democracies of India, Australia, Japan and the US.

In the second ministerial meeting of the Quadrilateral Security Dialogue, held in Tokyo on 06 October 2020, India emphasised on the centrality of freedom of navigation and rules based international order. "Our objective remains advancing the security and economic interests of all countries having legitimate and vital interests in the region. It is a matter of satisfaction that the Indo-Pacific concept has gained increasingly wider acceptance. The Indo-Pacific Ocean's Initiative that we tabled at the East Asia Summit last year is a development with considerable promise in that context."[192] Commenting on the Quad foreign ministers meet, China has cautioned the member states against any coalition formation. "We hope relevant countries can proceed from the common interests of countries in the region, and do more things that are conducive to regional peace, stability and development, not the other way around."[193] In a not so veiled acceptance of institutionalization of Quad, the outgoing US President on 22 December 2020 presented "Legion of Merit' to the other three leaders of the Quad. Analysis of the citations for the award provides adequate reference for the contribution made by the three leaders of India, Australia and Japan towards formalizing the initiative. The arrangement has crystallized into some definite shape and will require the challenges of present and future to test the strength and vitality of alliance.

Bilateral Relations

The Defence White Paper 2009, 'Defending Australia in the Asia Pacific Century: Force 2030', demonstrated complete maturing of Australia's approach to India, firstly rising influence of India, in the region as a growing power, and the joint commitment to combat regional and global terrorism and maintaining a rules-based global security order. Despite differences on a host of issues and pre occupation with the respective aspects concerning each country, India and Australia's shared interests, shared values, close regional integration, expanding bilateral economic relationship, agreed views on reforming multilateral institutions, and people-to people links, "means that there is now an impetus to develop an India-Australia strategic partnership."[194] The requirement for both the countries therefore is to seize the opportunities which will lift the bilateral relationship to the pedestal of strategic cooperation and build upon the existing mechanisms. 'Creative middle power diplomacy' is one such mechanism adopted by Australia to develop strategic relationships with the other likeminded powers. It was one of the seven national security policy principles announced in the 2008 National Security Statement, and can be described as "an active foreign policy capable of identifying opportunities to promote Australia's security and to prevent, reduce, or delay, the emergence of national security challenges."[195]

The role of state visits and visits by diplomats provide a boost to the bilateral relationship. The centrality of India in the region has also been supplemented by the growing diplomatic engagements of India in the region. Increased diplomatic engagements call for realigning the existing networks so as to facilitate concentration and singular focus on the changed preferences. In order to provide directed and coordinated efforts of engagement in the region, the Ministry of External Affairs (MEA), Government of India created an Indo Pacific division in the ministry in 2019. The vision and reach of the division having domain overlaps and to facilitate focused interest and initiatives in the region, MEA has further realigned the diplomatic efforts by creating a new division, the Oceania division, which has mandated task to focus on the larger Indo-Pacific in an apparent indication of the importance of the region for the country. The new division has subsumed the erstwhile divisions of ministry to include southern division, which looked after a swathe of countries from Thailand to Australia and New Zealand and the Indo-Pacific division.[196] With the creation of the new division, India has signaled the significance of the region for India and the growing importance of Australia in the strategic matrix of Indo Pacific. The new division will have all the south pacific islands under its proposed charter and with the growing alignment of interests between India and Australia, is further mandated to boost the strategic and geo political congruence between the two countries.

In the case of India and Australia, the bilateral relationship was also held hostage to the limited number of visits. The bilateral discussions and agreements are also directly linked with the frequency of visits. During the visit to Australia in 2014, the Prime Minister of India referred to this skewed trend in the bilateral relationship between the two countries. "It has taken a Prime Minister of India 28 years to come to Australia. It should never have been so. Australia will not be at the periphery of our vision, but at the centre of our thought. I see a great future of partnership between India and Australia and, a shared commitment to realize it."[197]

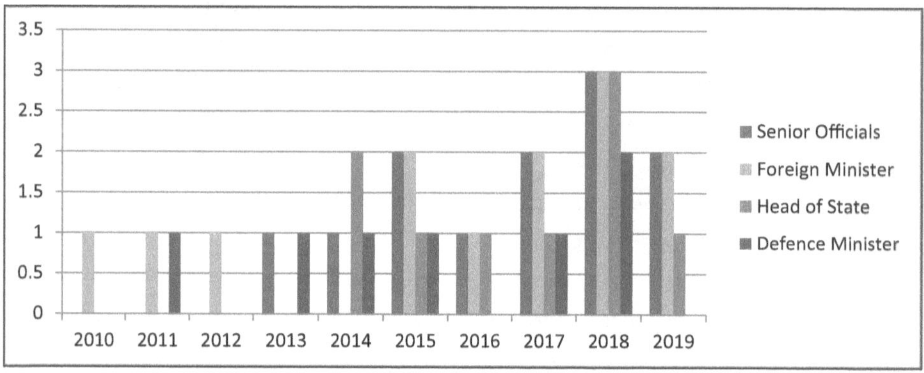

Fig 3: Surge in the Bilateral Visits[198]

As the bilateral visits result in mutual understanding and signing of cooperation treaties/agreements, the effect of the limited bilateral visits can also be seen in the treaties/agreements signed between the two countries. In the period between 1940 to 2010, only 12 agreements/treaties were signed between India and Australia, on the other hand, between 2010 and 2020, 31 agreements have been signed between the two countries.[199] This asymmetrical matrix has witnessed serious amelioration which is increasingly manifesting in the trajectory of the bilateral relationship.

Non Traditional to Traditional Security

Non Traditional Security (NTS) issues have played an important role of a catalyst in the development and expansion of emerging and envisaged regional security architectures across the Geo-Political construct of Indo Pacific. The Non Traditional Security issues possess a remarkable uniqueness of transgressing national boundaries and bearing a distinct non-military character and thus have facilitated the nation states to seek substantial levels of security integration. They are consistently, "transnational in scope, neither domestic nor purely interstate, come with very short notice, and are transmitted rapidly due to globalization and the communication revolution."[200] NTS issues are invariably politically neutral and therefore form an ideal test bed in which cooperative vulnerabilities and opportunities can be tested and implemented, "a growing trend of security integration across the Indo-Pacific, centered on ASEAN, and characterised by a 'staggering growth in regional multilateralism."[201] India and Australia having shared commonalities of similar geostrategic locations have important interests in the interlaying region in the South East Asia, a sub set of the larger Indo Pacific. The development and the realization of the importance of concept of 'Comprehensive Security' have resulted in nontraditional security issues gaining more, if not equal importance vis-à-vis traditional military concerns.

India and Australia have also not been untouched by this paradigm shift, with India's 'Look East' and Australia's 'Look West' policies converging on the East Asian region geographically and the Asia Pacific region strategically.[202] As the concept of Indo Pacific is primarily related to the convergence of Oceans, the importance of the aspect of maritime security cannot be understated. This aspect comprises of both military (Traditional) and non military (Non Traditional) aspects, whereby Naval threats and challenges are typical military concerns, arms trafficking, vulnerability of SLOCs, piracy, narco terrorism and cyber being classified as typical nontraditional threats. The emerging concept of Indo Pacific has offered unique opportunity to both the countries to exploit the characteristics of NTS issues to come together and establish focal points for regional cooperation."As India extends its reach and influence into areas of shared strategic interest, we will need to strengthen our defence relationship and our understanding of Indian strategic thinking. In the near term, we are looking for opportunities to expand high level defence dialogue, building upon annual talks between the chief of the defence force and his Indian counterpart... We should also increase practical cooperation in areas such as defence information sharing, counter terrorism and peacekeeping."[203]

India and Australia have realized the common strategic need for maintaining secure sea lanes for facilitating the smooth transport of oil and other commodities, dealing with the issues of maritime security like smuggling of small arms, drug trafficking and illegal migration, restricting influence of extra regional powers in the Indian Ocean Region, and equipping to face new challenges to regional security such as the threat of religious fundamentalism spilling on to the dangerous contours of terrorism, impel a greater interaction between these two countries.[204] NTS issues have been lucrative enticements for India and Australia to coordinate their efforts towards resolution of these and in turn achieve regional stability. "As a result of the emergence of non-traditional security concerns, there are common interests, among these nations that impel them to deal with the new challenges hereby leading to more cooperation rather than competition."[205] Another critical factor which has facilitated coming together of India and Australia in the realm of NTS is the fact that NTS issues are easier to handle than the strategic issues. The addressing of the strategic and defence related issues (Traditional Security), involves taking crucial decisions which may or may not be in sync with the strategic outlook/preferences of a country. Often NTS issues lack political baggage and are therefore less likely to "raise the same level of sensitivity that more traditional security issues are apt to generate."[206]

Further supplementing the efforts towards resolution of NTS issues, Indian Prime Minister during his address to the Joint session of Australian Parliament in 2014 had reiterated the importance of cooperation in the field. "Our region has seen huge progress on the foundation of peace and stability. India and Australia can play their part in it by expanding our security cooperation and deepening our international partnerships in the region. Responding to the region's disasters, combating proliferation, acting against piracy, we can work together on a full range of security challenges."[207] In order to address concerns regarding illicit trafficking and drug abuse between the two countries, during this visit of Indian Prime Minister to Australia, a MoU for combating narcotics trafficking and developing Police cooperation was signed between the two nations. The agreement intends to prioritise tackling of illicit trade, diversion of precursors and assets forfeiture. During the same visit as part of cooperation on NTS issues, both the nations had also signed an agreement for establishment of a framework for security cooperation to reflect the deepening and expanding security and defence engagement, both in traditional and nontraditional fields. During the state visit of Australian Prime Minister to India in 2017, India and Australia providing further boost to the cooperation in NTS fields signed MoUs on Cooperation in combating International Terrorism and Transnational Organized Crime and Promotion and Development of Cooperation in Civil Aviation Security.

Providing a comprehensive outlook to the bilateral relationship and incentivizing the cooperation in the field of NTS, India and Australia signed MoU on Framework Arrangement on Cyber and Cyber-Enabled

Critical Technology during the first ever virtual summit between the Prime Ministers of the two countries in June 2020. Carrying forward from here both the countries have also decided to hold a unique and singular summit on the emerging, critical and cyber technologies in 2021. "The Australian Government is supporting the establishment of the Sydney Dialogue, which will be held for the first time virtually in the second half of 2021. While significant international conferences and dialogues exist for traditional areas of security and economics, there is currently a gap for political leaders, industry experts, academics and civil society representatives to meet and discuss the most pressing issues around cyber and critical technology."[208]

The aspects of NTS are an important component of an all encompassing and holistic relationship between India and Australia and therefore, consideration of contemporary and emerging cyber technologies is critical for both the countries in the field of NTS. Providing fillip to the bilateral relationship, the proposed Sydney dialogue summit is focused on the theme of Indo Pacific and is slated to have India as a core topic. India on its part is alive to the importance of technological cooperation for the diplomacy and accordingly the political mileage offered by the technological convergence. There is a quantum potential in the technological convergence between India and Australia which can be exploited for the furtherance of the bilateral relationship. "Technology is clearly very political. It is today very much a core part of diplomacy. It is something which every foreign Ministry is going to be focused on in many ways in a very Central way."[209]

The CSP 2020 has brought convergence between both the countries on another important aspect of cooperation in the supply of strategic minerals and has provided fillip to the increasing connect in the realms of NTS. As part of CSP 2020, Australia has conveyed that India could consider it as a stable, reliable and trusted supplier of high-quality mineral resources to India and that both sides jointly decided to diversify and expand the existing resources partnership.[210] Both the countries have signed a MoU under the provisions of which Australia will supply critical minerals, which are vital for the contemporary technologies in India. "The MoU identifies specific areas where Australia and India will work together to meet the raw material demands of the future economy, particularly the increased global demand for critical minerals. India presents growing opportunities for Australia's critical minerals, especially as the nation looks to build its manufacturing sector, defence and space capabilities."[211] This mutual understanding and the agreements in the arenas of NTS, not only substantiates the all encompassing and holistic bilateral relationship between both the countries but also provide a take off point for increased congruence and connect in the domain of traditional security.

The Australia–India Security Declaration: 2009

Year 2009 was a watershed year in the history of strategic relationship between India and Australia. In November of 2009, the Prime Ministers of both the countries agreed to take the relationship to the next level of strategic understanding and intensify their contacts with each other, "India and Australia were 'natural partners' and should become strategic partners."[212] A Joint Declaration on Security Cooperation to set out shared strategic perspectives and further create a framework for the development of bilateral security cooperation was signed during the summit. The signing of Joint Declaration on Security Cooperation, has helped to shed historical baggage being carried by both the countries and has facilitated both to come closer in the realm of traditional and NTS issues. "Affirming that the strategic partnership between India and Australia is based on a shared desire to promote, regional and global security, as well as their common commitment to democracy, freedom, human rights and the rule of law, India and Australia have decided to create a comprehensive framework for the enhancement of security cooperation between the two countries."[213]

The broad mechanics of the security declaration signed contains the elements of information exchange and policy coordination on regional affairs in the Asia region and on long-term strategic and global issues; Bilateral cooperation within multilateral frameworks in Asia, in particular the East Asia Summit and the ASEAN Regional Forum; Defence dialogue and cooperation within the framework of the MoU on Defence Cooperation signed in March 2006; Efforts to combat terrorism; Cooperation to combat transnational organised crime; Disaster management; Maritime and aviation security and Police and law enforcement cooperation. India and Australia, as part of the security declaration have also agreed to work towards developing an action plan with specific measures to advance security cooperation.

Both nations have tried to build up their relationship within the overall ambit of multilateral forums and have accepted the importance of these institutions in strengthening their relationship. "Regional and multilateral cooperation is an important strand of the India - Australia relationship. The two leaders reaffirmed the key role being played in the Asian region by bodies such as the East Asia Summit, the ASEAN Regional Forum and the Asia Europe Meeting."[214] This security declaration was a notable step for both the countries in establishment of a framework for the further development of the security relationship, to include formalisation of regular consultations and dialogues between senior ministers, senior military and diplomatic representatives and joint working groups on maritime security operations and counter-terrorism and immigration.

Visit of Indian defence Minister to Australia: June 2013

In a first ever official visit of Indian Defence Minister, former union minister of Defence AK Antony had visited Australia in June 2013. In continuation of India-Australia historical relations and defence -to-defence and military -to-military cooperation, the visit proved to be very beneficial as far as India-Australia bilateral relations are concerned. "The Ministers exchanged ideas concerning regional and international security as well as defence cooperation and exchanges between Australia and India. They agreed to continue to contribute to the peace, stability and prosperity of the Asia-Pacific region and to promote cooperation in the Indian Ocean region."[215]

The defence ministers of both the countries agreed for some mutually acceptable practical measures that will further enhance bilateral defence cooperation between the two nations by continuing to have regular bilateral Defence Ministers' Meetings; to promote exchanges between the defence establishments and the Armed Forces of both sides, including through the regular conduct of the Defence Policy Dialogue, Armed Forces Staff Talks and professional military exchanges and to promote the sharing and exchange of professional knowledge and experiences through participation in training courses in each other's military training institutions.

Australia-India Declaration and Security Framework: 2014

The Australia-India Declaration and Security Framework of 2014 was a notable step forward in the further development of the bilateral security relationship, as in particular it articulated a sea change in India's view of

Australia as an important regional partner. "As Australia has become more engaged in this part of the world, we welcome its growing role in driving this region's prosperity and shaping its security. India and Australia can play their part in it by expanding our security cooperation and deepening our international partnerships in the region."[216]

As an appropriate tribute to the similarities and complementarities between both the nations and the increasing need of each other for each other, a New Framework for Security Cooperation (NFSC) was signed on 18 November 2014 during the state visit of Indian Prime Minister to Australia. The security declaration also reflected India's willingness and eagerness to operationalise defence and security relationships throughout the Indo-Pacific region and the relative importance of Australia in these calculations. The Action Plan provided a broad framework within which bilateral engagements and mechanisms are envisaged for cooperation. The declaration exhorts both the nations to work together in multilateral forums, to include the East Asia Summit, ASEAN Regional Forum, ASEAN Defence Ministers' Meeting Plus (ADMM+), the Indian Ocean Rim Association (IORA), Indian Ocean Naval Symposium (IONS), the United Nations and the G20. "The Prime Minister of India and the Prime Minister of Australia reaffirm that the Strategic Partnership between India and Australia is based on converging political, economic and strategic interests; a shared desire to promote regional and global peace, security and prosperity; and a commitment to democracy, freedom, human rights, and the rule of law. They have decided to establish a Framework for Security Cooperation to reflect the deepening and expanding security and defence engagement between India and Australia."[217]

The action plan as part of the framework provides for annual summits and foreign policy exchanges and coordination through annual meetings of Prime Ministers, including in the margins of multilateral meetings: Foreign Ministers framework Dialogue; Senior officials talks led by India's Secretary (East) in the Ministry of External Affairs and the Secretary of Australia's Department of foreign Affairs and Trade and 1.5 track Australia-India dialogue. In the area of defence policy planning and guidance, the framework calls for regular meetings of defence ministers; an annual 1.5 track defence strategic dialogue and a service to service engagement to include regular high level visits, annual staff talks, joint training and regular exercises as decided. The framework also called for close cooperation in regional and multilateral forums, including the EAS, ARF, ADMM Plus, IORA, IONS, the UN and its specialized agencies and the G 20 and support for India's bid to be permanent member of the UNSC.

As part of framework, cooperation in defence technology is envisaged through visits by Australian and Indian defence material delegations and through efforts to foster joint industry links. As Defence technology has been an inalienable aspect in India's relationships with the Soviet Union/Russia, France, Israel, and the United States, inclusion of Defence Technology in the Framework will definitely boost the relationship between the two countries. Australian strengths in Radar Technologies, undersea applications and naval shipbuilding can be exploited by India. The agreement also envisaged direct cooperation between the government defence research organisations, India's Defence Research and Development Organisation (DRDO) and Australia's Defence Science and Technology Organisation (DSTO). There is an immense potential of cooperation between the two nations in this aspect. The memories of an untoward incident in 2014, which involved deportation of two boat loads of Tamil asylum seekers by Australia, are a stark reminder of grey areas in the field. The potential for practical cooperation between Australian and Indian border protection authorities was underlined by the visit of an Indian Coast Guard vessel to Darwin in December 2014, "the first such visit of the Indian Coast Guard to Australian waters."[218]

India's quick response mechanism and subsequent cooperation with the regional naval forces, post Tsunami of 2004 has been established as a benchmark in the Humanitarian Assistance and Disaster Relief (HADR) operations. This event also is taken as turning point in India's understanding of the benefits of cooperation with other maritime democracies in the Asia Pacific. "The Action Plan envisages commitments for greater cooperation in Humanitarian Assistance and Disaster Relief (HADR), collaboration in the East Asia Summit on disaster management; and cooperation and exchanges on peacekeeping issues, including between peacekeeping institutions."[219] There is much room for India and Australia and other Indian Ocean states to work together in HADR. For example, India and Australia could work together to develop a system for responding to natural disasters in the Indian Ocean region, "similar to the FRANZ trilateral cooperation arrangement in the South Pacific which helps Australia, France, and New Zealand and others to coordinate their relief operations after cyclones and other natural disasters."[220] The framework for Security Cooperation signed between the two countries is significant from several aspects. "It represents an intention to intensify the engagements that have been developing over the last decade or so. It may also indicate a desire by the Modi Government to move past some of India's previous inhibitions in the defence relationship with Australia."[221] The significance and importance of the framework can also be ascertained from the fact that the "Framework" has been included in Defence White paper 2016, released by the government of Australia, "In line with the Framework for Security Cooperation, the Government will seek to further mature our defence relationship with India in support of our shared strategic interests."[222]

Comprehensive Strategic Partnership 2020

In a first of its kind initiative, Indian and Australian Prime Ministers jointly participated in an India-Australia Leaders' virtual Summit on 04 June 2020. In order to strengthen bilateral ties and to prepare them for futuristic challenges, India and Australia committed to elevate the bilateral Strategic Partnership concluded in 2009 to a Comprehensive Strategic Partnership (CSP). "We have built a durable, future-looking relationship. India and Australia are natural partners, well positioned to build a more secure and prosperous future for own peoples, the Indo-Pacific and the wider world. The CSP reflects a historic high point in our relationship. The elements include defence and maritime security, cyber -security and technology, science and research and critical supply chains."[223]

The CSP mirrors the India and Australia's vision of a free and rules-based Indo Pacific region duly supported by inclusive global and regional institutions and shared interests and vindicates the respective engagements of both the countries in the Indo Pacific. During the virtual summit, a joint statement on CSP and a joint declaration on Shared Vision for Maritime Cooperation in the Indo Pacific were announced. The shared vision reiterates the stated position of both countries to harness opportunities and meet challenges together in the commons of Indo Pacific. With the shared maritime geographies and a deep and long-standing friendship, India and Australia have committed themselves to work together towards realisation of this shared vision and ensure freedom of navigation and over flight in the

Indo Pacific region, and maintaining open, safe and efficient sea lanes for transportation and communication.[224]

Two plus Two Dialogue

The bilateral relationship between India and Australia is also witnessing an upward swing due to the increased levels of diplomatic engagements. Foreign Ministers' Framework Dialogue (FMFD) is another initiative and is playing a fundamental role in the advancing of bilateral agenda. The dialogue in its present format is held annually, alternatively in India and Australia. In another vindication of converging strategic interests of India and Australia, both the countries are involved in Foreign and Defence Secretaries' Dialogue (2+2) since 2017. The third edition of 2+2 dialogue was held in New Delhi in December 2019. These meetings provide opportunities for both the countries to review the status of their bilateral relationship in the context of emerging scenarios.[225] Continuous engagement of India and Australia in 2+2 dialogue underscores the growing alignment between the defence and foreign affair perspectives of both the countries and provides a subtle but stable platform for defence diplomacy. Under the aegis of Comprehensive Security Partnership and as a sign of growing bilateral alignment both the countries have also decided to upgrade their relationship.

Military Diplomacy

Defence diplomacy over a period of time has attained the status of a special instrument of foreign policy and facilitates the bilateral relationship of two countries to become more close and intimate, yet allowing respective countries to retain strategic autonomy. As per Defence Strategic Update 2020, released by Australia, the Indo Pacific is becoming the main theatre for greater strategic competition between major powers, making the region tenser, more contested, and more prone to conflict and the region is in the midst of the "most consequential strategic realignment since the Second World War."[226] As part of the initiative, both the countries are working towards closer defence cooperation; providing impetus to the military diplomacy, which has been an increasingly prominent characteristic of India Australia bilateral relationship. The recent accretions in the bilateral and minilateral defence engagements of

India have been recognised globally and a due notice of these engagements has also been taken by China. The expansion of defence diplomacy by India has also been acknowledged by the Asia Power Index 2020 released by Lowy Institute, Australia. "On the one hand, it is up by one place in defence networks, reflecting progress in its regional defence diplomacy, notably with the quadrilateral security grouping, which includes Australia, Japan and the United States."[227]

As part of CSP, India and Australia have signed seven bilateral agreements, out of which centrality and significance of Mutual Logistics Support (MLSA) is particularly important. "The MLSA assumes greater importance in light of India and Australia's limited naval capabilities. Normally, a scarcity of resources puts severe limitations on a country's ability to project power in the distant waters, leaving its far-off assets at the mercy of other actors. In the case of India and Australia, such a limitation does not match their ambitions in the region; it also puts them at a disadvantage vis-à-vis a belligerent China. For this reason, the MLSA holds considerable significance."[228] The agreement mandates allowing of reciprocal access to military facilities for logistics support to include food, water, petroleum (fuel), spare parts and other components. The agreement will provide logistics arrangements during joint military exercises, Humanitarian Assistance and Disaster Relief (HADR) operations and Passage exercises (PASSEX) of Navies of both countries. The agreement has paved way for future such agreements between the two countries. The strategic significance of this agreement is immense in terms of up gradation of strategic relationship. "A shared understanding and foundational agreements on logistic support shared SOPs and communication protocols will enable both countries to optimally utilize their resources not only towards effective surveillance of the region against a developing threat but also to combating the non-traditional threats to maritime security that abound in this region."[229] The agreement is also important from the perspective of facilitating the interoperability between the armed forces of two countries. The logistics support agreement between India and Australia is integral to the community of law-abiding nations working to uphold the prevailing order in the Indo-Pacific.[230]

AUSINDEX

The foundations of any strong and mutually reliable bilateral relationship hinge on two important aspects of defence and economic cooperation and the strategic location of India in Indo Pacific is facilitating up-gradation of existing strategic relationships. "Its long tradition of democratic values and abiding commitment to freedom of navigation and free trade makes India a key strategic partner of Australia."[231] As part of this up-gradation, India and Australia decided to take the relationship in the defence cooperation to newer heights by instituting a biennial naval exercises code named AUSINDEX. "The Bilateral Maritime Exercise between India and Australia 'AUSINDEX-15' was conducted on the East Coast of India, in September 2015. The maritime exercise was a tangible sign that will strengthen defence co-operation between the two countries as envisaged in the Framework for Security Co-operation announced by the Australian and the Indian Prime Ministers in 2014."[232]

India and Australia conducted the third edition of bilateral maritime exercise - AUSINDEX 2019 in the Bay of Bengal. Over a period of time, the series of bilateral maritime exercises have been transformed into an extended Indo-Pacific Endeavour deployment, a perfect demonstration of maritime diplomacy tool and the exercise witnessed a first ever largest deployment of Australian forces to India.[233] Besides AUSINDEX, India and Australia are participating in a series of other bilateral military exercises, to include AUSTRAHIND, Exercise Pitch Black and Kakadu series. The increased level of defence diplomacy between India and Australia has manifested in the almost four fold increase in bilateral defence exercises between the two countries. "During (exercise) Malabar, we saw the type of cooperation envisaged by the MLSA. However, attention focused on Malabar has masked the four-fold increase in defence activities over the past six years between India and Australia, which includes the AUSINDEX, which is Australia's biggest and most complicated bilateral naval exercise; and Exercise Pitch Black, involving Airway Forces."[234] Overall, by the reckoning of the Australian government, there has been an increase from 11 defence exercises, meetings, and activities in 2014 to 29 in 2017, and 38 in 2018.[235] Besides international signaling towards the intent of strategic partnership, these exercises are facilitating closer cooperation at tactical level, exchange of best practices and interoperability of processes and drills.

Table 1: Major Defence Exercises Between India and Australia[236]

Exercise	Conducting/Hosting Entity	India/Australia's Participation
Exercise Kakadu	A joint-enabled, biennial exercise hosted by the Royal Australian Navy and supported by the Royal Australian Air Force	India, since 20 16
Exercise Talisman Sabre	A bilateral combined training activity between Australian Defence Force and United States military	India, Observer in 2019
Rim of the Pacific (RIMPAC)	A biennial international naval exercise hosted by the US Navy	India, since 2012
MILAN	A biennial multilateral naval exercise hosted by the Indian Navy	Australia , since 2003
Exercise AUSTRA HIND	A joint military exercise conducted between India and Australia	Held in 2016-2017 and 2017-2018
Exercise Pitch Black	A biennial multi-national warfare exercise hosted by the Royal Australian Air Force	India, in 2018
AUSINDEX 2019	A biennial bilateral maritime exercise between India and Australia	Held in 2015, 2017, 2019

Malabar Exercises

Malabar Exercises between India and the US, pitched at a basic level of naval drills have been conducted since 1992. The series have become an annual feature since 2002. In 2007, a multilateral version of these exercises, involving Australia, Japan, Singapore, India and the US were conducted. In June 2007, days before the first-ever official-level security consultation between the US, India, Japan and Australia, China issued demarches to each of the participants seeking to know the purpose behind their meeting.[237] No further multilateral exercises have been held after 2007 but 2015 onwards, Japan has been made as a permanent member of the Malabar exercises.

Australian Defence Minister Marise Payne during her visit to Tokyo in April 2017 raised the issue of Australia's participation in Malabar exercises as an 'observer' and that Australia was "very interested in a quadrilateral engagement with India, Japan and the United States."[238] In a subtle but clear sign on the firming up of military dimensions of QSD, Australia was invited for Malabar naval exercises 2020, an indication that shared national security concerns over China's perceived expansionism in the region is bringing the two countries closer together.[239] In a sign of increasing reapproachment and strategic alignment between the two countries, Australia joined Malabar series of Exercises after 13 years. This bilateral engagement in the garb of multilateral arrangement is very significant and stands out as a major step towards closer defence cooperation between India and Australia. "The undeniable success of Malabar this year helps to tell a broader story - that Australia, India, Japan and the US are working together quadrilaterally, trilaterally and bilaterally to demonstrate a common purpose, to support a secure, open and inclusive region."[240]

The geostrategic undertones of the Indo Pacific construct are aligning to provide opportunities for both India and Australia to play a dominant role in the region. The region is not based on exclusivity but rather on inclusivity as the enthusiasm and readiness of other nations of ASEAN and nonresident powers indicate. In spite of a decent progress in the Quad deliberations in the recent times, the concept is still in infancy stage and will need more time and commitment from members to crystallize. The strategic partnership between India and Australia, facilitated by converging defence and diplomatic compulsions will be of great significance in the emerging geostrategic landscape of Indo Pacific.

The foundation of a strong bilateral relationship cannot be laid in isolation and requires a holistic integration of all the stake holders. Bilateral relationship is about engagement and building relationships based on strong and redundant networks of people to people relationship to include individuals, families, community groups, institutions of higher learning's and technological and scientific research institutions. In the case of India and Australia, besides government to government reapproachment and congruence of strategic and geo political interests, people to people links have also played an important and significant role in strengthening and sustaining the relationship. The strength and stability being provided to the bilateral relationship by the people to people relationship is of historical importance and promises a strong possibility of further cementing the relationship.

CHAPTER 3

TRANSNATIONAL EDUCATION & KNOWLEDGE PARTNERSHIPS: A SYMBIOTIC THREAD

"Steps should be taken for the exchange of technicians and students, which will not only assist us both but will further cement the relationship between the two countries."[241]

It is a proven fact that the knowledge base of any economy is invariably synonymous with the times of origin of civilisation itself and the mutual relationship between knowledge and economy has indeed been very intricate and absolute. Societies in the history have benefitted from the knowledge of its inhabitants and have allowed others also to benefit from the same. Alfred Marshal, a pioneer in the field of economics was instrumental in linking the concept of knowledge with the economy, when he propounded that production or economy is directly proportional to the knowledge base of the society. "Knowledge is our most powerful engine of production". In another pioneer work, M. Abramowitz brought out disconnect between knowledge and the production function in the early 20th Century. "Knowledge was neither directly measured nor incorporated in the production function. Researchers attempted to account for it through the unexplained portion of economic growth. The unexplained portion was labeled technical change, human factor and organization, measure of our ignorance or residue."[242]

In the contemporary times the rapid upsurge of innovative global research networks, coupled with unique modes of scholastic mobility involving all stake holders to include students, scholars, programs, education providers, research, and policies has shuffled the theory and practice of International higher education and research to a never seen before incarnation. Coupled with the emergence and vitalization of new instruments and mechanisms in the contemporary diplomacy, people to people relations have assumed a significant portion of modern day diplomacy. The rise and increasing adaptation of these mechanisms is ensuring that the traditional diplomacy which was earlier restricted to the domain of state only is increasingly being challenged, thereby giving importance to the informal diplomatic channels. Therefore, these potential diplomatic agents beyond the traditional government only approach require careful deliberation in the contemporary bilateral engagements between the states. These diplomatic agents are playing a critical part in promoting the bilateral relationship between India and Australia also. As part of this chapter an endeavour has been made to bring out the importance of the transnational flow of students, researchers, and other academia duly facilitated by government to government agreements, which is providing a tremendous boost to public diplomacy between India and Australia and facilitating the strengthening of bilateral relationship of India and Australia.

Collaborations in the field of International higher education between the countries, are increasingly being considered as potential agents of diplomacy which possesses an immense potential to foster the people to people relations. The knowledge partnerships in research and innovations have proved themselves very useful in facilitating the building and strengthening of bilateral relations between two countries, whereas as a corollary the strength of bilateral relations has correspondingly promoted the relations in the fields of higher education, research and innovation. In order to promote people to people relations, the public diplomacy strategies therefore, have been tweaked by the countries and correspondingly bilateral relations in the fields of higher education and research have become an invariable part of public diplomacy, thereby making international students an important part of the entire process. The commonly accepted definition of international (or mobile) students, defines them as students who have crossed a national border and moved to another country with the objective of studying. Operationally, Organization for Economic Co-operation and Development (OECD), has defined international students as who are not usual residents of their country of study, i.e. those who have recently moved to the destination (host) country from somewhere else.

Felt Need for International Education: India

A lot of research has been carried out to delineate the aspects underscoring the need to go abroad for higher studies. An obvious relationship between international education and migration is an established fact. A large number of push and pull factors also play a critical role in crystallizing the decision to go abroad for higher studies and in deciding a country and institution, in which to study. As per findings of an Education Report titled 'The Value of Education: Learning for life', conducted by Hong Kong and Shanghai Banking Corporation (HSBC) India in 2015, India has the world's highest proportion of parents, 88 percent who are willing to send their children abroad for post-graduate studies, ahead of Turkey (83 percent) and Malaysia and China (82 percent).[243] The same study also concluded that higher costs of overseas education are one of the key barriers for Indian parents when it comes to sending children overseas for education and at least 92 percent of Indian parents, who are open to the idea of an international university education, would consider paying more for it than they would to educate their children in India.[244] This study underscored the significance of international degrees for both, the prospective international students and their parents in India and has rightly put into perspective the obsession of foreign degree for Indian students.

It is a known fact that the knowledge economy of a society is invariably linked with the inhabitants, which includes the natives as well as people who get attracted by the prospects of superior and well established credentials of the knowledge economy of that particular society. An international student while initiating the process of selecting a final study destination undergoes three separate and distinct stages. Initially the prospective student decides to study internationally rather than locally, influenced by a series of 'push' factors within the home country. After the finalization of the decision to study abroad, in the second stage the 'pull' factors for the selection of the host country start getting manifested. In the third and the final stage, a prospective international student, selects an institution. An assortment of supplementary 'pull' factors, to include, an institution's prestige for quality, array of courses offered, government to government agreements, spread of alumni among others, further collaborate and facilitate selection of a particular institution. Due to the existence of institutional mechanisms forged at governmental levels, significant pull factors were offered for Indian students by the universities in the USA and European countries, particularly UK and Germany, in the later part of the last century.

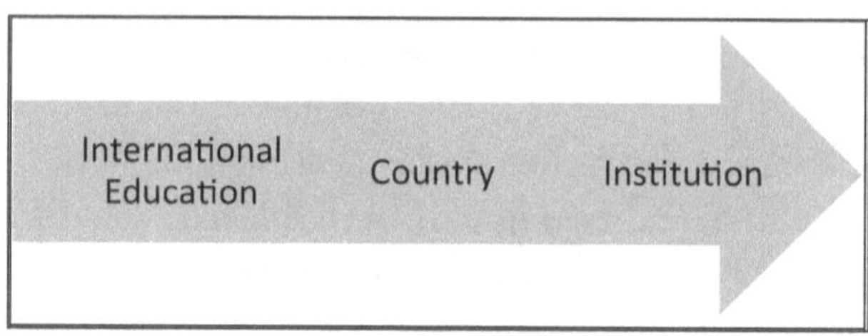

Fig 4: Three Stage Process

Australia, as part of its Public Diplomacy strategy, also endeavoured to utilize the opportunities in the field to supplement the diplomatic efforts. Towards this direction a large number of efforts and initiatives were institutionalized by the country. "To highlight her commitment to building deeper and broader links through, the New Colombo Plan (NCP); Australia Awards; Australian Volunteers for International Development (AVID); Australian NGO Cooperation Programme (ANCP); the Direct Aid Programme (DAP); sports cooperation; growing two-way tourism; investing aid in the sustainable development of our close neighbours; and strengthening regional political and institutional architecture."[245] It is due to these continued efforts that transnational flow of information and ideas has become core to the public diplomacy strategy of Australia.

Internationalization of Education: Australia

As far as the bilateral relationship between India and Australia is concerned, the inherent push and pull factors; push from India and pull from Australia are intricately linked as manifested in the rapid rise of international students from India in Australia. A glance at historical evolution of internationalization of education in Australia reveals that due to restrictions imposed by the White Australia policy and other associated acts; the number of international students allowed was also very restricted. Based on one odd individual agreement between Australia and the concerned country, some relaxations allowed the flow of international students to Australia. The end of the World War II, witnessed independence of a large number of countries and the corresponding aversion to the colonial aspirations also manifested. Alongside the aversion, the urge and the need for social and economic upliftment of the newly independent societies by provisioning of developmental aid, also witnessed an exponential increase in the immediate aftermath of the Great War.

The Colombo Plan, formulated at the Commonwealth Heads of Government Meeting (CHOGM) at Colombo in 1950 was one such instrument, under the aegis of which Australia for the first time sponsored the overseas students for study in Australian institutions. The original signatories to the agreement included Australia, Canada, Ceylon, New Zealand, Pakistan, the United Kingdom, Malaya and North Borneo, the scope of which was later expanded to include 25 countries in total. Starting 1973, a series of wide ranging reforms in the internationalization of education was launched by Australia. With a view to provide more opportunities to Australians in tertiary education, the government capped the number of private international students to 10,000 and tuition fees for Australians as well international students were abolished. Realizing the importance of higher international education, in a fresh initiative in 1979, the cap of 10,000 private international students was removed and some initiatives for providing subsidy to international students in form of visa fees and later Overseas Student Charge (OSC) were also introduced.

Based on the recommendations of Committee to Review Australian Overseas Aid Programme and Committee of Review Private Overseas Students Policy, some tweaking of existing policies was announced in 1985 which catered for unlimited number of international students over and above the authorized limit of allowance of subsidized students, subject to respective university entry requirements and payment of full fees. This decision came under serious scrutiny from academicians and overseas, who abhorred the very idea of linking of trade, aid and education. In an ultimate step towards internationalization of education, the government in 1989 completely scrapped the subsidized component of the education for international students and beginning 1990 all international students or their sponsors were supposed to pay complete fees for the respective courses. This landmark event in the internationalization of higher education, proved to be a catalyst in the transnational flow of students and researchers albeit one sided only, from India to Australia. The lifting of capping on the number of international students and the provision of admitting international students by the universities in Australia forthwith metamorphosed into an opportunity for countries of South East Asia including China. These nations because of their intimate relations with Australia were able to realize the significance of higher education opportunities available in Australia.

Transnational Education: Significance of Cooperation

As discussed in chapter one, till 1980s and even in early part of 1990s, the bilateral relationship between India and Australia was marred with issues of mutual distrust and dissonance and the Australian perspective during this period continued to be dominated by an active East Asian outlook, relegating India into background. However, the potential of India in the field of internationalization of education was not lost on the planners in Australia and in anticipation of the promising future of bilateral cooperation in this field, the Australian Government appointed its first education counselor to its High Commission in India in the early 1990s. The mandate of the appointment included application of the 'whole of government' approach to the holistic spectrum of educational exports. Starting here onwards this phase in the internationalization of higher education and transnational flow of students from India to Australia can be divided into three distinct sub phases.

Initially, the primary focus of the efforts of Australia was concentrated on increasing the enrolment of students from India for higher education, thereby yielding the entire process, purely commercial overtones. These endeavours did not result in the optimum exploitation of inherent potential of collaboration in the field of higher education between the two countries, as they were not supported by an institutionalized mechanism of academic and cultural exchange agreements at the governmental levels, leading to the non realisation of the targets of enrolments from India. As a result, the percentage of Indian students to the overall International students arriving in Australia for higher studies was very miniscule in the last few years of the previous century and early years of the present millennial. The later part of this phase is also characterized by a decline in the percentage of Indian students to the overall arrival of international students primarily due to the free fall witnessed in the bilateral relations attributed to the nuclear tests carried out by India in 1998.

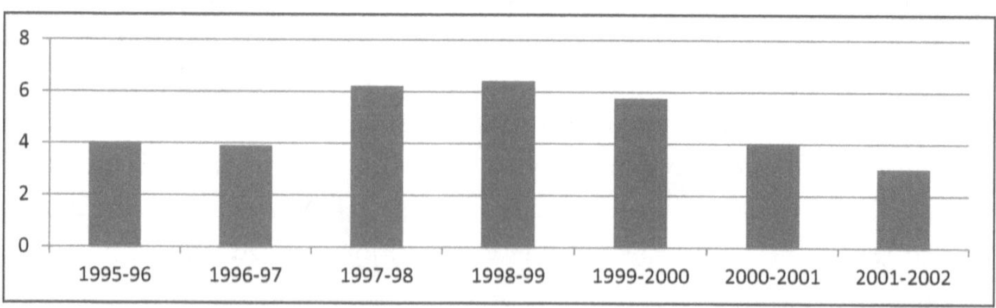

Fig 5: Percentage of Indian Students to Overall International Students Enrolment (1995 to 2002)[246]

The second sub phase of the transnational flow of Indian students to Australia can be assumed to have started in 2002 and continued till 2013. This phase initially witnessed a rise of students from India but the unfortunate events of series of racial attacks on India students in Australia, coupled with the economic recession of 2008, played a major role in the reduction of Indian students. The racial attacks not only threatened Australia's international education sector but also strained relations between Australia and India and triggered riots and mass protests in Sydney and Melbourne. "I speak on behalf of all Australians when say I say that we deplore and condemn these attacks, I said to Prime Minister Singh that the more than 90,000 Indian students in Australia are welcome guests in our country."[247] In the aftermath of these racial attacks, the then Deputy Prime Minister of Australia Julia Gillard visited India and an honest and sincere mechanism was endeavored to be launched to address the Indian concerns on the issue. "The Australian Government is committed to taking its relationship with India to the front rank of our international partnerships, the principal aim of my visit is to reinforce Australia's image as a culturally diverse, welcoming and safe country for Indian students, business people and other visitors. I will have the opportunity to thank the Indian Government for its support as we have responded strongly to the challenges faced by Indian students in Australia."[248]

In a survey carried out by the Australian think tank Lowy Institute in 2010, to the response to the question, "Do you personally think Australia's relationship with India has been damaged or has not been damaged following the recent attacks on Indian students in Australia?", 28 percent of respondents had agreed that the relationship has been damaged a lot, whereas 45 percent of respondents categorized it as damaged somewhat.[249]

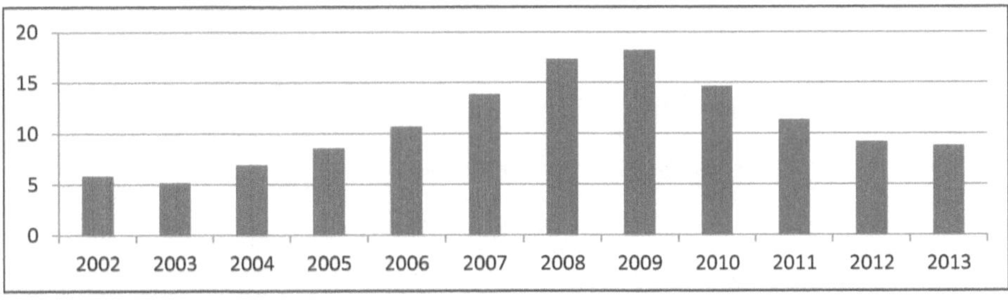

Fig 6: Percentage of Indian Students to Overall International Students Enrolment (2002 to 2013)[250]

The third and ongoing sub phase of the transnational flow of Indian students to Australia started from 2014 onwards and has witnessed exponential increase of Indian students in Australia. As compared to phase one of the process, this phase has been characterized by a series of Memorandums of Understanding (MoU) and bilateral agreements, in the fields of students mobility, students welfare and international education between India and Australia. In October 2012, a MoU on Student Mobility and Welfare was signed during state visit of Australian Prime Minister to India, which was followed by a MoU on Cooperation in Technical Vocational Education and Training (TVET) signed during the state visit of Prime Minister of Australia to India in September 2014. In order to strengthen the people-to-people contacts and facilitate and regulate the regulations between the two countries with respect to social security benefits and coverage, an agreement on Social security was signed during the state visit of Indian Prime Minister to Australia in November 2014. During the virtual summit between the Prime Ministers of India and Australia in June 2020, another MoU on cooperation in Vocational Education and Training (VET) was signed. In addition during the period a large number of individual agreements and MoU between institutes of higher learning on student exchange programmes and cooperation have been signed.

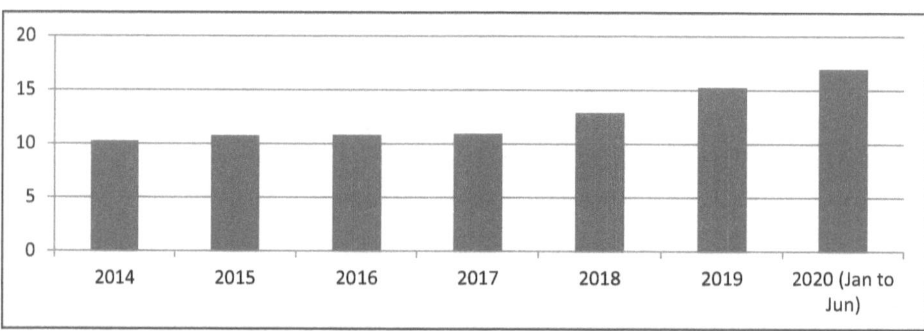

Fig 7: Percentage of Indian Students to Overall International Students Enrolment (2014 to 2020)[251]

Coming back to the attractiveness of Australia for higher studies for Indian students, Mazzarol, Kemp and Savery in a seminal study in 1997 on 'pull' factors, facilitating decision of a prospective student to select a particular study destination brought out certain factors which influence the decision. The study identified six factors to include, knowledge and awareness of the destination country in the home country of the student, personal recommendations that the study destination receives from parents, relatives, friends and education agents, cost related aspects, environment, geographical proximity and social links were identified as an important framework for understanding the influences that motivate a student's selection of a host country.[252]

Table 2: Importance of the Knowledge & Awareness of the Host Country as an Influencing Factor in Motivating Student Destination Choice[253]

Factors	Percentage of Respondents
Ease to obtain information on host country	89
Knowledge of host country	82
Quality of Education in host country	96
Recognition of qualifications of host country	90

This study in isolation provides an insight into the mind of a prospective international student and delineates the pull factors which influence the decision to select a destination country for higher education. A holistic analysis in conjunction with the other available India specific studies pertaining to the selection of a destination country for higher education reveals that Australia indeed scores high as a destination country for higher education by the prospective students from India.

A series of four country studies carried out on behalf of Australian Education International (AEI) and the Department of Education, Training and Youth Affairs (DETYA), from 1996 to 2000, had enabled an investigation of the factors likely to influence international student choice of study destinations. As part of this series, the India specific study yielded greater insights into the factors responsible for facilitating finalization of choice of destination country for higher studies. Providing a fillip to the theory of 'push' factors, an overwhelming 93 percent of respondents had graded overseas courses higher than the local courses, whereas 59 percent of students had expressed their intentions to migrate. In the same study, a greater percentage of respondents had graded quality of education in the host country as an important factor.

Another study, after the unfortunate events of 2009, carried out by the AEI with support from the Department of Immigration and Citizenship (DIAC) and Australia Trade and Investment Commission (AUSTRADE) in six of Australia's largest source countries of international students, had examined the perceptions of students studying in Australia. In the survey, the Indian Education Agents and prospective students gave predominant importance to quality of education and the cost of education, in the decision making process for international education. [254] The same survey also concluded that more than half of the prospective international students from India, think that tuition fees and living expenses at Australia are competitive than those of Canada, UK and the USA. The aspects of time taken by the universities to process an application and issuance of visa were also dampeners for other countries, whereas Australia was ranked relatively high by the prospective Indian students. [255] Education agents, perform a very critical and essential role in facilitating the flow of students for international higher studies. In a report prepared for Australia Education International (AEI), government websites with education information have been ranked relatively high by Education Agents, in order to know about costs of studying in foreign countries.[256]

Table 3: Perspectives of Education Agents

Aspect	Education Agents	Students
Time taken by a University to process an application	1	1
Time taken to process Visa	1	1
Amount of information needed to apply (01- least)	2	1
Quality of Education System	2	3

The quality of holistic education offerings plays an extremely important role in the international education decision making process by the prospective international students, parents and education agents. The quality of international education offered by the Australian education facilities is eminently responsible for attracting international learners to Australia's shores. A large number of universities in Australia are providing quality for international learners in terms of the quality of the courses and the institutions, the global recognition of the qualifications and corresponding improved employment outcomes, which is exerting a significant pull factor for the learners from India. The quality and reputation of Australia's education institutions is well established on institutional and other global rankings. In the Times Ranking 2020 of World Universities, there are six Australian universities in top 100, thereby corroborating the international standards in teaching, research and international outlook being practiced in these institutions.[257] The international acceptance of these universities is substantiated by the percentage of international students in these universities which varies from 38 to 48 percent. This international recognition of Australian Universities has also resulted in doubling of Indian students in Australia, at the expense of the US, where the percentage of Indian students has witnessed declining trends.

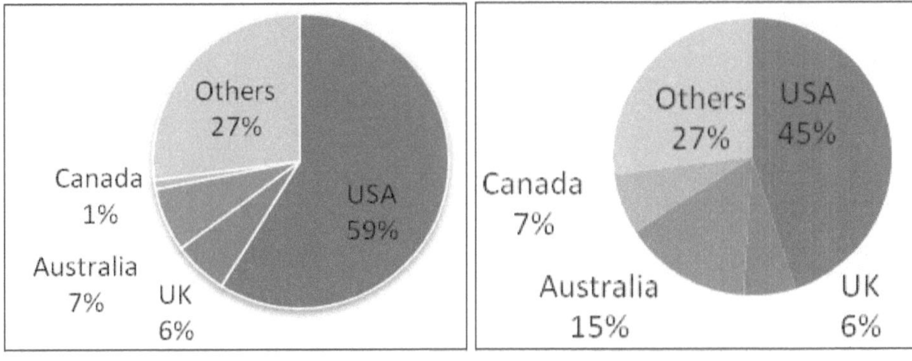

Fig 8: Change in Preferences of Indian Students: 2000 to 2017

Thus, it can be inferred that in sync with the results of the survey, the destination choice of Indian students has increasingly been centered on Australia. The relative ease of obtaining information on the host country along with the knowledge of the host country gleaned from friends, peers and distant relations, has played a preeminent role in deciding Australia as the destination choice for higher studies. In the initial years of the establishment of higher education relations between India and Australia, the aspects like university rankings, equivalence of qualifications and fund requirements played spoil sport, which have gradually been resolved over the period of time. This factor gets highlighted in the year on year increase in the number of Indian students applying for higher studies in Australia.

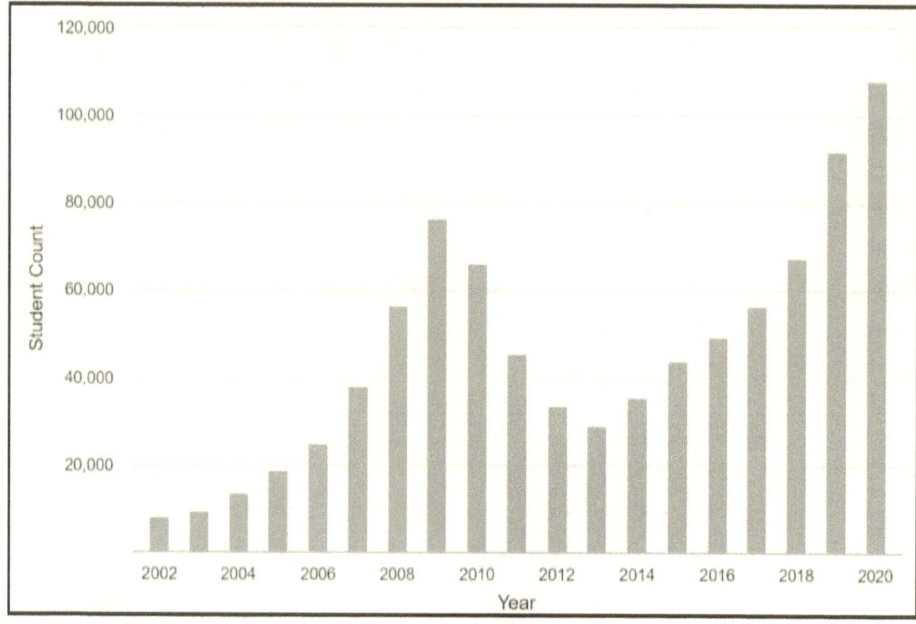

Fig 9: Rise in the numbers of Indian Students in Australia

Another significant aspect of the bilateral relationship between India and Australia is the factor of Indian Diaspora which has been discussed in detail in the next chapter of the book. As diaspora is directly linked with the aspects of migration, the streams of study selected by the international students from India are therefore also linked with the twin aspects of migration and diaspora. There has been an exponential increase in the number of students from India who are pursuing higher education in Australia.

Opportunities for Indian Students

In Australia, the international students are predominantly enrolled in five distinct types of sectors, to include higher education sector, Vocational Education and Training (VET) sector, the English Language Intensive Courses for Overseas Students (ELICOS) sector and the schools sector. ELICOS provides a popular pathway for international students moving into the VET and higher education sectors and most of the international students opt for this avenue to move out to other sectors in the higher education. The analysis of data provided by AEI reveals that in 2015, 30 per cent of international students who commenced a higher education course had previously studied in the ELICOS sector, while 37 per cent of international students who commenced a VET course did so through an ELICOS pathway.

Like other international students, Higher education sector has also been a favorite among the students from India. In the initial days of cooperation in the transnational education between India and Australia, due to the duration and other qualitative requirements, the Master of Business Administration (MBA) in Australia of those times, was not suited for the students from India. As a result at the inception of educational relationship between India and Australia, in the late 1990s, the students from India preferred engineering and computer science subjects for higher education. The challenge for university planners in Australia therefore translated to assess the extent to which degree offerings could be modified to suit a potentially huge market in India, while at the same time meeting a demand in Australia for a quite different degree.[258] With the educational relationship between India and Australia advancing over a period of time, the basic details have been sorted out and the strength of Indian students studying in Australia continued to increase.

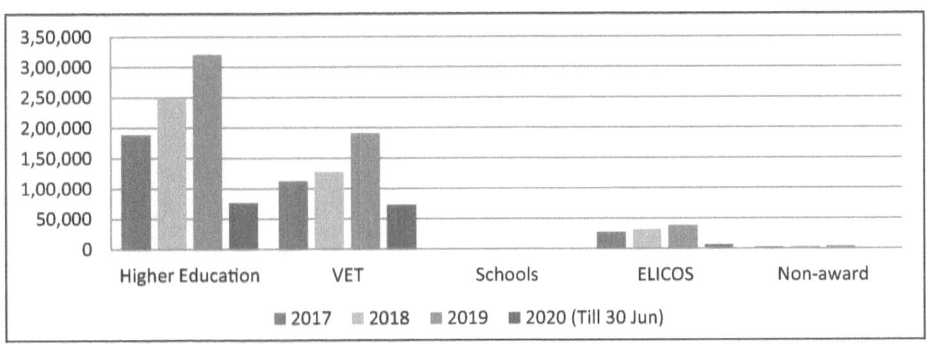

Fig 10: Commencements by Indian Students in Different Sectors: 2017 to 2020[259]

As a result not only higher studies in business administration and management, but the entire spectrum of higher studies opportunities being offered in institutes of higher education in Australia has undergone qualitative and quantitative innovations, specifically addressing the requirements of students from India. Corresponding with the strengthening of the bilateral relations between the two countries, the educational relationship has also continued to prosper, thereby facilitating rise in commencement and enrolment of Indian students in different sectors of higher education system in Australia.

From Education to Migration

Historically, in sync with the Australia's skilled migration framework, most Indian students at least till 2005 were heavily subscribing to Post Graduate programmes in Information Technology (IT) related and accounting subjects, as these occupations were identified under the framework where graduates were in high demand. Enrolments, therefore, of international students including Indians in programmes that enabled students to obtain residence increased exponentially, so much so that in 2004-05, out of total Indian students graduating from Australian university programmes, who obtained permanent residency, more than one third of these students were computing professionals (36%) and over a quarter were accountants (28%), with just 5% of them being tradespersons.[260] An analysis of the history of student migration to Australia from India makes it obvious that the enrolment of students in a particular course of instruction or level is directly proportional to proposed or introduced changes in the qualification recognition framework for migration purposes.

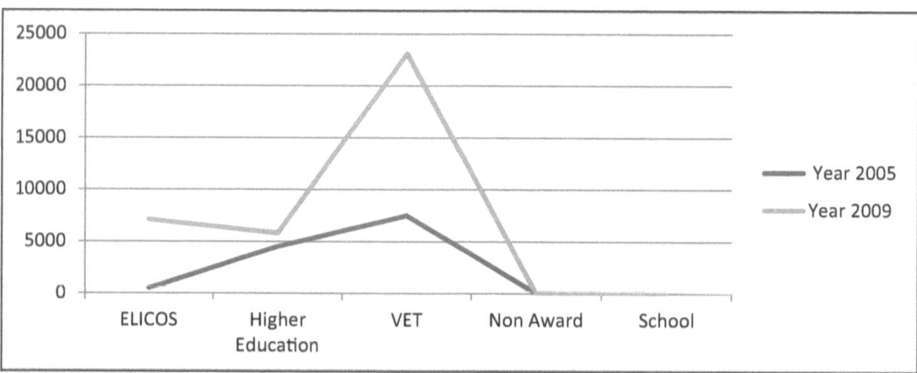

Fig 11: Commencement of Indian Students by Sector: 2005 & 2009[261]

In 2005, Australia, increased the number of points required by international graduates to obtain permanent residency in the along with the inclusion of some additional trades, like cooking and hairdressing in the occupation list. "At present, cooking and hair dressing attract the maximum 75 points for a trade and virtually guarantee a visa after the 30 points for age and 15 points for

English proficiency are added for the required total of 120. These courses are so popular that enrolment in commercial cookery and hairdressing has nearly tripled in the past two years, with many graduates not practicing their trade once they have attained a visa"[262] and by 2008, 14400 Indian students were studying in private colleges in programs grouped under the 'Food, Hospitality and Personal Services' classification, accounting more than a quarter of all students in these programmes. In 2009, the Immigration Department of Government of Australia reported that, "the number of student visa holders from India increased by 44.6 per cent from 63,558 on 30 June 2008 to 91,887 on 30 June 2009, making it the top source country"[263] for overseas students coming to Australia in that year. In 2019 (Jan - Dec), there was an increase of 30 percent of Indian students from the previous year (Jan - Dec). Out of fresh enrolment of 78,506 students in 2019, the majority commenced their studies in higher education and VET sectors. The dominance of higher education and VET sectors is continuously being witnessed in the total enrolment of Indian students.

Table 4: Temporary visas selected categories, 2015-16 to 2018-19[264]

Temporary visa category	2015-16	2016-17	2017-18	2018-19	% change since 2017-18	% change since 2015-16
ELICOS	18	32	39	115	194.9	538.9
Schools	83	84	112	120	7.1	44.6
Vocational Education and Training	4,303	2,790	5,377	9,673	79.9	124.8
Higher Education	24,417	30,795	42,920	55,481	29.3	127.2
Postgraduate Research	600	605	756	889	17.6	48.2
Non-Award	136	116	180	149	-17.2	9.6
Foreign Affairs or Defence	34	68	85	22	-74.1	-35.3
Total: International Student visa grants	29,591	34,490	49,469	66,449	34.3	124.6

The intricate link between higher education and skilled migration in Australia, with specific reference has been a subject of intense research and the link has also been conclusively proven. This aspect has critical bearing on the issue of Diaspora, which has facilitated the bilateral relationship between the two countries.

Institutionalized Collaborations

The Government endorsed agreements form a bed rock of the bilateral relations. The relations between India and Australia in the fields of education and research have also been promoted and diversified by the virtue of these agreements. In this part of the chapter an endeavour has been made to study the bilateral relationship through the prism of cooperation in the fields of education and research. The significance of VET Sector in the bilateral relationship has been adequately covered in the earlier part of the chapter. The sector has witnessed unprecedented demand from prospective students from India and holds immense potential to take the bilateral relationship to new levels. "The work that both India and Australia industry skill councils have done ... We have seen an exchange of mutually beneficial standards in the skills landscape which are bound to build strong resources for both the countries."[265]

The Economic Strategy for India 2035[266] categorized the impact of cooperation in this field on bilateral relationship in three distinct spheres, Technical Vocational Education & Training (TVET) at the government level, partnering with Indian training providers to offer courses for both onshore and offshore employment and working directly with large Indian corporate sector to meet their skills needs. A Memorandum of Understanding (MoU) on cooperation in TVET between the National Skill Development Corporation (NSDC), Government of India and the Department of Industry, Government of Australia was signed in September 2014. The MoU prescribed exchange of information and policy ideas on areas of mutual interest to include, TVET systems in both countries, competency standards development, assessment and certification, particularly skills assessments for migration and/or occupational purposes, industry participation in TVET policy development, training delivery, assessment and certification, and formal work-based training such as apprenticeships. [267] The initiative was one of its kinds and has been considered very successful in providing a great boost to the people to people contacts between the two countries. Though the one sided movement of Indian students to the established VET ecosystem in Australia is experiencing an year on year increase, almost exponential growth, the initiative for providing

TVET competency standards development in India by Australia seems to have lost steam. As per the information hosted on the portal of Ministry of Skill Development and Entrepreneurship, Government of India, the status of TVET MoU with Australia is being depicted as dormant due to withdrawal of funds from Sector Skill Councils (SSC) in Australia by the Australian Government, and therefore the process of developing transnational standards has been depicted as unable to be proceed.[268] In order to further the people to people relationship between India and Australia, it is imperative that this collaboration is taken forward and issues, if any are resolved at the earliest. The huge demographic dividend offered by India provides a significant untapped potential towards further cooperation between India and Australia in the field of TVET.

The first agreement between India and Australia in the field of Education and Research was signed as part of a Cultural Agreement on 21 October 1971. Under the provisions of this agreement, both the countries agreed to exchange of scholars and cooperation in the field of science, besides other fields. Through another bilateral agreement of 1975, India and Australia had agreed to promote opportunities for cooperation in the fields of scientific and technological research. With the stream of biotechnology having been established as holding a promising opportunity for cooperation between the two countries, both countries signed an agreement between the Department of Biotechnology (DBT), Government of India and the Australian Department of Education, Science and Training, Government of Australia in March 2006. With an upswing in the bilateral relationship between India and Australia, a large number of agreements have been signed for cooperation in the fields of education and research, which are facilitating an increased cooperation, synergy and a warm people to people relationship. It is therefore imperative to have a critical understanding of the existing arrangements and agreements which have transformed the bilateral relationship to newer levels.

One of the most important arrangements which have facilitated the knowledge partnership between India and Australia is the Australia India Strategic Research Fund (AISRF). With an objective to facilitate Australian researchers from public and private sectors to collaborate with Indian scientists in leading-edge scientific research projects and workshops, AISRF was launched by both the countries in 2006. The fund had commenced with an initial commitment of $20 million by both the countries over five years.

The commitment was increased to $50 million by each country over five years in November 2009. The AISRF over a period has transformed into Australia's largest fund dedicated to bilateral research and as one of India's largest sources of support for international science. The fund has facilitated the increment in the uptake of leading edge science and technology by supporting collaboration between Australian and Indian researchers in strategically focused, leading-edge scientific research and technology projects, while at the same time strengthening strategic alliances between Australian and Indian Universities and researchers.

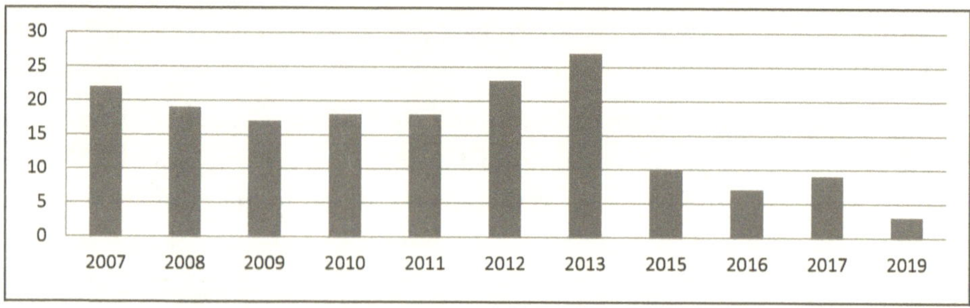

Fig 12: Number of Projects Approved Under AISRF [269]

Since its inception, the AISRF has supported a large number of joint projects, workshops and fellowships in key areas of priority to Australia and India, involving some 100 top universities and research institutes in both countries. The relevance of the fund for both the countries can also be gauged from the type of research projects undertaken under the initiative. The fund has financed research across many priority areas to include agriculture, biomedical devices and implants, food and water security, clean energy technologies, marine sciences, information and communication technology etc. An overwhelming number of projects have been sanctioned/carried out as Joint collaborative projects providing fillip to the crucial people to people contacts in a bilateral relationship. As on date, Government of Australia has committed approximate AU $ 70 Million under the initiative[270], there by indicating the significance of initiative for the bilateral relationship. The success of the fund in promoting the crucial people to people contacts between the two countries can be gauged from the fact that the initiative has supported more than 300 opportunities including joint workshops, collaborative activities and fellowships.

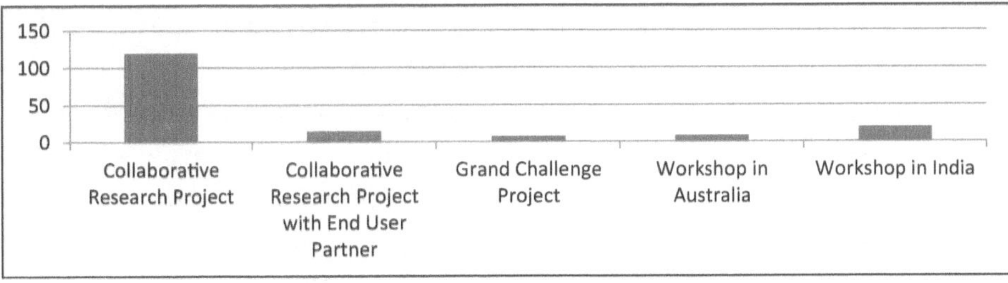

Fig 13: Type of Activities Carried out under AISRF [271]

Regular review of any initiative is imperative to gauge the success rate and also to carry out any mid course correction if required. In a comprehensive review of the initiative carried out by the Department of Industry, Innovation and Science, Government of Australia against the criterion of appropriateness, effectiveness, efficiency, integration, performance assessment and strategic policy alignment, the original strategic policy objectives of the AISRF have been established to be relevant and the review recommended the retention of the initial objectives as the core focus of the fund. The review also summarized the positivity of the ongoing bilateral relations fostered by the AISRF and a generalized finding from the stakeholders that the AISRF is a direct contributor to positive diplomatic relations. The report has also concluded that the AISRF is supporting bilateral engagements between India and Australia, via the long-term maintenance of these bilateral initiatives and its outcomes of deep engagement between the two countries in science and innovation as well as intercultural engagement and understanding.

In another initiative to facilitate fundamental and socially relevant research in the Indian context, Ministry of Human Resource Development, Government of India had launched Global Initiative of Academic Networks (GIAN) in 2015, under which an International academician could visit an Indian Institute for two weeks to share experiences. In an improvement to GIAN, Department of Science & Technology, Government of India, launched Visiting Advanced Joint Research Faculty Scheme (VAJRA) in 2017, under which an International Academician/Scientist was able to spend longer duration in India. Scheme for Promotion of Academic & Research Collaboration (SPARC) has further improved upon the existing scheme and has endeavored to propose a collaborated eco system. Besides catering for long term long term visit by the International Faculty (2 to 8 months), it also endeavours to fund the travel and sustenance of Indian students at the University/Institute of the International collaborator.

The scheme has facilitated close cooperation between the scientific communities of India and Australia and has furthered the bilateral cooperation by promoting people to people contacts at functional levels. Analysis of data for the approved projects available at the home page of the initiative reveals that the total collaborations with Australia comprise of approximately 14 percent of the total collaborations carried out with 28 countries. The cooperation between the two countries, under the aegis of the scheme has been carried out in five critical areas of Action Oriented Research, Convergence, Emergent Areas of Impact, Fundamental Research and Innovation Driven research. Among the Australian Universities identified for the collaboration, the SPARC initiative has collaborated with all the major universities of the country, spread with the thrust areas of the initiative. "There are 26 universities from Australia involved in SPARC. Out of the total of 157 applications received in the first call for applications, 54 joint research projects from Australian and Indian institutions have been approved under SPARC totaling US $ 4.9 million. Out of the 1,839 courses that have been approved under GIAN, 104 courses were taken by Australian faculty. "[272]

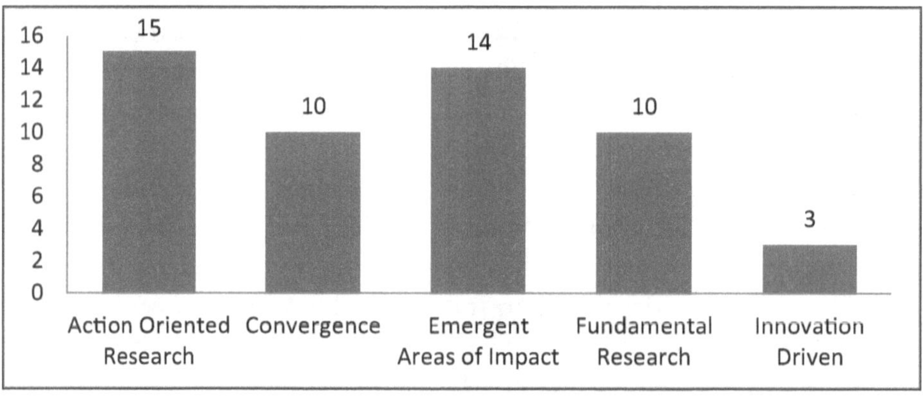

Fig 14: Dimensions of Approved Projects with Australia[273]

Realizing the huge quantum of potential offered by the aspect of collaboration in the educational field, on 08 April 2010, the Education Ministers of India and Australia signed a Joint Ministerial Statement reaffirming the commitment of the respective Governments' to continue to expand collaboration in education, training and research. To support this expansion, establishment of the Australia India Education Council (AIEC) was agreed upon, the inaugural meeting of which was held in New Delhi in August 2011. The AIEC is a bi-national body chaired by the Education Ministers of India and Australia. The council is mandated to work out and implement the modalities for expanding collaboration between the two countries in the fields of education, training and research.

The AIEC has representation from academia, policy makers and industry which is facilitating the strategic direction of the bilateral education, training and research partnership and to develop strategic advice to focus and shape collaborative efforts. The AIEC is co-chaired by Australia's Education Minister and India's Minister for Human Resource Development. Due to the efforts of AIEC, the transformation of bilateral relationship through enhancement of people to people contacts has materialized. The joint research partnerships between higher education institutions of India and Australian institution have been made possible and the collaborations in the areas like Joint Research Projects, Joint supervision of PhDs, student/faculty mobility and award of Joint Degrees/PhDs has been facilitated. As a result of the initiatives taken by the council, the pathways degrees awarded by Universities in Australia have been recognized for continuation of further education in India and also for job opportunities, boosting the relationship between the two countries further.

In another initiative of 'Dynamic Mix', the council has devised a programme to acknowledge and celebrate the success stories of contribution of people of Indian descent to the Australian society. The series has aimed to inspire more cross collaboration between Australia and India and is an excellent initiative to further the people to people relations between the two countries. The council has also been in forefront in the allocation of grants for the projects which are novel and innovative and in turn are fostering deeper people-to-people and institutional links between Australia and India. A study of selection of projects for 2019 reveals that the funding has carried out a vide section of projects throughout the length and breadth of India. The projects are of mutual importance to both the countries and have been specifically selected for their symbiotic value.

Table 5: AIEC: 2019 Grant Round Outcomes[274]

Project	Funding
Innovative economic opportunities through sharing sustainable farming systems knowledge	$66,131.00
Jaipur Literature Festival in Adelaide	$60,000.00
Digital Transactions in India: Platforms, Markets and Users	$54,980.00
Connecting Women Social Entrepreneurs in India and Australia	$64,575.00
India-Australia Internet of Things (IoT) Training Academy	$33,500.00
Developing a digital platform for hospital management education in India	$62,339.00
Transfer of mitigation technologies for heat stress in farm animals	$38,825.00
Developing Indo-Australian Collaboration for Sustainable Mining in India	$52,723.00
Developing India-Australian Collaboration towards a Horticulture Centre of Excellence	$44,120.00
Young Indians' Plan for the Planet Program	$116,700.00
Develop 3D printing, Bio printing and AI medical applications between India-Australia	$95,000.00

Youth of any country form an inalienable part society. As part of the society, the youth are ambassadors of any country and are the major component of people to people relations between any two countries. The bulk of the international students are the youth, thereby making them an important part of the deliberations. One of the important facets of growing people to people contact, Australia India Youth Dialogue (AIYD) is a youth-led dialogue between the young and emerging leaders of Australia and India. "The AIYD embodies the people-to-people links which are the foundation of the strong partnership between Australia and India. Bringing together some of Australia and India's brightest young minds, More importantly, it helps build ties and understanding amongst the generation which will drive this relationship into the future."[275]

The initiative hosts fifteen of the best and brightest young minds from each country at an annual conference, held in India and Australia in alternate years. The dialogue facilitates free and frank exchange of ideas and perspectives between the youth ambassadors of both the countries with an ultimate aim of strengthening of bilateral relationship. The AIYD has facilitated to complement the strategic partnership between the two countries by undertaking some of the path breaking initiatives:[276]

➢ Cultivating and fostering the relationship between Australian and Indian youth in a meaningful manner.

➢ Providing a deeper cultural insight and understanding of the similarities and differences between the respective nations.

➢ Providing support to deal with problems and trends in the relationship and potentially providing solutions for those problems.

People to people links play an important role in the development of closer bilateral relationships and cannot be negated. AIYD is playing the bridge between India and Australia to further the people to people contacts. The composition of dialogue itself is important indicator of the importance of dialogue. Bilateral relationship is not dependent on one or two aspects, but is a complex to include trade, services and diplomacy which all require continued focus. The AIYD boasts of an impressive alumni list, numbering 180 young leaders from both India and Australia. The alumni group consists of young executives, journalists, politicians, sportspersons, NGO leaders, entrepreneurs, amongst a whole host of professions.[277]

AIYD has been successful in the youth engagement between the two countries. It has played an important role in increasing the cultural awareness about each other. In a survey carried out by AIYD, it has been revealed that increasing the level of cultural understanding on both sides of the relationship was a key to developing closer ties and the activities of AIYD have been broadly successful in the endeavour.

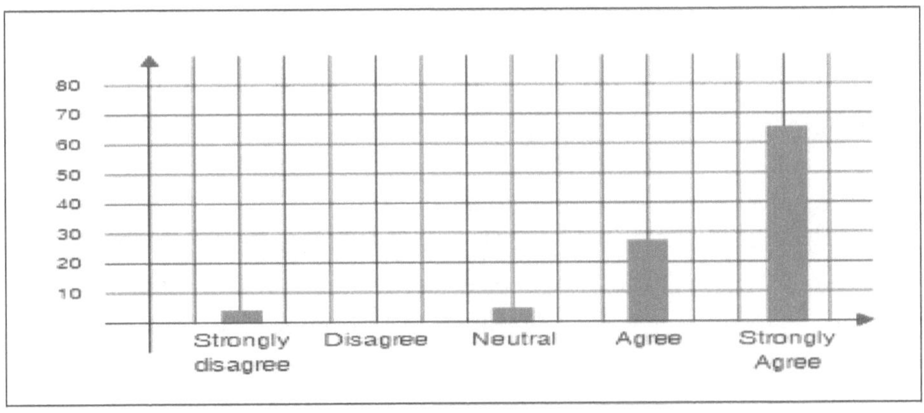

Fig 15: Role of AIYD in Promoting Bilateral Relationship: Results of Survey[278]

The AIYD Alumni Grants programme is an integral component of AIYD and facilitates to encourage and empower AIYD alumni to collaborate with their counterparts on projects with strong potential to enhance and strengthen the Australia-India relationship. The seed funding for the collaborative projects in the Australia-India space is catered under the scheme. AIYD is contributing significantly and positively to the India Australia bilateral relationship and the activities and alumni of dialogue are committed to the potential significance of the Australia-India relationship

Any study of transnational education and knowledge partnership between India and Australia will not be complete without mentioning the stellar contribution rendered by the Australia India Institute (AII). The institute was established in 2008, with an express purpose of study of India and the bilateral relationship. The Institute is funded by grants from the Australian Government, the State Government of Victoria and the University of Melbourne, and is hosted at the University of Melbourne.[279] The institute has played an exemplary role in facilitating the development of bilateral relations and perceptions between and about, India and Australia. The Institute has developed a strong reputation in foreign policy, research, education and the arts. Its publications, international conferences, public seminar series, events and programs, are changing Indian perceptions of Australia and have created opportunities for partnerships across key areas of the relationship.[280] This part of the book will not be complete without alluding to the some of the path breaking initiatives being undertaken by the institute to foster and promote the bilateral relationship between India and Australia.

In an initiative to promote bilateral relationship, the institute has realized commitments from some of the prominent Australian universities, to include the University of Melbourne, University of New South Wales, La Trobe University, Deakin University, University of Sydney, University of Western Sydney, Queensland University of Technology and the University of Western Australia, to facilitate funding of New Generation Network (NGN) of Post Doctoral scholars. Since 2015 onwards, this assistance has been worth over $3.5 million, thereby marking a major effort in the furthering of bilateral relations to the Australia India relationship. The Australia India Leadership Dialogue (AILD) is another flagship event of AII and has been instrumental in facilitating the government and non-government exchanges between influencers and decision-makers in both the nations. The dialogue was launched in 2015 and has been held alternatively in each country since then.

The last dialogue was held in Melbourne in December 2019. The wide and varied arena of dialogue includes but not restricted to governance, geopolitics, water security, trade, economics

Carrying forward the momentum generated by the Comprehensive Security Partnership 2020, an Australia-India Framework Arrangement on Cyber and Cyber-Enabled Critical Technology Cooperation has been signed by the two countries. The proposed cooperation is structured on the basics of an Australia-India Cyber and Critical Technology Partnership (AICCTP), a partnership which is worth $12.7 million. Concentrating in Indo Pacific, the area of shared interests for both the countries, the partnership in the critical cyber enabled technologies is further expected to configure the trends in technological advancements at the global level generally and in the particular aspects of India Australia bilateral relationship.

Exploiting the Potential of Universities

Towards promoting and ensuring the cooperation in knowledge partnerships and as part of a joint initiative to confront global food security issues, Western Sydney University (WSU) of Australia has entered into an agreement with the Indian Council of Agricultural Research (ICAR) and thirteen state agricultural universities in India. As part of the initiative the WSU will invest $5 million to leverage new research and developments and will primarily focus on the issues of protected cropping and related aspects of horticulture and agriculture, as well as collaborative teaching and learning. "We are delighted to formalise partnership agreements with ICAR and such prestigious Indian agricultural institutions. This is the beginning of vitally important relationships between our countries that will contribute to addressing global food security challenges. This highly innovative Indian-Australian collaboration will be driven by world's best research, teaching and learning."[281]

The dominance of resources sector in Australian economy is a well established fact. The resources sector accounted for 73 per cent of Australia's goods exports in 2018-19, and the sector was responsible for 35 per cent of the country's GDP growth in the same period. The sector has been identified as one of the lead sectors in the India Economic Strategy 2035 by Australia. It is therefore logical for the institutes of higher learning engaged in resources sector in both the countries to forge strong partnerships. In a series of partnership agreements between the two countries, the Australasian Institute of Mining and Metallurgy (AusIMM) and the Indian Institute of Technology (The Indian School of Mines) have signed a three-year agreement to connect Australia and India's communities of resources experts. "By working together, we will be able to provide even more value to the mining professionals and economies of our nations. This partnership allows us to exchange knowledge and collaborate on professional development programmes and will help advance the skills and professionalism of people working in the resources sectors of India, Australasia and further abroad."[282]

In another initiative of cooperation between the two countries in the resources sector, a MoU between Indian Government and the Australian state of Queensland has been signed to facilitate improvement in the mining safety in both countries. The MoU is facilitating a critical relationship between the Directorate General of Mines Safety (DGMS), of the Government of India and the Safety in Mines, Testing and Research Station (SIMTARS), an Australian research group that works to improve the conditions of mines and provide safety training to workers. The two groups will work together to establish a safety management system, train employees in best safety practices, and organise a number of meetings, including conferences and seminars. SIMTARS will also be responsible for improving and modernising the research and development facilities of the DGMS. The SIMTARS' expertise in the areas of mutual concern has been projected to yield greater benefits to mining operations in India and will facilitate further synergy in the bilateral relationship.

Besides agreements at government to government level, a large quantum of collaboration between Australian and Indian universities is also facilitating the promotion of bilateral relationship. Some Australian universities have a long-standing presence in India and have developed strategies at an institution -to-institution level, while others have focused on collaborations that are established between researchers in the two countries.[283] These collaborations are addressing multiple social and developmental issues simultaneously, by bringing together universities, government, civil society and industry in order to understand and solve specific problems and in the process incentivizing the people to people contacts. Australian tertiary education sector is known for international research collaboration. Australian universities, both in Group of Eight (Go8) and outside the framework, have strong research collaborations with Indian universities in place. The unity of effort thus developed between academic and non-government organisations of India and

Australia is facilitating capacity building at the levels of universities and Non Governmental Organisations (NGO) levels in both the countries.

The overwhelming dominance of Indian Institutes of Technologies (IIT) in these collaborations and co-authored papers with Australia is a foregone conclusion because of the majority of collaborations being in emerging domains of Science Technology Engineering and Mathematics (STEM) and IITs being in top league of institutions in India. In the recent times, a large number of high ranking private universities in India have signed MoUs with Australian universities and have provided boost to the research collaborations. Melbourne India Postgraduate Programme (MIPP) of Melbourne University has played a key role in facilitating bilateralism. A joint initiative of the University of Melbourne and a select group of IITs from India, MIPP is catering for access to research facilities and the opportunity to contribute to the development of educational, cultural and industry links between the two countries.

As an established practice, Australian universities were hosting India specific Centers in the respective institutes, which were facilitating studies and research pertaining to India, but in a first of its kind development, O.P. Jindal Global University (JGU), one of India's Institutions of Eminence has established, Centre for India Australia Studies (CIAS), the first and only centre embedded in an Indian higher education institution that is focused on the India-Australia bilateral relationship. [284] Furthering the existing knowledge partnership between the two countries, JGU has also signed MoUs with the leading Australian universities to include, Macquarie University, University of New South Wales, University of New England, University of Newcastle, University of Sydney, University of Technology Sydney and Western Sydney University.[285]

An agreement to boost academic and educational exchange and research collaborations between University of New South Wales (UNSW) Sydney and Manipal Academy of Higher Education (MAHE) has also been signed, wherein both the institutions have jointly committed $5 million in seed funding up to 2025 to deliver tangible outcomes and ensure the success of the partnership.[286] Similarly, New South Wales based University of Wollongong, in its MoU with IIT Kharagpur and IIT Bombay, had initiated a project with the Council of Scientific and Industrial Research and the Government of Gujarat for the development of an International Centre for Excellence in Mining Automation and Safety (iCEM).[287] In a recent initiative the university has also signed a MoU with Dedicated Freight

Corridor Corporation of India Limited (DFCCIL) to provide additional rail freight transport capacity.[288]

Though, these collaborations are facilitating increased people to people contacts, thereby providing fillip to the bilateral relationship, there are some issues of concern which demand immediate resolution for the knowledge partnership between India and Australia to reach greater heights. In a research carried out by AII on the research collaboration between Indian and Australian universities, it was revealed that out of the 397 individual partnerships, only 40.5% can be confirmed as active research collaborations, with a majority of the MoUs being inactive or having no public status at all.[289] The same study has identified availability of time, patience, inadequacy of established follow up mechanisms and funding constraints as the major reasons for the non performance of these collaborations. The temporary setbacks notwithstanding, a large number of agreements have been signed or are in the process of finalization. These burgeoning partnerships in the knowledge sector will definitely facilitate faculty and student exchanges, dual degree programmes, joint teaching, joint research, joint conferences and joint publications.

New Education Policy (NEP) 2020 released by Ministry of Human Resource Development, Government of India has laid emphasis on use of technology and its integration with the existing pedagogies being adopted. The New circumstances and realities require new initiatives. The uncertainty induced by the pandemic in 2020, has necessitated the availability and deployment of alternative modes of quality education when there is a likelihood of disruption of traditional and in-person modes of education. "In the meantime, the existing digital platforms and ongoing ICT-based educational initiatives must be optimized and expanded to meet the current and future challenges in providing quality education for all."[290] India and Australia has huge potential for cooperation in the field of Education Technology, which encompasses a wide spectrum of activities to include use of computers, online classes, and online submission of assignments by the students, online degree platforms and corresponding mobile learning applications. The social reach of the internet facilitates the endeavours undertaken by the Education Technology. In a report on 'Indian Tech Education Market Insights: Opportunities for Australia[291], commissioned by the Australian Trade and Investment Commission, Government of Australia, identified sectoral opportunities in the fields of professional education sector in India, which estimated that this sector is expected to grow at a CAGR of 30%.

With a proven track record in education technology Australia, can provide necessary assistance in development and delivery of online and offline educational content, skilling, and blended learning which can further advance the intimate bilateral relationship. Both countries are already working on the partnership, which will facilitate further boosting of people to people contacts. "Had a virtual meeting with Mr Barry O Farrell, Australian High Commissioner to India. Both sides expressed commitment to take forward India-Australia education relations under the National Education Policy. "[292] It is therefore evident that bilateral relationship between India and Australia is being boosted by the strong foundations provided by the people to people links. This furtherance of the relationship has also been officially recognised. "People to people links are transforming the relationship. Educational links are deep and strong. Prime Ministers welcomed cooperation between Australian and India universities and in particular joint PhD programmes to encourage research."[293]

As the Australian universities' international standing and high-end research credentials are time tested and their linkages with Indian universities are being facilitated, the education sector provides immense opportunities for Australia and India to collaborate. The Australian export and collaboration in the education sector will continue to be a standout component of Australia-India relationship in the region in the times to come. The relationship between higher education, migration and the diaspora is intricate and all encompassing. In the case of India and Australia, the transnational education is furthering migration which in turn is facilitating the Indian diaspora in Australia. Diaspora is a critical aspect of people to people relationship and a very dynamic catalyst of bilateral relationship. The Indian diaspora is playing a crucial role in the bilateral relationship between India and Australia and deserves a detailed discussion.

CHAPTER 4

DIASPORA & TRADE: DEFINING THE DEPENDENCY

"The expanding linkages between our people are enriching all aspects of bilateral ties. The Indian diaspora in Australia is now the fastest-growing large diaspora. In recognition of the growing contribution of Indian-Australians to the bilateral relationship, we will continue to work to deepen diaspora and community -level contacts."[294]

The term 'Diaspora' happens to have been derived from a Greek word, meaning dispersion. The term owes its origin to the concept of worldwide dispersion of Jewish people (Golah meaning Exile) outside their homeland. Though the term diaspora is generic, the people forming diaspora do not aggregate into a homogenous group, but are characterized by demonstrating all the cultural and religio-linguistic diversities of respective groups. Heterogeneity is the most distinct characteristic of these groups. As far as definition of these groups is concerned, the commonly accepted definition of diaspora includes only the first generation of migrants, whereas the contemporary diversity and mobility of migrants is defying the traditional understanding of the concept of migration and migration settlements. As a result, in the present context, the term migration is not restricted to the contemporary generation of migrants but has transformed into an all inclusive and holistic concept, to include all generations of migrants.

Accordingly, Indian diaspora is also an all encompassing term, which can be used to describe the people who have migrated from territories that are within the borders of republic of India. In the context of India also, the concept of 'Indian diaspora' has witnessed an expansion of scope of terminology and is no longer limited to the first generation of permanent migrants born in India. In its expanded version, the term diaspora also include permanent residents born outside India and temporary visa holders from the country to include temporary workers and international students. Belongingness to a common ancestry serves to facilitate in provisioning of an identifiable and verifiable cultural background for the Diasporas to identify with. As shall be seen in the subsequent part of the chapter, the proportion of Indian diaspora in Australia has increased significantly over the past decades. Different definitions define diaspora differently, based upon the underlying datum of generations considered for definition. For the purpose of this book, however, the extended definition of diaspora, has been assumed to include first generation of Indian migrants, Indians born in other countries, Indians born in Australia, temporary workers and international students.

Perspectives on Historical Immigration

During the colonial era (1788–1900), three distinct types of international immigrants came to Australia; as transported convicts, through subsidised passage schemes or as free settlers (self-funded). As can be expected the immigration policies of the time were naturally skewed in favour of the British immigrants. The majority of immigrants of those times belonged to British ancestry, but some free settlers also came from other European and non-European countries. Ironically though the immigration to the new colony was being promoted by a plethora of means, the migration was not completely free and was accompanied by a nominal fee for the voluntary migration. The fee structure levied for the immigration, however was not very high and was structured to ensure facilitate maximum migration to the newly established colony. "Any person of sound health who could secure a relative or friend in Australia to nominate him and his family could immigrate on the payment of £10 for an adult, £5 for a child between sixteen and nineteen years of age, and free for a child under the age of sixteen years. In addition, under the Commonwealth scheme, Australia provided accommodation at their end for selected British migrants and paid their fares as well."[295]

Though the migration to Australia from Europe in general and Britain in particular continued to dominate, the famous gold rush of mid nineteenth century witnessed a large influx of non- European immigrants, particularly from China. The conflicting demands of requirement of labour for a rapidly booming economy along with an apparent threat of expanding communism generated a pressure on the planners of the time and the huge Asian influx of migrants was equated with a dilemma of 'populate or perish'. This apparent dilemma of the then Australia was captured by the author Lachlan Strahan, who considered both options. "As an ethnocentric slogan that in effect was an admonition to fill Australia with Europeans or else risk having it overrun by Asians."[296] Surrendering to the dilemma and to counter the growing non European population, the colonial government of Victoria was the first one to enact restrictions on 'alien' immigration by the way of the Chinese Immigration Act 1855.

On 01 January 1901, the Commonwealth of Australia was proclaimed with the six British colonies, New South Wales, Victoria, Queensland, South Australia, Western Australia and Tasmania. As one of the first acts passed by the new Federal Parliament, The Immigration Restriction Act of 1901, also colloquially known as 'White Australia Policy' was implemented which primarily aimed at excluding non-Europeans from settling in Australia. Borrowing precedence from South African Natal Act of 1897, the immigration restriction policy introduced a 'Dictation Test', which required certain category of applicants to pass a written test in a European language, certainly putting them at disadvantage with respect to European applicants. These restrictions were further supplemented by the Naturalisation Act of 1903 (Commonwealth), which further precluded people from Asia, Africa or the Pacific Islands from applying for naturalisation process.

In spite of these, the demand of labour for the new colony had not subsided and the dilemma proposed by Lachlan Strahan was still very much applicable. The requirement to populate the continent in the aftermath of World War II forced the country to have a rethink on the option of populate or perish. In order to populate, the government set up a target to increase the population by two per cent each year, along with one per cent coming through immigration. In order to institutionalize immigration, Australia was the first country in the world to establish a Department of Immigration in 1945. Coupled with this, the Nationality and Citizenship Act 1948 (Commonwealth), introduced the concept of Australian Citizenship for citizens of Australia as till that time Australians were eligible to hold the status of British subjects.

Alongside these developments, the racially-selective immigration programmes continued to be a dominant factor of immigration to Australia and till as late as middle of the last century, immigration was being guided by the principle that the intake of immigrants should be carefully considered. "The immigration programme should be balanced between assisted and non-assisted immigrants, British and non-British immigrants, and between northern and southern Europeans within the non-British intake."[297] Due to the racially motivated profiling for immigration purposes there was widespread antagonism in the world and the efforts to dismantle White Australia policy picked up pace. Adjusting to the realities of the contemporary world, the government introduced the Migration Act of 1958, which abolished the much abhorred Dictation Test and restrictions on migration of non Europeans started getting gradually relaxed. The dismantling of 'White Australia' policy, followed by the introduction of Migration Act of 1958, provided a broad framework for the effective functioning of immigration system and the foundation of a utility based immigration programme was laid. "Applications for migration would be accepted from well-qualified people on the basis of their suitability as settlers, their ability to integrate readily and their possession of qualifications positively useful to Australia."[298]

Over a period of time, a number of commissions and inquiries have facilitated the overhaul of Australia's immigration policies. As a result of recommendations of these commissions, racially motivated immigration policies were amended in favour of multiculturalism and the management of immigration became more focused on the objective of increasing the wellbeing of the Australian community. [299] Based on the recommendations of another highly critical report of the existing immigration policies, the Committee to Advise on Australia's Immigration Policies, also known as FitzGerald report, revisions to the Migration Act 1958 and Regulations was carried out in 1989, which were also described as "the most fundamental changes to Australia's immigration laws ever introduced in a single package."[300] Major reforms included capping the level of immigration through the points-tested components of the family and 'economic' streams, introduction of a floating pass mark and changing the process by which temporary immigrants were granted permanent residency. In another series of changes in the immigration policies and to cater for increasing public debate on security and multiculturalism, in 2007, the residency requirement to gain citizenship was increased from two to four years and a requirement to hold permanent residency for 12 months was introduced.[301]

The immigration policies of Australia have generally been very responsive to existing economic and social conditions in Australia and in keeping up pace with the environmental and social realities, periodic changes in the policy provisions related to the immigration have continued to be introduced. The immigration quotas have witnessed an increase or decrease as per the prevailing situation. Due to the concerns about increasing unemployment; the government of the time had reduced planned immigration in the early 1970s. By 1975, the number of places was 50,000 annually, the lowest it had been since World War II.[302]

Keeping pace with the changed environmental realities and other associated considerations, the immigration policies of Australia have undergone a considerable number of amendments over a period of time and are up to a large extent aligned to the contemporary requirements and realities. The immigration department has played a major role in facilitating and promoting immigration of eligible and qualified people to the country. Since 1945, when Australia's first immigration department was established, approximately seven million permanent migrants have settled in Australia.[303]

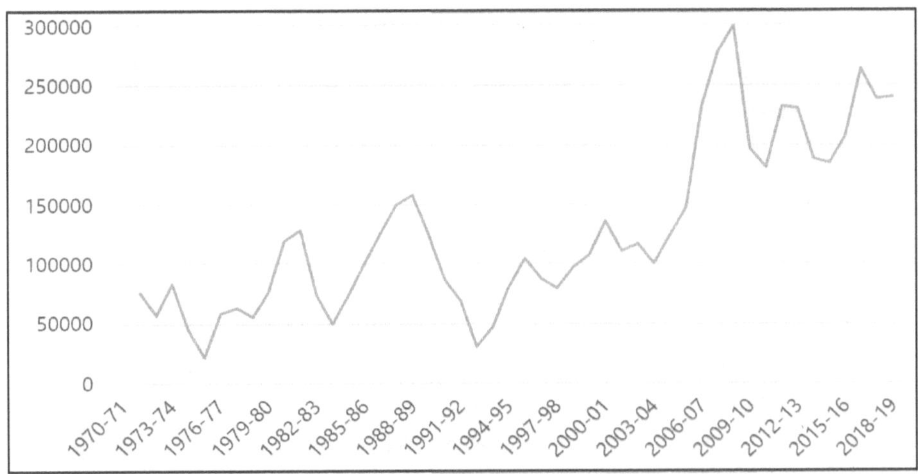

Fig 16: Net Overseas Migration to Australia – 1971-72 to 2018-19[304]

The first migration of Indians to Australia can be traced to the movement of labourers and convicts in the early 19th century. The late 19th century was witness to the opening up of camel trade between India and Australia and Indian cameleers from North West India accompanied expeditions and pastoral ventures in the virgin lands in Australia. The immigration restrictions imposed due to 'White Australia' policy in the early part of 20th century effectively blocked the Indian immigration to Australia for the next five decades. The census of 1921 recorded 2000 Chinese 'born in Australia', 230 'Hindus' and 3000 'Mahommedans', as well as 3500 Chinese and 600 Hindu 'half caste', whereas Sikhs did not get an entry.[305] While the White Australia Policy reduced the immigration of non-Europeans, the arrival of various European groups like British, German, Italian and Greeks increased. In spite of an increase of 75.01 percent in the population of Australia from 1901 to 1933, the percentage of population born in India witnessed a decline from 0.9 percent to 0.7 percent, thereby corroborating the adverse effects of 'White Australia' policy on migration from India.

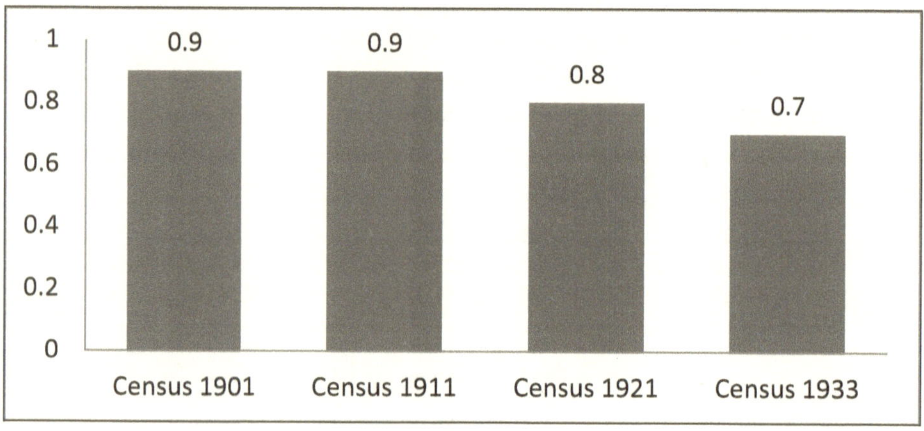

Fig 17: Percentage of Australian Population Born in India[306]

The abolition of the White Australia policy in 1972, the introduction of the Multiculturalism policy in 1973 and the Racial Discrimination Act of 1975 (RDA) were the hallmark initiatives which facilitated the recommencement of migration to Australia. As the existing restrictions were lifted, the Indian born British citizens and Anglo Indian arrived first, followed by a more sustained migration flow of professionals from India.[307] The Indian immigrants during this period were dominated by highly-qualified professionals in well-paying jobs in medicine, engineering and business. Two decades, from 1970s to 1990s witnessed the overwhelming dominance by the immigrants from India in the net overseas migration. The subsequent grant of permanent residency during this period was predominantly on the basis of their skills or through familial connections.

Introduction of temporary skilled migrant visa program (Sub Class 457) in 1996 was another important step which facilitated migration from India. This sub class visa allowed Australian businesses to sponsor temporary migrants with specialized skill sets that were deemed to be in short supply in Australia. The entitled migrants under this category were allowed to work and stay in Australia for up to four years. This proved to be a game changer in the dynamics of migration to Australia from India and tremendously boosted the Indian migration to Australia. Though, the 457 visa programme has since been replaced by a new Temporary Skill Shortage (TSS) visa, with effect from March 2018, which is also helping the cause of migration from India.

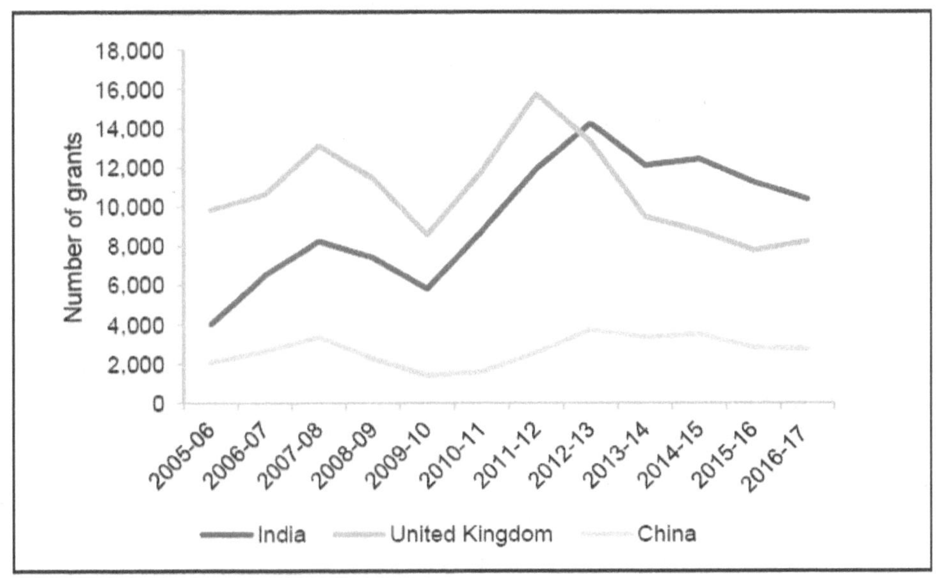

Fig 18: Primary 457 Visa Grants by Year: Top Three Countries[308]

Higher Education and Migration

A common perception related to the concept of migration, is the educational level of the prospective migrants. Migrants are generally associated with escaping from illiteracy, poverty and civil strife in the remote regions of the world. But more often than not, the reverse holds true in case of international migration, specifically in the cases of economic migration. Migrants in search of a better future usually have a more pronounced initiative, attitude and boldness than the average person, with some skills and financial resources needed to plan and fund a long-distance journey as it is the case for international migration.[309] In addition, individuals from families or communities that have already positively experienced migration in previous years are more inclined to migrate as their travel abroad is regarded as of possible benefit to the origin society.[310] Migration related to education has not always been looked positively from the perspective of the country of origin. The negativity associated with the loss of qualified people from the country of origin to the country of residence has precluded association of any advantage to the process of migration. The concept of 'Brain Drain' has been considered adequate to explain the migration related to education, as the migration of educated people from low and middle income countries to the developed countries has always been associated with a net loss of human qualified resources for the origin countries and a gain for the host country.

As discussed in the previous chapter, the link between higher education and intended migration is unique and intertwined. In order to take advantage of the significant economic benefits accrued by the international education sector, Australia has successfully endeavored to institutionalize the mechanism to attract overseas students through immigration policy measures which in turn provided a pathway to the permanent residency. As a result, the contemporary era has been witness to the rapid growth in the numbers of temporary migrants, including students, transitioning to permanent residency through the skill stream of the Migration Programme.[311] As brought out earlier, in the case of Australia, the enrolment in the higher education sector and the immigration process have been dynamic and constantly evolving, depending upon the policy changes on the subject announced by the government from time to time. The educational options available to the international students provide different pathways for immigration and permanent settlement. Therefore, it can be observed that immigration policies evolved over a period of time have generally helped the educational industry in Australia. In the case of students from India, the educational industry has proved to be great help in establishment of a strong Indian diaspora in Australia. "Australian immigration policy has facilitated the growth of the educational industry by offering the option of permanent settlement to those successfully completing courses in areas of high demand."[312]

The strong link between immigration policies and international education industry has also not been without its share of controversies. These institutionalized measures had some serious inadvertent ramifications and resulted in the exponential increase in the number of enrolments in the VET sector and confirmed the apprehensions that programme was being exploited as a pathway to permanent residency. The subsequent attempts by the various governments to delink the overseas student programme with the skilled migration coupled with the attacks on Indian students and global financial crisis severely dented the international confidence in the overseas education programme of Australia. In order to contain the damage and resurrect the image of Australia as a destination for international higher education, various Australian governments did initiate certain programmes to encourage increased enrolments in the VET sector and restore confidence in Australia's international education sector as a whole. As a result of these holistic, sincere and dedicated efforts by the authorities in both countries, an introduction of a system of checks and balances has ensured that Australia did not witness a return to the explicit linkages between the overseas student program and permanent skilled migration.[313]

Indian Diaspora

In any society the accepted notion of diaspora is highly dependent on the individual perspective. The generally accepted perspective of diaspora invariably establishes a link between the individuals in the country of residence with the country of origin. It has however been empirically proven that this link cannot be taken for granted. The significance attached by individuals to their country of lineage can be highly variable and subject to individual preferences, education and social and economic antecedents. On the other hand the established relationship between the territoriality and citizenship has also been put under severe strain by the ease and convenience of global mobility. The earlier notion of an individual doing something for their country of lineage only if located within the geographical limits of the country is no longer valid. "One to one relationship between territoriality and citizenship can no longer be sustained. The issue is no longer where people are physically located, but what contribution they are able to make to the social, cultural and economic development of the (multiple) countries with which they identify."[314]

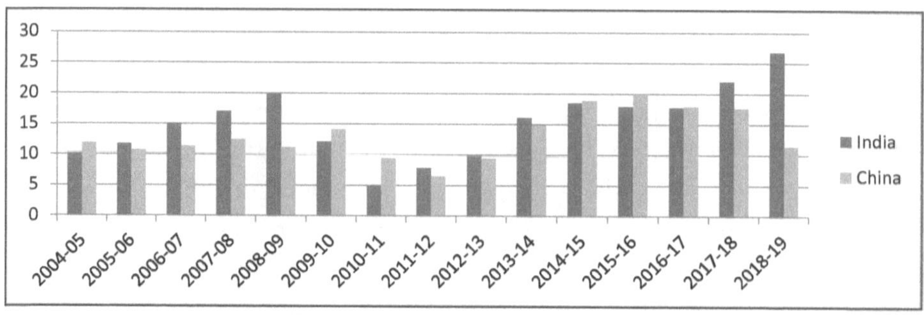

Fig 19: Percentage of Net Overseas Migration to Overall Migration: India and China [315]

The exponential increase in the proportion of Indian diaspora in Australia in the recent times has augured well for the bilateral relationship between India and Australia. Statistically also it is increasingly evident that the proportion of Indian diaspora in the Australian society is on an upswing. Census data of 2016 released by the Australian Bureau of Statistics (ABS) revealed that the Indian diaspora comprised of 2.8% of Australia's total population, whereas the India-born population constituted 1.9% of the country's total population. In another report on Indian diaspora, commissioned by Australian Council of Learned Academies (ACOLA), the first generation of migrants born in India is the largest source for India diaspora in Australia, representing 65% of the total Indian diaspora population, followed by international students (11.1%), people born in other counties acknowledging Indian ancestry (10.8%), Australian-born Indians (9.6%) and temporary working visa holders (3.4%).[316]

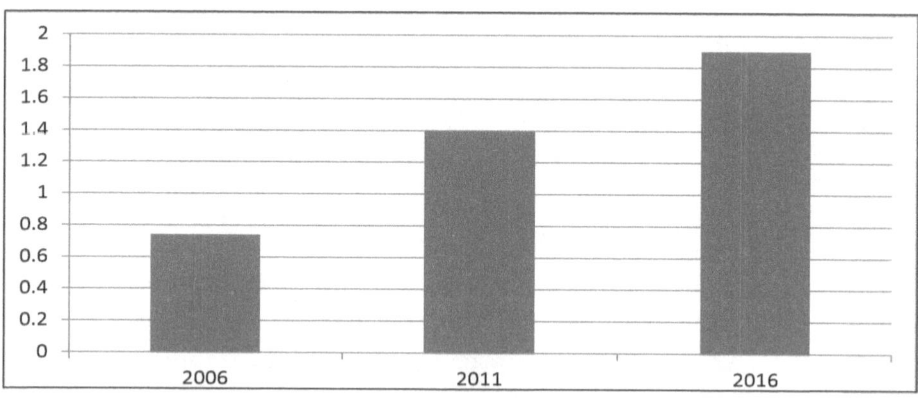

Fig 20: Percentage of India born Population in Australia in Census Years [317]

In terms of bilateral relationship between India and Australia, the Indian diaspora has played a crucial role. The diaspora has contributed immensely in terms of social, cultural and economic development of Australia in general and India in particular, as shall be seen in the later part of the chapter. In spite of being diffused culturally, this diaspora possess a highly activated network which has facilitated the strengthening of bilateral relationship. During the state visit to India in 2017, Prime Minister of Australia underscored the significance of contribution made by the Indian diaspora in facilitating and uplifting the bilateral relationship between India and Australia. "A major pillar of strength in our partnership is the connect between our societies. Australia is also home to nearly half-a-million people of Indian origin. Their prosperity and vibrant culture enrich our partnership."[318] Indian migrants over a period of time have established themselves as a strong community in Australia. In the data provided by the Department of Home Affairs, Government of Australia the predominant position of Indian migrants in all the fields, to include international education and point based skilled migration gets amply vindicated.

Table 6: Significance of Migration from India: 2015 to 2019[319]

Ranked position of Migrants	2015–16	2016–17	2017–18	2018–19
Population in Australia	4	4	4	3
Points Tested Skilled Migration	1	1	1	1
Employer Sponsored	1	1	2	2
Total Skill stream	1	1	1	1
Total Family and Child stream	2	2	2	2
International students	2	2	2	2
Temporary Resident (Skilled Employment)	1	1	1	1
Visitors	8	8	7	6

Biculturalism

Various studies and research carried out in the field of diaspora studies have suggested a number of typologies, which describe the nature of ties of diaspora to the homeland. The very impression of diaspora and the corresponding linkages with the country of origin and the country of residence have conflicting perspectives. Depending upon individual experiences and preferences, a member of a diasporic community may or may not identify oneself with the country of origin, but the advantages accrued by global mobility and global awareness in the contemporary times are facilitating the animated identification with the country of origin. In the instant case of India Australia relationship, the Indian diaspora has been making deliberate efforts to stake claims to India, the country of family origin and do possess an emotional attachment to what their country of family origin represents to them. A study carried by the Institute for Culture and Society, University of Western Sydney and the Asia Literacy: Language and Beyond Expert Working Group had brought out that the Indian diaspora in Australia was bounded by objective, subjective and normative links to India. The Indian diaspora in Australia identified with India and values their attachment with their country of origin and corroborated the underlying hypothesis that, "people are now able to live simultaneously in more than one nation-state and have multiple senses of belonging and affiliation."[320]

Broadly four distinct typologies of relationships with the country of origin are maintained by the diaspora communities. In the economic field, diasporas have the potential to enhance international economic development and 'brain circulation' within and between knowledge economies whereas in political field the diasporas are a site of political organisation for or against the interests of homeland governments or as advocates for the interests of the diaspora in Australia and/or in other receiving countries.[321] In family and kinship, diaspora are a vehicle for the provision of transnational family care giving and support and in the cultural aspect, diaspora play an important role in the continuance of religious and cultural practices of the country of origin.[322]

The members of Diasporas have varied experiences with respect to the extent to which the cultures of India and Australia share an overhang or are in a conflict zone. These varied experiences, though based on individual perceptions can be explained by the process of biculturism. Collins English dictionary defines biculturism as, "characteristics of a two culture society". Over a period of time, the Diasporas which have embraced more than one culture and have transformed into biculturalism can adequately explain the varying degrees of overhang or conflict between the cultures. Indian diaspora in Australia definitely falls in this category. Though only 1.90 percent of Australian population is born in India, the overall cultural differences between the two societies possess a quantum differential. This aspect gets further acerbated due to the fact that Australia itself is multicultural society, having immigrants from all over the world. The basics of cultural difference between the two societies can be explained in a qualitative manner, but for the purpose of this book, the tangibles as provided by Hofstede Insights have been referred to, which substantiate the existence of subtle cultural differences between the two societies.

Table 7: Hofstede Insights: India and Australia[323]

Aspect	Rankings	
	India	Australia
Power Distance	77	38
Individualism	48	90
Masculinity	56	61
Uncertainty Avoidance	40	51
Long Term Orientation	51	21
Indulgence	26	71

In the case of India and Australia, the process of biculturalism has indeed contributed significantly in facilitating the convergences of the cultural and religious differences between Indian diaspora and the multiculturalism of the Australian society, thereby further facilitating and promoting the bilateral relationship between the two countries.

The multilingualism advantage offered by the Indian diaspora is another inherent and a competitive advantage, which is facilitating faster integration of Indian diaspora into the Australian society. In spite of English being a singular and dominant language of international communication, the variety offered by various Indian languages is definitely endowing to the reciprocity and collaboration. The multi linguist potential offered by Indian diaspora assumes greater significance in the light of Australia being a multicultural and multilingual society. Indian diaspora in Australia being multilingual has proved to be a substantial resource for the learning and transmission of Indian languages. On the other hand various studies have also proved that the multilingual capabilities of any diaspora in a country of residence have a distinct tendency of getting forfeited within three generations or less due to the strain imposed by the over powering dominance of English. But with the majority of Indian migrants in Australia belonging to the first generation, there is an intense potential available which is facilitating benefits to Australian society domestically and is enhancing its competitive edge regionally and internationally. The awareness and deeper understanding of Indian languages and the concepts of bilinguism and interlinguism duly promoted and sustained by the Indian diaspora in Australia are helping engagement between both the countries. The Indian diaspora in Australia is as diverse as culturally as India is, thereby facilitating the pluralism and engagement with the diversity and is helping to build a coherent Australian society. As is the case with the languages, religion is also offering multi faceted opportunities to the cause of India Australia relationship. This religious diversity as existing in India since times immemorial is helping the Australian society in ways more than one. The learning about faith of co inhabitants in a society promotes reaching out and cements relationships. The improved relationships in a society facilitate obviating the negative consequences of fear, hostility and biases, which further promotes the bilateral relationships.

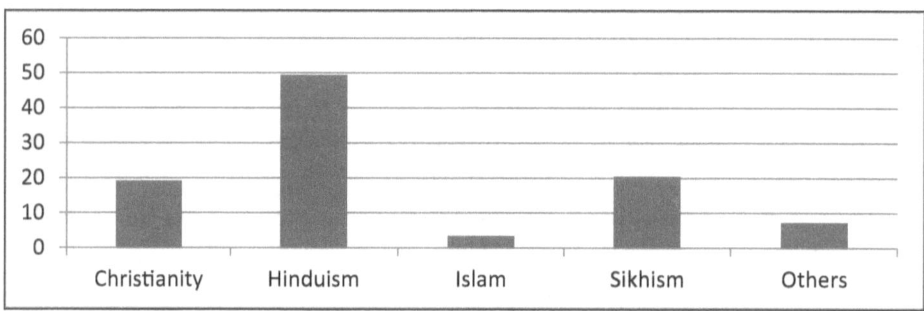

Fig 21: Religious Diversity of Indian Migrants (In Percentages) [324]

As is evident Indian diaspora is contributing immensely to the Australian society. Though technically oriented professionals have witnessed an upswing, analysis of skill stream migration data reveals that migrants from India are dominating other professions which are held in high esteem in any society. In order to bring out the impact of Indian diaspora on the Australian society by way of diverse professions, the author carried out an analysis of past four years of skill stream migration from India. The analysis reveals the complete domination of technical fields to include software and applications programming, Information & Communication Technology (ICT) Business and System analysis and ICT Support and Test Engineers.

Table 8: Top Ten Professions for Skilled Migration (India): 2015-2018[325]

Professions	2015-16	2016-17	2017-18	2018-19
Software and applications programmers	3849	3914	3781	3733
ICT business and systems analysts	965	1,085	1036	1011
Cooks	1352	1076	553	781
Computer Network Professional	-	735	537	625
Accountants	541	402	446	485
Cafe and Restaurant managers	491	415	-	278
Chefs	-	-	-	270
Database and systems administrators, and ICT security specialists	-	-	338	495
Registered Nurses	657	562	562	728
Industrial, Mechanical and Production Engineers	435	482	432	439
Electronic Engineers	-	331	244	-
Civil Engineering Professionals	-	-	260	270
Call Centre & Customer Service Managers	312	-	-	-

Contribution to Academia & Research

In the 2016 Census conducted by ABS, 79.8 per cent of the India-born aged 15 years and over had some form of higher non-school qualification compared to 60.1 per cent of the Australian population. Of the India-born aged 15 years and over, 6.5 per cent had no qualifications and were still attending an educational institution. The corresponding rate for the total Australian population was 8.5 per cent.[326] The relatively higher educational levels of Indian migrants are certainly facilitating the contribution of migrants from India in the Australian academia and research. The important stake holders in the process of knowledge partnership, namely Indian researchers and people associated with academia are playing an important and critical role in the burgeoning academic research between the two countries.

Massive expansion in the transnational flows of people and ideas and international scholarly collaborations has been witnessed in the case of India and Australia. The diffusion of expertise, ease of international travel and the advancements in the information communication technologies has made the transnational flow of people and ideas actually possible. Coupled with this, the growing acknowledgement and facilitation of these collaborations by the apex levels at the respective governments has also aided the research and academic collaborations between India and Australia. A number of studies on the subject have concluded that the pool of scholars in the diaspora can make positive economic and knowledge based contribution to the country of residence as well as country of origin. As the contribution and efforts of Indian research community in the overall research in the basic sciences across the world is being increasingly recognised and acknowledged, the corresponding effect is also being felt in the Australian society. This increased collaboration is facilitating the crucial people to people relationship, thereby providing a crucial fillip to overall bilateral relationship.

Brain Drain or Brain Circulation

The introduction of the concept of 'Brain Drain' can be attributed to the large scale movement of highly skilled and qualified people to another country where the working conditions and remunerations are relatively better. The concept up to a large extent mirrors the phenomenon of 'human capital flight' as the bulk migration of financial capital is affected. This large scale migration deprives the country of origin of these migrants, the employment of skills and qualifications gained by them in the country of origin. The reverse process of 'Brain Gain' is true for gains accrued by the recipient country as it employs the skilled and qualified people and provides a catalyst to own economy.

In recent times, the concepts of brain drain and brain gain have been replaced by a new concept, called as 'Brain Exchange' or 'Brain Circulation'. The concept of brain drain was totally unidirectional and facilitated one sided movement of highly skilled and qualified migrants from developing to developed economies. The brain circulation however pertains to the bidirectional and transnational flow of knowledge and people, as a result of which both, the country of origin and the country of residence are benefitted by the skills and qualifications of these migrants. The concept of brain drain or brain gain had an element of negativity attached to it, depending upon the perspective. The concept of brain circulation on the other hand is all inclusive and provides a sense of positivity to both sides. This element of positivity facilitated by brain circulation is definitely providing boost to the bilateral relationship between India and Australia. The government of India has also undertaken certain initiatives to tap the incentives of brain circulation offered by the skilled migration to Australia. "At a policy level, a rise in the awareness of the importance of knowledge-based activities in the development process has certainly triggered the interest of home countries to try and involve skilled migrants in various strategies that lead to a strengthening of their scientific and technological capacities, based on the understanding that they can make long-distance contributions."[327] With a substantial number of Indian origin people in Australia, the diaspora has been a force multiplier in furthering the bilateral relationship between the two countries. The Indian diaspora in Australia has expanded India's value proposition and facilitated in enlarging the brand value of homeland in Australia.

Economic Impact of Indian Diaspora

A number of studies have established the relationship between immigration and the contemporary economic conditions. The immigration has generally been found to be directly proportional to the economic health of a nation. Whereas this has been found true for developed economies, the reverse has generally been true for developing or underdeveloped economies. As a corollary, the migration has been found to be directly proportional to the economic conditions in these economies; migration has seen upward trends when the economy has deteriorated in developing and under developed economies. In case of Australia, immigration had touched very high levels, during the growth period of the 1950s and 1960s and the trend of immigration has generally followed the trends of economic activity.

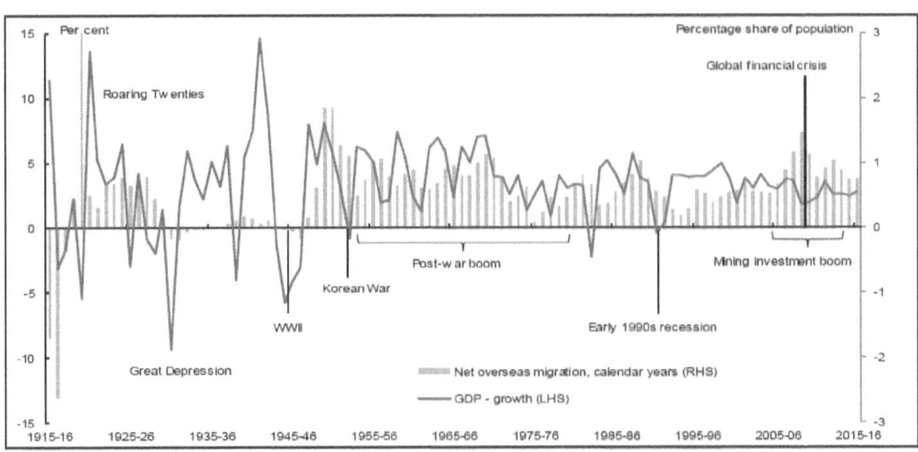

Fig 22: Real GDP Growth and Net Overseas Migration - Australia [328]

Existence of a large amount of empirical evidence suggests that migration definitely fuels the economic growth of the recipient country. In case of Australia, skill stream migrants constitutes for approximate 70 per cent of total migrant intake, thereby contributing to Gross Domestic Product (GDP) per person, by offsetting Australia's ageing population, improve labour force participation and productivity, and help businesses to source skills that are difficult to develop at short notice.[329] In addition, migration under skill stream category contributes to the positive fiscal impact through associated sub category of family stream and the contribution to the innovation ecosystem in the host country by bringing in the diversity and best practices of respective societies. In a study carried out by the Productivity Commission of government of Australia in 2016 it has been estimated that GDP per person would be around 7 per cent higher in 2060 under a business as usual case compared to a zero Net Overseas Migration (NOM) scenario, or an average of 0.15 per cent higher growth each year. In sync with the findings of the Productivity Commission's finding, the International Monetary Fund (IMF) has also estimated that Australia's current migration program will add between ½ and 1 percentage points to annual average GDP growth over the period 2020 to 2050 through its effect of limiting the economic impact of Australia's ageing population.

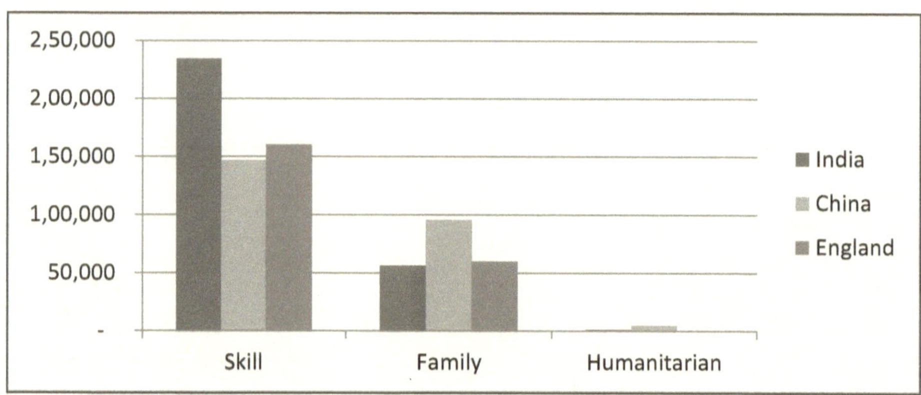

Fig 23: Visa Type by Country of Birth: Permanent Migrants [330]

Since a large proportion of migrants are constituted of skilled migrants, therefore, unemployment among migrants is very low. The unemployment rate of the skill stream (including both primary and secondary applicants) is comparable to unemployment rates in the general population after migrants have been in Australia for only 18 months.[331] As per the data released by ABS, Indian migrants have almost 81 percent of employment rates of the total skilled migrants from India.

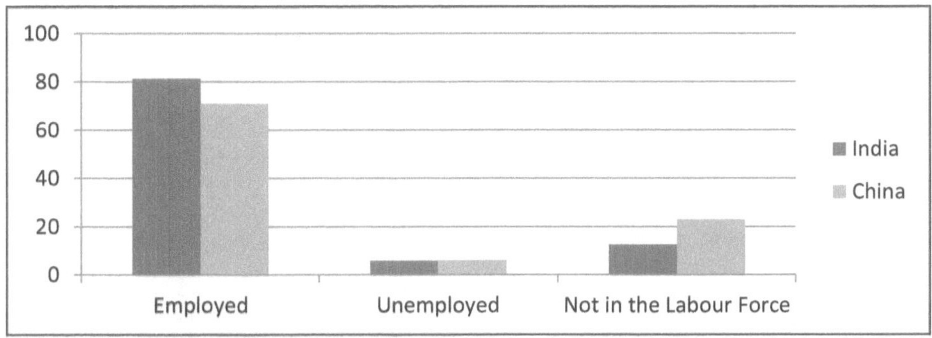

Fig 24: Percentage of Labour Force (Skilled) to Total Population of Skilled: India & China [332]

One of the major reasons for the high proportion of Indian migrant's relatively high labour force participation rates is the adaptability and English language. As far as working proficiency in the English language is concerned, Indian migrants score very high among the migrants from other nationalities, thereby providing a leading edge to the migrants from India. In Australia, 96 percent of Indian migrants can speak English reasonably well, whereas the corresponding figures for migrants from China and balance of the world were 67.32 percent and 88.94 percent respectively.

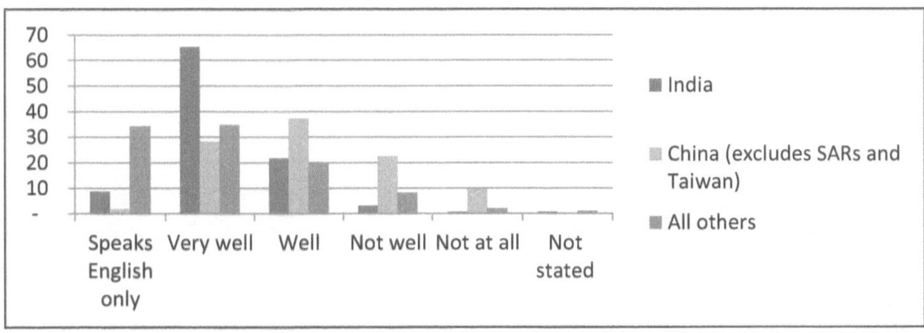

Fig 25: Percentage Proficiency in spoken English/language by Country of birth, Permanent Migrants [333]

Studies also suggest that the skilled migrants tend to contribute more to the society in terms of revenue through taxation, than what they receive in terms of government benefits. The median age of migrants from India being lowest also correspondingly reduces the requirement of government services and benefits to these migrants, which in turn leads to the positive contribution of Indian migrants to the Australian society. Even migrants in the family stream, who accompany skilled migrants and are not brought into Australia for their skills, have been estimated to have a positive fiscal impact over their lifetimes, as they also arrive relatively early in their working lives. As a result the under the employee category, the skilled migrants from India have the highest proportion of total income generation, followed by family visa stream.

Table 9: Proportion of Total Income of Indian Migrants by Visa Stream and Type of Income[334]

	Skilled (%)	Family (%)	Humanitarian (%)
Employee	73.1	21.6	2.8
Business	62.5	27.3	7.2
Investment	61.0	37.1	1.3

Indian diaspora is also contributing significantly to the Australian economy. The migrants from India contributed 16.6 percent of total income generated by all the migrants in Australia under the employee category for 2016-17, only behind migrants from the United Kingdom who contributed 18.4 percent of total income by migrants in Australia in 2016-17. At the time of the 2016 Census, the median individual weekly income for the Indian-born in Australia aged 15 years and over was $785, compared with $615 for all overseas -born and $688 for all Australian-born, whereas the total Australian population aged 15 and over had a median individual weekly income of $662.

Table 10: Proportion of Income by Top Five Countries of Birth 2016-17 [335]

Category	United Kingdom (%)	India (%)	China (%)
Employee	18.4	16.6	8.0
Business	17.2	15.9	9.0
Investment	25.2	6.6	8.1

Due to domination of Indian migrants under the skills category of visa, the corresponding taxation by migrants from India is also relatively high (16 percent, AU $ 18 billion), only behind migrants from the United Kingdom, who contributed 19 percent (AU $ 21 billion) in taxation in 2016-17. As part of the holistic analysis of immigration the country of origin of the migrants also gets long term benefits. In case of India Australia bilateral relationship, also this corollary holds true for India. Remittances continue to be an important indicator of the strength and significance of diaspora. India being the world's largest recipient of remittances is particularly more affected by the fluctuations in the trends of flow of remittances. In 2019 itself, as per a report of the World Bank, India is estimated to have received $83.1 billion in remittances from people working overseas, about 12% of the total expected global inflows.[336]

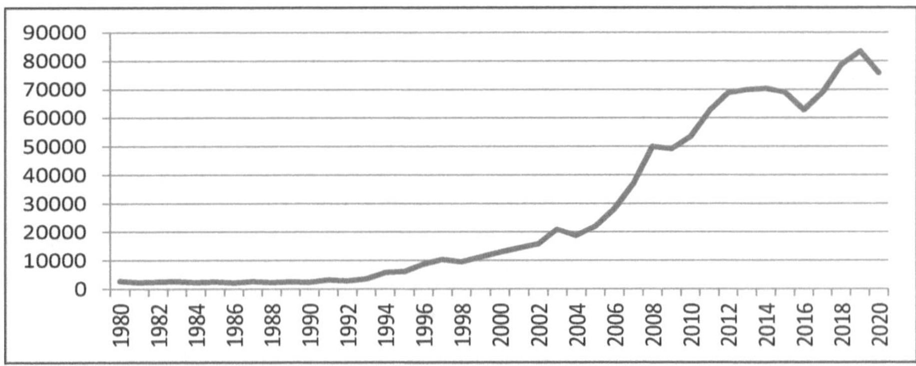

Fig 26: Time Series Migrant Remittance Inflows: India (US $ million) [337]

As per a report on India's inward remittances commissioned by Reserve Bank of India (RBI), total inward remittances from Australia to India were 0.7 percent of total inward flows of remittances in 2018.[338] In 2018, India was the second largest recipient of remittances from Australia, only behind China. With an Indian diaspora in Australia set to be the largest diasporic community in the country, the outward remittance flow from Australia to India is expected to see an upward trend.

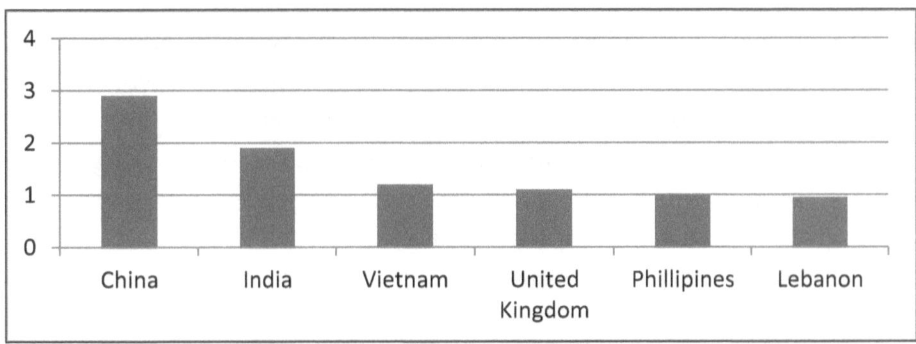

Fig 27: Bilateral Remittances Flows from Australia ($ Billion)[339]

Diaspora Engagement Strategies

As per United Nations report on International Migration 2019, India was the leading country of origin of international migrants, with 17.5 million persons living abroad. Most countries in Central and Southern Asia are net senders (negative net migration) for the period 2000-2010 and 2010-2020. The top sending countries during 2000-2020 were India (478 thousand per annum) and Bangladesh (445 thousand), followed by Nepal (179 thousand) and Pakistan (162 thousand). These four countries combined, accounted for 1.3 million or 84 per cent of the region's total net migration.[340] This Indian diaspora has made significant efforts in boosting India's economic growth and development. Due to the quantum of migration effected from India, concerted efforts have been initiated and maintained by the Government of India to target and engage the global Indian diaspora. A large number of initiatives and schemes have been introduced so as to facilitate persons of Indian origin to maintain ties with India. As part of diaspora engagement strategies in Australia, Indian government has ensured that all States and major cities in Australia have associations/organizations of Indian diaspora. Umbrella federations of Indian associations along with the ethnic publications, Indian language programmes on radio, Indian language schools, and Indian dance schools are the other avenues being exploited by India to ensure effective diaspora engagement.

The reach and contribution of Indian community in Australian society has also witnessed an incredible growth in the recent times. The Indian community in Australia has contributed in all the fields but the most prominent field, where Indian diaspora is leaving its imprints is in the academic field. In order to map the data base of academia of Indian origin in Australia, Ministry of External Affairs, Government of India has conceptualized a unique initiative known as 'Gyan Network'. The initiative ultimately aims to provide a collaborative environment that will facilitate a further sharing of information and resources between Universities in India and Australia.[341] The initiative encompasses six broad categories of areas of expertise, to include health sciences, pure sciences and computing, engineering, business, mining and social sciences.

On the other hand, though a similar influx of Australian diaspora in India cannot be claimed, a large number of alumni having studied from Australia and presently staying in India are a definite medium which are facilitating people to people links. "Because of their familiarity with their host country, former students often use the knowledge and networks to develop business linkages between the sending and host economies. Thus the export of educational services can be the precursor of expanded trade and investment relations between the host and sending country."[342] These alumni are playing a definite and an important role in promoting the bilateral relationship. The sheer number of students from India who have studied in various universities in Australia have the potential to be 'Alumni Ambassadors' and boost the bilateral relations. "Our ability to connect within our own region, the Indo-Pacific, is underpinned by enduring relationships forged through Australia's longstanding commitment to international education. These valued alumni relationships extend the reach and impact of our existing diplomatic network."[343]

With the help of an institutionalized programme like Australia Global Alumni Engagement Strategy, the bilateral relationship between India and Australia is manifesting in the strengthening of economic diplomacy between the two countries and facilitating the trade, investment and business linkages by adding depth to the bilateral relationship. Active cooperation in the capabilities and credentials in education, science, research and innovation between the two countries is also manifesting due to the adoption of the Alumni engagement strategy. The alumni have been instrumental in the sharing of unique experiences, insights and ideas, which are augmenting the value to the established notion of Australian research and innovation in the fields of science, technology, engineering and mathematics. The active involvement of alumni in promoting the bilateral relationship has the potential of bringing in dividends for both India and Australia. The alumni mirrors the positive reflections of the learning experiences gained by the alumni in Australia and are active contributors in supporting and facilitating an informed decision for selecting Australia as a destination for study, thereby corroborating the success to the successful archetype of systems thinking concept. These alumni having established successful businesses in India and maintaining links in Australia are a potent tool for nourishing the bilateral relationship.

Diaspora and Economics

At a macro level, diaspora and economics does not seem to have a relation with each other. At micro level however, the networks developed by the diaspora population provides a definite edge to the economic or trade relations between the two countries. The business associations established and manned by the diaspora in either country facilitate in increasing the volume of trade and overwhelm the boundaries of unknown. Diaspora business councils play a critical role in enhancing the business cooperation between two countries. In the case of India Australia bilateral relationship, diaspora communities are facilitating and promoting cross border investments and are responsible for establishing important social and economic connections between country of residence and country of origin of diaspora.

Research indicates that these social and economic ties foster a greater degree of familiarity between home and host country due to the provision of local information on foreign markets and customs.[344] The bilateral business councils and chambers of commerce are critical indices of diaspora contribution and facilitate business and trade links between Australia and migrant home countries. With the presence of leading business people in business councils and chambers of commerce, these organisations are helping in facilitating business flows within their respective diaspora communities. Acting as an interface between their countries of residence, these organisations are promoting and helping potential investors getting in direct contact with their local and informal diaspora network.

Following the recognition of huge trade potential between India and Australia, the Australia India Business Council (AIBC) was established during the visit of the then Prime Minister of India to Australia in 1986. The AIBC is a national membership organisation with active chapters in Sydney, Melbourne, Brisbane, Adelaide, Perth and Canberra and maintains close relationships with federal and state government agencies, the diplomatic corps and industry bodies, and showcases opportunities to the Australian business community through an active program of events throughout Australia.[345] Besides facilitating policy and business planning initiatives with major stakeholders including the Indian government, federal and State governments of Australia, major trade and investment bodies, the AIBC is also involved in organising targeted Australian business delegations to India, hosting Indian business delegations in Australia and also facilitating business networking events for members to build partnerships with India.

AIBC is providing a yeoman service to the cause of facilitating international business links and trade flows between India and Australia and in the process promoting greater economic, cultural and business ties between Australia and India through their local knowledge. "Australia India Business Council's advice to Indian companies that are investing here is that they have to become part of the community. We advise them that they have to support the community. So we are doing our bit to help make them part of the community for the longer term investment."[346] Indo-Australian Chamber of Commerce (IACC) was also established during the visit of Prime Minister of India to Australia in 1986 along with the AIBC and formally had come into existence 22nd June, 1989. The Chamber has in the past 28 years, led sixteen Business Missions to Australia and has helped over 400 Indian companies, mostly SMEs, to establish long term business relations and effective partnerships with Australian companies.[347]

Bilateral Economic Engagement Strategies

Bilateral economic relations are an important component of bilateral relationship between the two countries. This assumes importance more so as the contemporary global economic scenario does not allow restriction of economic activities. The advantages offered by developing and sustaining economic relations with likeminded countries offer numerous advantages. In the instant case of India Australia bilateral relationship, economic relations form an inseparable part of the engagement strategies of both countries towards each other. The enormous potential of bilateral relationship also finds resonance in the economics of the relationship. The India Australia bilateral relationship is also unique and singular in the respect that both countries have charted a futuristic course for their relationship in a written format with definite timelines.

Realizing the potential offered by long term engagement with India, an India Economic Strategy 2035, charting the road map and vision for India - Australia bilateral relationship till 2035 was commissioned by Government of Australia in 2018. The study was carried out under the chairmanship of former foreign secretary of Australia, Peter Varghese, a renowned champion of increased bilateral relationship between India and Australia. The strategy visualizes Australian Indian diaspora to be a national economic asset and has drawn out recommendations for engaging Indian diaspora in Australia. The strategy recommended that the entrepreneurial spirit and knowledge of the Indian market by the Indian diaspora in Australia will facilitate enhancement of the future productivity and resilience of the Australian business sector.[348] The report primarily champions for the more robust economic relationship between the two countries and has concluded that people to people relations along with alignment of geo strategic interests are important for India Australia bilateral relationship. "A long-term economic strategy towards India should rest also on two other critical pillars that support the people-to-people ties and geopolitical congruence. "[349]

Diversifying the engagement strategies for India into the federal structure of India, the report has rightly homed on to the federal structure of governance in India. The strategy besides concentrating on to the cooperation at the level of central government in India also aims to focus on the states of India. "While Australia needs to continue to engage with India as a national economy including on its macro settings, India's federal structure holds many of the levers that control the investment climate."[350] For the purpose of increased cooperation at state levels, the strategy has identified ten high potential states which can provide rich dividends for the bilateral relationship, to include Maharashtra, Gujarat, Karnataka, Tamil Nadu, Andhra Pradesh, Telangana, West Bengal, Punjab, Uttar Pradesh and the National Capital Region.

India Australia bilateral relationship is symbiotic and is providing a matrix of balanced incentives to both the countries. A large number of studies and papers on the subject have brought out that the bilateral relationship between Australia and China has been one sided and benefits of the relationship have been unilaterally taken over by China. Drawing a distinction between bilateral relationship between India-Australia and Australia-China, the report underscores the fact that India is not China and goes on to identify ten sectors where both countries can cooperate to the optimal level. The strategy has listed education as the 'flagship' sector', whereas resources, agribusiness, and tourism have been endorsed by the strategy as 'lead sectors'. The report has also charted the future course of action for cooperation between the two countries in the fields of infrastructure, health, financial services, sport, and science and innovation.

In an acknowledgment to the India Economic Strategy Report 2035 released by Australia, Confederation of Indian Industry (CII) in collaboration with KPMG has released the Australia Economic Strategy Report. "The report, based on independent research and inputs collected from personal interviews of the team with the ministries, governments, academia, think tanks etc., has identified potential areas of collaborations across sectors between the two nations."[351] This is apparently first time ever when a country specific holistic engagement strategy has been promulgated by the Indian Government, thereby indicating the significance attached to the relationship by the highest echelons of the Indian government. Other than the current economic engagements the report has charted a roadmap for engagement in other niche sectors to include labour intensive services, defence, sports and sports technology, textile and textile designing, digital gaming and animation, water management and commercial shipbuilding, space and education technologies. "The implementation strategies in the key opportunity areas, as highlighted in the report, would serve as critical action points for policymakers and governments of both countries. While the success of the strategy would depend on the interest taken by industry and governments of the two countries, the strategy, if implemented and disseminated with care and diligence would greatly enhance bilateral ties and will lead to a fostering of growth and development of closer ties between the two countries."[352]

Non-governmental interaction is an important part of any bilateral relationship. The interactions outside the ambit of governmental mandated interactions have tremendous scope for promoting the people to people links. These interactions largely being voluntary facilitate understanding of societal values and culture of each other, leading to the up gradation of bilateral relationship. In the case of bilateral relationship between India and Australia this crucial role is being played by the tourism factor. As per estimates of India Economic Strategy 2035, the number of tourists from India is expected to grow to 1.2 million by 2035, an upsurge from the 0.3 million in 2017. This increase will result in India to become the fourth largest tourism market for Australia, from the eighth largest market in 2017. In 2019, India was Australia's fastest growing market for visitor spends. India is Australia's seventh largest inbound market for visitor arrivals, sixth largest market for total visitor spend and second largest for visitor nights.[353] India's considerable diaspora coupled with the population of Indian students for higher education in Australia is expected to act as an enormous pull factor for Indian tourists to visit Australia. Tourism sector, with the current levels is playing a significant role in promoting people to people relationship between India and Australia. With projected increase in the tourism arrivals from India, this sector possesses an optimum potential for enhancing bilateral relationship between India and Australia.

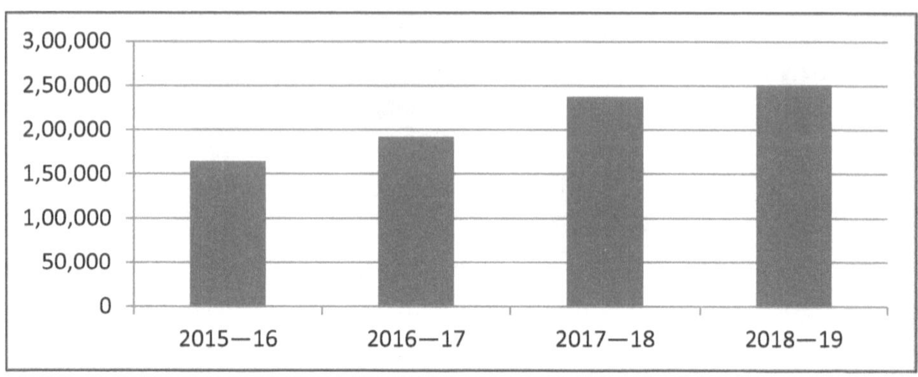

Fig 28: Grant of Tourist Visas to Indians[354]

Energy: Prime Mover of Relationship

Conservative estimates have pegged a massive surge in the energy demand of India. Notwithstanding the economic slowdown attributed to COVID-19, India economy is expected to be bouncing back sharply and a V shaped growth trajectory is very much anticipated. Coupled with the huge population incentive, projected energy requirements of India are very positive. "India's energy demand will grow by a Compound Annual Growth Rate (CAGR) of 3.1% from 2009 to 2035, which is more than double the world's energy demand at a CAGR of 1.3% for the same period. India's share in world energy demand will increase by 5.5% in 2009 to 8.6% in 2035 and the growth would come from all fuels."[355] The same forecast projects a threefold increase in the demand of coal and a massive 18 fold increase in the demand for renewable energy, "The demand for coal will almost triple from 280 (Million of Tonnes of Oil Equivalent) Mtoe in 2009 to 618 Mtoe in 2035 at a CAGR of 3.1%. The renewable energy demand is projected to increase from 2 Mtoe in 2009 to 36 Mtoe in 2035. Nuclear energy demand would reach 48 Mtoe in 2035 from 5 Mtoe in 2009."[356]

The bilateral relationship between India and Australia based on strong foundations of strategic and people to people relationship has a huge potential in energy sector to usher an era of stronger economic partnership. Energy partnership and resource sharing can become an integral and an inescapable aspect of this cooperation. Institutional measures adapted in coal extraction in India have resulted in the increase in the coal supply in the domestic sector. Coal, as on date continues to be the largest domestic source of energy supply and electricity generation in India. As a result of evolution and implementation of severe norms of air pollution in the country, upcoming coal fired power plants are of High Efficiency Low Emissions (HELE) category and correspondingly require high-quality coal for operations. With domestic coal characterised by low energy and high ash, India and Australia have high potential for a symbiotic resource sharing possibilities in the coal sector. In the energy sector, cooperation in the sharing of Liquefied Natural Gas (LNG) is another possibility of stronger bilateral relationship. India's import demand is likely to reach 80 Billion Cubic Meters (BCM) by 2040 and Australia's share is predicted to increase and become dominant by 2040. As on date Australia is the second largest exporter of LNG, while India is the fourth largest importer of LNG, a mutual possibility which can be harnessed by both countries.[357]

Cooperation in the field of Non Renewable Energy (NRE) sector also has a huge potential for increased bilateral trade between India and Australia. After signing of bilateral agreement for cooperation in the peaceful uses of Nuclear Energy in 2014, Australia can emerge as a major source of uranium for India. In the area of Solar Energy, Australia has proven expertise, which can provide a strong foundation for bilateral cooperation between India and Australia. Australia is also working on tapping wave energy and could help India initiate its own such endeavor. India could also benefit from Australian expertise in forecasting and solar scheduling.[358]

The arbitrariness and an apparent overlooking of established international norms and order by the rise of China economically as well as militarily, in the Indo-Pacific region, are also forcing India and Australia to look at more relevant cooperation. Overdependence of China in the economic realm and a convergence of geo political interests with India are facilitating a proposed diversification of existing trade and economic relationships by Australia. Energy and resource sector has a massive potential of cooperation between the two nations in the field of energy cooperation. "Going forward, I think energy is going to be the defining feature of our relationship, particularly since you have already played an important role in providing adequate supplies to our coal based thermal plants. We are now looking at increased engagement on uranium; Gas is going to be the next enabler for cleaner technology for our power production. "[359]

Bilateral Trade

Australia India Business Exchange (AIB-X) in 2020 conducted the visit of one of the largest trade missions to India, with an underlying theme of Trade, Tourism and Taste of Australia. The business delegation was aptly led by Australian Trade, Investment and Tourism Minister. On the face of it, this visit by a business delegation may be termed as a standalone regular visit but the significance of the visit lies in the India Economic Strategy- 2035, which is primarily aimed to address the gaps and exploit the possibilities existing in the bilateral relationship between India and Australia. The strategy has set a target for India to become one of Australia's top three export markets, to make India the third-largest destination in Asia for Australian outward investment, and to bring India into the inner circle of Australia's strategic partnerships.[360]

The changing dynamics of Australia China bilateral relationship and increased synergy between India and Australia on a host of issues are facilitating Australia to safeguard its economy against excessive reliance on China, and further diversify to other emerging markets with optimal potential. The present day two way trade between India - Australia is very miniscule as compared to two way trade between Australia and China. In 2019, the two way trade between Australia and India was $30 billion and at the same time, the two way trade between Australia and China was more than $200 billion.

Though trade between two countries is an important indicator of strength of bilateral relationship and the dictum holds true in case of bilateral relationship between India and Australia. Trade dynamics between both the countries are complex and the similarity index in agriculture and other associated issues have played a significant role in prolonged negotiations on conclusion of Free Trade Agreement (FTA) and the recently signed Regional Comprehensive Economic Partnership (RCEP), from which India had opted out. Differences in perception over protectionist regimes in specific commodities have not allowed fructification of these negotiations. A particular characteristic of bilateral relationship between India and Australia is that, in spite of increased convergence of interests, the independence of strategic interests has been retained by both the countries. Therefore, minor differences of opinion in the trade negotiations have not derailed the bilateral relationship. In fact, it has been repeatedly emphasised by both the countries that FTA details are being worked out and that both the countries are open to a FTA.

Free Trade Agreement

Capitalizing on the rapid development of the economic relationship between Australia and India, both countries had agreed way back in 2008 to carry out a feasibility study for a FTA. The aim of the study was to objectively analyse the requirement of a comprehensive FTA between India and Australia covering goods, services, investment, intellectual property, sanitary and phytosanitary issues, technical barriers to trade, competition policy and government procurements.[361] The feasibility study had concluded that a bilateral FTA was actually feasible and recommended that both countries should actively consider finalizing a FTA between them. "The feasibility study had also indicated that that the welfare of the two countries would increase with the conclusion of an FTA. The welfare gains for both the countries could be in the range of 0.15 and 1.14 per cent of GDP for India and 0.23 and 1.17 per cent of GDP for Australia. An Australia-India FTA could result in a modest positive impact on total global economic output."[362]

Based on the recommendations of the feasibility study, India and Australia started the discussions in the right earnest for concluding a Comprehensive Economic Cooperation Agreement (CECA) in May 2011. Since then though there have been nine rounds of negotiations between both the countries, CECA has alluded them. Due to the inherent differences in interpretation of trade and services along with associated tariff barriers have precluded signing of such a bilateral agreement. "If anyone has seen a draft of bilateral trade agreement, it is very fat and it is very complex document. And so, they do take time to conclude. Often, you reach a point in bilateral trade negotiations, and even in multilateral trade negotiations, where it actually becomes politically challenging to cross a line. So, invariably, those things get resolved through lots of discussions and negotiations and they do need to give a political license to negotiators to go beyond a certain point."[363]

In spite of delay in signing of CECA between both the countries the key negotiation at different levels is continuing. Both the countries realize the enormous benefits offered by such a trade agreement between both the countries. "We will continue making progress in CECA… While Australian investors will make their own commercial decisions, increasing Australian investment stocks in India deepens our economic integration." [364] India also realizes the delay in concluding CECA with Australia as though all other aspects of a holistic and comprehensive bilateral relationship with Australia have been addressed, this aspect is still lagging." There is a discussion on a free trade agreement, a bilateral free trade agreement as well because, as you know, we didn't sign the RCEP (Regional Comprehensive Economic Partnership)."[365] The respective economic engagement strategies commissioned by both the countries also lay a futuristic road map for concluding a much required comprehensive economic cooperation agreement. These strategies have provided a fresh impetus to the stalled efforts in concluding the trade agreements.

Foreign Direct Investment

A number of theories have posited the complementary and substitute links between the Foreign Direct Investment (FDI) and the bilateral trade. Empirical evidences do exist which prove the repetitive corresponding relationship between the bilateral trade and FDI, which in turn provides a reinforcing propensity for both. Ironically, at the present levels the reverse is true in case of bilateral trade and FDI configurations between India and Australia. Both, the bilateral trade and FDI are reinforcing each other but certainly not in a positive manner and the bilateral relationship behold a greater scope of improvement. The Australian direct investment relationship with India has been weak for a long time. Just 0.24 per cent of India's total equity inflows since 2000 have been sourced from Australia.[366] India hosted a modest 0.3 per cent share ($ 1.8 billion) of total Australian direct investment stocks in 2017.[367]

The FDI inflows to each country from the other one have generally followed the strength sectors in each country, whereas the investors have avoided treading into the hitherto unknown sectors.

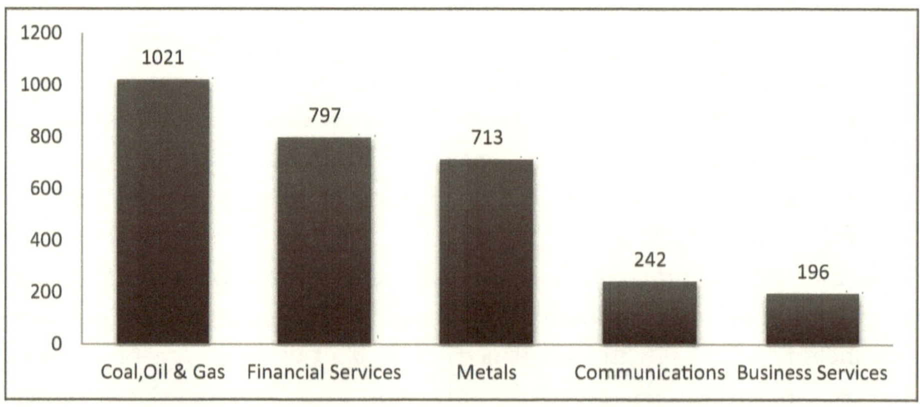

Fig 29: Pattern (2003-2019) of FDI from India to Australia (US $ Billions) [368]

In India, coal oil and gas, followed by financial services investments in alternative/renewable energy and metals have been the largest source of Australian FDI investments, but these investments are in no way near to the Australian FDI in other countries.

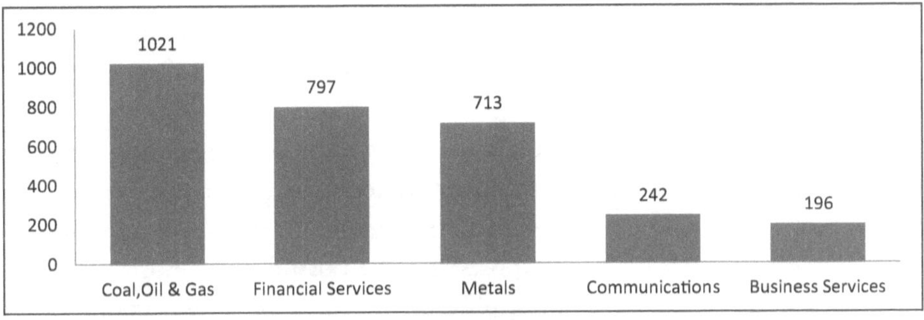

Fig 30: Pattern (2003-2019) of FDI from Australia to India (US $ Billions) [369]

Regional Comprehensive Economic Partnership (RCEP)

RCEP claimed to be the modern world's largest trading bloc was signed on November 15, 2020 with 15 nations deciding to establish a mega regional trading partnership. The members include ASEAN 10, Australia, China, Japan, New Zealand and South Korea. India, though one of the most important member of the bloc, had decided to stay away from the agreement due to the non inclusion of her concerns in the agreement. "India had been consistently raising fundamental issues and concerns throughout the negotiations and was prompted to take this stand as they had not been resolved by the deadline to commit to signing the deal. Its decision was to safeguard the interests of industries like agriculture and dairy and to give an advantage to the country's services sector. The current structure of RCEP still does not address these issues and concerns."[370]

The developing multilateral, trilateral and bilateral arrangements due to the geo strategic compulsions and the common detest against arbitrariness exhibited by China in the commons of the region would have been greatly benefitted by the participation of India in the trade deal. "Despite such circumstances, China's participation on the RCEP bloc indicates that several other member nations have decoupled geopolitics and economic interests as a policy imperative."[371] As brought out earlier, Australia is having serious and growing tensions with China on a large number of issues. In spite of these simmering tensions, Australia joining the trade deal has surprised many. "We make decisions on the basis of our national interest. As a trading nation, Australia supports open markets and encourages expanded trade and investment. RCEP is to be the world's largest FTA, which brings together nine of Australia's top 15 trading partners into a single economic framework. So, Australia saw sense and national interest making that decision." [372]

Major observations of India related to the trade pact are concerned with China only. As part of the deal India was required to provide certain risk prone exposure to China. Indian concerns included inadequate provisioning of protections against surge in exports and the possibility of evasion of rules of origin, thereby facilitating dumping of products by certain countries by routing through third country with lower tariffs. It was expected that India Australia surging bilateral relationship might get affected adversely by the reticence of India in exiting the deal. However, the strong foundations of relationship coupled with common understanding of the cause have ensured that Australia is on board with India regarding the observations and objections proposed by India. "The ministerial declaration of 15 November says that the door remains open for India to join the RCEP. But that declaration also noted that India will be able to participate as an observer at future RCEP meetings, and in any economic cooperation activities, even though it hasn't joined the RCEP. So whatever India ultimately decides, Australia will respect the decision and will continue to support India's engagement in the trade and economy of the Indo-Pacific. "[373]

The bilateral economic relationship between India and Australia though held hostage for quite some time with issues of self interest and mutual concerns has started to look up. The release of economic engagement strategies by both countries for each other is very significant from this point of view. Binding themselves with a futuristic road map for increased economic and trade cooperation will augur very well for both the economies. "India is a great friend of Australia and a strengthened trade relationship between the two countries would provide mutual benefits for both the countries."[374]

CHAPTER 5

LOOKING AHEAD: PROGNOSIS OF RELATIONSHIP

"Both the countries are historical and vibrant democracies, both the nations have an envious set up of political and civil liberties, and both share their respective ideals about greater economic interdependence and political stability in Asia and around, yet so far they have been unable to achieve "a quantum leap in the relationship."[375]

When the then Prime Minister of Australia John Howard said above words in 2013, nobody could have imagined the import of the words. In the past seven years, a quantum leap in the bilateral relationship between India and Australia has indeed been achieved in all aspects of relationship. The historical mistrust apart, there is no apparent reason for this relationship to not achieve further magnitude and amplitude in the years to come. Though starting from a zero a lot of ground has been covered in the bilateral relationship and a large number of issues of concern from both sides have been reconciled. This reapproachment and alignment has also been facilitated by other developments in their immediate environment in which the traction of the geopolitical construct of Indo Pacific has played a major role. Within the constraints of contemporary and futuristic geostrategic and geopolitical environment this relationship will certainly achieve greater heights.

As I pen down the last chapter of the book in the winter of 2020, the more I observe and follow the developments in the context of the bilateral relationship between India and Australia, the more I am convinced that alignment of interests is for real. This relationship is based on a strong and stable foundation of mutual understandings in the fields of Defence, Diplomacy and Diaspora. Though in the previous chapter, I endeavored to touch upon the context of trade and economic relationship, but am confident that with the positive leanings of the top leadership on the subject, it is a matter of time before a comprehensive economic cooperation agreement is signed between both the countries. In the conclusive chapter of the book, I have made an attempt to prognosticate the bilateral relationship between India and Australia. Based on the three underlying crucial aspects of Strategic Congruence, People to People Relationship and Trade, some definitive propositions have been recommended. These recommendations are not exhaustive but may be considered as indicative, which if considered and implemented have the potential to provide further increment to the burgeoning bilateral relationship.

Military Exchange Programmes

For an enduring strategic partnership it is imperative that the foreign affairs and defence planners of both countries are aware of each other's way of functioning so as to facilitate interoperability and to understand the nuances of functioning of these departments. In the contemporary diplomatic engagements, bilateral understandings ensure that selected officials from Foreign/External Affairs' and Military in each country travel to other country for short duration courses of instructions as part of military exchange programmes. The relationships developed during the process facilitate mutual confidence and respect and strengthens both countries in the process.

Table 11: Temporary Visa for Foreign/Defence Students: Australia

Country	2015-16	2016-17	2017-18	2018-19	Total
India	34	68	85	22	209
China	16	13	24	15	68
Philippines	268	290	277	211	1046
Vietnam	494	395	522	336	1747
Nepal	74	126	143	111	454
Indonesia	1629	1970	1488	1126	6213
Pakistan	207	200	214	139	760

An analysis of the short term visa granted by Australia to applicants from India for foreign affairs and defence students as part of student exchange programmes reveals that the strength of these exchange students is very minimal as compared to the potency of the bilateral relationship. On the other hand, the visas granted to students under exchange programmes in the fields of defence and foreign affairs from countries like Philippines, Vietnam, Indonesia and Pakistan is phenomenally higher. It is therefore proposed that in order to achieve greater strategic alignment through people to people contacts, more number of students under exchange programmes from India in foreign affairs and defence are nominated to Australia.

Strategic Minerals

Strategic minerals can be defined as those minerals which are considered vital for the contemporary technologies, but their supply being limited or non availability in the country, makes their requirement all the more critical. These minerals are essential to support critical defence, medicine and infrastructure requirements. Australia Economic Strategy has identified 49 minerals which can be considered very vital for India's economic growth and out of these 21 minerals reserves exists in Australia which can sustain India's requirements. The report has further identified 13 minerals as 'High Potential Geological Opportunities', which have the potential to provide crucial boost to the bilateral cooperation in the field. Australia counts in top three countries of the world in the production of Cobalt and Zircon and can be a top provider of these critical minerals to India. As India provides a crucial push to 'Make in India' programme and the resultant boost is provided to the manufacturing sector, electric mobility vehicles, space exploration and defence capabilities, there exists a window of opportunity for both the countries to exploit the relatively advantageous position of Australia in the sector. The institutionalized bilateral cooperation between the two countries in the field of rare earths is presently not developed up to the optimal potential and further close and intimate bilateral framework can complement the surge in the strategic cooperation and more so in the light of the Comprehensive Strategic Partnership Agreement signed between the two countries in 2020.

Cooperation in Defence Technology

After a path breaking journey of witnessing an active cooperation in NTS and traditional security domains, cooperation in defence technology is another unexplored field which has tremendous potential to boost the bilateral relationship between India and Australia. As part of Comprehensive Strategic Partnership 2020, both countries have agreed to implement arrangement for cooperation in Defence Science and Technology. As India pushes for Cyber command, data security and cyber security assume critical importance for existing and futuristic defence capabilities of Indian defence establishment. The MoU signed between India and Australia for cooperation in defence science and technology has the potential to usher an era of greater and enhanced collaboration in the fields on nontraditional security. Australia has been ranked in top ten of the Global Cyber Security Index, whereas India has been ranked 47 on the Index (2018 rankings), thereby indicating the differential in the current capabilities and indicating the significance of potential of cooperation in the field. Both the countries can explore the possibilities of cooperation in the field, both as institutionalized and informal arrangements.

Knowledge Partnerships

The dynamics of a strong knowledge partnership in making has already been discussed in detail earlier in the book. These knowledge partnerships not only help to facilitate access to niche technologies to both the countries involved but also help to foster people to people links, a very important and critical facet of bilateral relationship. Under the aegis of knowledge partnership programmes, both India and Australia have made substantial progress in formulating agreements and arrangements in the field. In spite, there is still scope of further engaging each other in sharing knowledge partnerships. With almost 1000 universities in India, not even one tenth universities have partnered with universities in Australia. The point of quality of research and academic merit notwithstanding, a deliberate effort to target more Indian universities for academic collaboration with Australian universities will provide a distinct differential to the relationship. A deliberate, dedicated and sincere mechanism to engage existing and prospective Indian students on Australian universities campuses will go a long way in promoting people to people contacts, an essential prerequisite for furthering the bilateral relationship between India and Australia. On similar lines, providing depth and breadth to the alumni engagement strategies will facilitate Indian students to retain their close connections with Australian institutions of higher learning. Knowledge partnerships provide an opportunity to the research scholars and academicians to promote the knowledge and understanding about each other. There is a clear and identified felt need to expand the scope of contemporary knowledge partnerships between India and Australia. STEM subjects though have been identified as the pillars of the knowledge partnerships and an extensive collaboration matrix in the STEM subjects is operational, it is recommended that a similar collaboration matrix for knowledge partnerships in the fields of humanities and economics is identified and developed.

Migration and Mobility Partnership Agreement

As discussed in detail in the previous chapter of the book, people to people links between India and Australia are performing an important role in the furthering of the bilateral relations between the two nations. Indian diaspora is set to be largest diaspora in Australia in the near future. The contribution of this diaspora to the Australian society is immense and the corresponding brain circulation is helping Indian society as well. In order to institutionalize the migration and mobility between the two countries, it is desirable that a migration and mobility partnership agreement is finalized between the two countries at the earliest. As part of the Comprehensive Security Partnership 2020, both India and Australia have underscored the importance of contribution of diaspora in furthering the bilateral relationship and consented to initiate a discussion at senior levels for the proposed migration and mobility partnership agreement. Institutionalizing of migration and mobility arrangements between both the countries will further complement the links at people-to-people levels, and facilitate augmentation and regulation of mobility of students, researchers and skilled professionals. This type of agreement besides ensuring and incentivizing the circular migration thereby facilitating brain gain for India will also systematize the cooperation on issues related to illicit migration and human trafficking between the two countries and will provide an institutionalized experience to the prospective international students, academics and researchers from India.

University level MoUs

In order to facilitate strengthening of existing collaborations and to provide wider reach and variety to the prospective students from India, it is essential that opportunities are provided to the maximum number of students from India. With a very diverse higher education landscape in India, it is recommended that the individual agreements between the universities in Australia and India are encouraged. This type of arrangement besides providing opportunities to a larger clientele will also facilitate Australian universities to diversify and approach students in the Indian hinterland, thereby empowering a larger number of students from India. Coupled with this the provisions of twinning in the NEP can be further explored to provide depth to the knowledge partnerships. This will facilitate strengthening of collaborations of mutual concerns and will catalyze the bilateral relationship.

Offshore Campuses

NEP unveiled by the Ministry of Education, Government of India in 2020 provides for the Institutes of Eminence (IsoE) in India to open up their campuses in foreign countries. Under the guidelines issued by University Grants Commission (UGC), an IoE can set up to three offshore centers in five years, subject to a maximum of one per academic year. The concerned IoE will have to work as per a ten year strategic plan and a three year rolling implementation plan, subject to necessary regulatory approvals from the concerned agencies. As on date there are twenty IsoE in India, both in public and private sector, thereby providing immense opportunities and potential for both countries to promote the essential people to people contacts.

Australian Universities have been demanding access to Indian education system in terms of approvals for setting up of offshore campuses in India. The NEP 2020 has provisions for opening up of offshore campuses of foreign universities in India. Though the policy provisions have been formulated, the actualization of these proposals will require considerable efforts from both India and Australia. The present twinning arrangements between the universities of both countries though is sustaining the stop gap measures, the existing business models of Australian universities will have to undergo certain changes in order to be successful in India. As the policy for opening of foreign universities in India has already been formulated, it is recommended that necessary amendments in the existing models of Australian universities are brainstormed in advance.

Bilateral Higher Qualification Recognition Framework

With India implementing the NEP 2020, there is an increased need for India and Australia to work towards a convention/agreement on higher education qualifications recognition in each other's country. The framework will provide necessary impetus to the brain circulation by promoting circular migration and will also facilitate closer understanding between the institutes of higher learning in both the countries. There are existing policy provisions for recognition of Indian higher education qualifications in Australia in form of Australian Qualification Framework (AQF) and corresponding recognition provided by Association of Indian Universities (AIU) and University Grants Commission (UGC) in India. A bilateral higher educational qualification specific framework between both the countries is the need of the hour as it will provide support to the proposed off shoring of campuses by the institutes of higher learning in both the countries. The framework will also facilitate the students in both the countries to avoid the dubious educational consultants, a practice more prevalent in India. This framework in the larger scheme of things can be upgraded as one stop destination for the aspirants of international higher education in both the countries.

Sub Federal Convergence

Both India and Australia boast of an incredible federal set up as governance structure. There exists optimal potential to exploit the nuances of federal structure to promote the bilateral relationship. This may be true more in case of India than Australia that each sub unit of federal structure is a sub economy in itself. With highly variable infrastructure and growth requirements, there exists a strong case for recommending engagement at state and even at the city level in India by Australia. This will facilitate state governments in India to identify the areas of cooperation with Australia depending upon their respective requirements and potential for growth in the bilateral relationship. Therefore, it is recommended that agreements and partnerships between Indian states and states with Australia are promoted and institutionalized.

In order to build a strong relationship at the sub federal level, it is imperative that the dynamics of investment and the peculiar requirements of each stake holder are identified and worked upon. There is not much difference observed in these aspects in case of states in Australia but the states in India are highly different and diverse in these aspects. Therefore, it is recommended that peculiarities of Indian states in terms of investment patterns, growth dynamics and the economic compulsions are delineated, which will provide a much required boost to the relationship. The India Economic Strategy 2035 has also correctly identified this aspect of bilateral relationship and has targeted Indian states which are increasingly being exposed to the competitive federalism and will play a significant part in the India's economic future. The current and past researchers studying in both the countries have a significant role to play in the sub federal convergence. The alumni of Australian universities in India can provide an enduring foundation for developing and sustaining the sub federal convergence between the two countries. Similarly, a better and deeper understanding at the states level can also be explored by exploiting the people to people links established by the Indian students currently studying in the Australian campuses.

Tourism

As discussed in chapter four of the book, tourism traffic between India and Australia has a huge potential in promoting the bilateral relationship between India and Australia. Tourism provides fillip to the crucial aspect of people to people relationships which in turn helps to facilitate the bilateral relationship. The existing Indian diaspora in Australia along with the huge international student population from India will continue to provide a strong pull to the potential tourist's inflows from India. Similarly theme based tourism like Incredible India coupled with Alumni engagement strategies can provide a strong pull for the Australian tourists into India. Though a MoU to enhance and strengthen the people to people contacts between the two nations through tourism was signed between the two countries in 2014, the terms of the MoU have since elapsed and there is an explicit requirement to institutionalize the provisions of the MoU. The aspects of cooperation between the stakeholders involved in tourism between both the countries and promotion of bilateral flow of information still requires streamlining. Australia Economic Strategy released by India in 2020 has listed certain potential sub sectors where active cooperation between India and Australia can be achieved in tourism sector. The strategy has delineated developing India as a transit destination for the East Coast of the US and Europe for the travelers from Australia, access to tourism infrastructure in Australia and the increase in the frequency of direct flights between India and Australia which can further the two way tourist flows between both the countries. The hospitality industry particularly in India can learn a lot from relatively developed sector in Australia and there is a scope of bilateral cooperation in terms of on job training, internships and short duration institutionalized visits from trainees in the hospitality sector from India to Australia. Coupled with this, there exists a potential to develop twinning arrangements for higher education and research in the field of tourism and hospitality between both the countries. A fresh MoU on cooperation in the tourism and hospitality sectors between both the countries is the need of the hour. It is recommended that the provisions of the proposed MoU are comprehensive and institutionalized, particularly in view of the multiple complementarities in other fields of cooperation between India and Australia.

Regulation of Visa/Migration Climate

The existing climate of Visa/migration in Australia is very well regulated in form of Office of Migration Agents Registration Authority (OMARA), which is guided by the policy provisions of the government on the subject and is subject to an established system of checks and balances. The functioning of the agency is very transparent as all the data with respect to the agents registered with the agency are available on the portal of the agency. There is an established grievance redress mechanism and escalatory matrix available to the clients. On the other hand, the visa/migration climate in India is not regulated to that extent and there is an apparent lack of oversight mechanisms, leading to the duping of prospective international students and visa frauds in some cases.

As a prospective aspirant for international education from India in most of the cases applies for Australian universities in an individual capacity and is invariably handicapped by the absence of an institutionalized mechanism duly supported and backed by the governments in both the countries, there is a case in point for establishing an institutionalized mechanism for both the countries to evolve a dedicated mechanism for the same. Another area for concern in the evolving international education environment in both the countries is the growing convergence and establishment of an integrated regime for travel and educational consultants. The establishment of a dedicated agency backed by government support can go a long way in preventing the often reported visa frauds, which besides causing financial and mental agony to the student also brings a bad name to the international education sector.

Foreign Direct Investments

An analysis of bilateral trade between India and Australia will reveal that the investment relationship between the two countries is much less developed and talked about than the existing bilateral trade ties. The trade relationship between

India and Australia as such has a huge potential for further development and is a different topic altogether. But in the context of the bilateral relationship between India and Australia, it is imperative for both the countries to provide a push to the bilateral investment configuration which in turn can further facilitate the bilateral relationship to a large extent. With the unilateral cessation of Bilateral Investment Treaty (BIT) by India and the consequent lack of an alternate institutionalized arrangement for the Foreign Direct Investment (FDI) between the two countries, the required surge in the FDI by either country has not been achieved. It is therefore strongly recommended that an institutionalized arrangement for FDI is established between both the countries at an earliest possible opportunity, which can provide the impetus to the trade relationship.

Free Trade Agreement

Though the negotiations for formalizing a FTA between India and Australia are in the pipeline for past about a decade, yet no concrete arrangements for a formal trade agreement between the two countries has been achieved. There are various concerns of both sides which are required to be resolved prior to the actualization of the free trade pact, yet both sides realize the importance of this crucial linkage and the significance of the realisation can be gauged from the fact that respective economic engagement strategies released by both sides have provided adequate emphasis to this crucial economic linkage. The differential in the developmental levels between India and Australia is an issue which cannot be resolved and is therefore required to be acknowledged and accordingly tackled. The economic environment in both the countries in terms of investment regimes and growth priorities are mutually non convergent and therefore require deeper mutual understanding. Both India and Australia are presently at a threshold where they have evolved a mutually comprehensible understanding and a FTA between them is a matter of time. It is therefore recommended that a FTA on mutually acceptable terms is finalized between the two countries in an earliest possible time frame, which in turn can further facilitate the bilateral relationship.

REFERENCE

1. Opening Remarks of Prime Minister Modi at India-Australia Virtual Summit, 04 June 2020, Ministry of External Affairs, Government of India, Available at *Prime Minister's Opening Remarks at India-Australia Virtual Summit (mea.gov.in)*, (Accessed on October 26, 2020).

2. Mohan, C. Raja, *Samudra Manthan: Sino-Indian Rivalry in the Indo-Pacific*, Washington, Carnegie Endowment for International Peace, 2012.

3. Viotti, Paul R. & Kauppi, Mark V. *International Relations and World Politics: Security, Economy, Identity*, Prentice Hall, New Jersey, 1997, p 127.

4. Peter Mayer & Purnendra Jain (2010) Beyond Cricket: Australia–India Evolving Relations, Australian Journal of Political Science, 45:1, 133-148, DOI: *10.1080/10361140903517759*.

5. David Scott, "Australia's Embrace Of the 'Indo-Pacific': New Term, New Region, New Strategy?" *International Relations of the Asia-Pacific, http://irap.oxfordjournals. org* (Accessed June 30, 2020).

6. Strong and secure: a strategy for Australia's national security, *Australian Policy Online*.

7. Peter Verghese, "*Our Journey with India*", *http://dfat.gov.au/news/speeches/Pages/ australia-india-institute-oration-our-journey-with-india.aspx* (accessed September 23, 2020).

8. Transcript of the Prime Minister John Howard joint doorstop interview with the Prime Minister of India Dr Manmohan Singh, New Delhi, 06 March 2006, Available at: *http://www.pm.gov.au/.news/interviews/Interview1809.html* (Accessed July 26, 2020).

9. Prehistoric Links among Australia, South East Asia and India, D. Devahuti, *The South East Asian Review*, Vol 1, Number 1, August 1976.

10. Geoffrey Blainey, *The Tyranny of Distance*, Macmillan Publishers, London, 1968.

11. David Lowe (ed.), *Australia and the End of Empires: The Impact of Decolonization in Australia's Near North, 1945–65*, Deakin University Press, 1996. p.5.

12. Government of India, Ministry of Information & Broadcasting, *Jawaharlal Nehru's Speeches*, September 1946-May 1949, Vol. 1, New Delhi, 1949, p 236.

13. Statement of Anderson Hume in Australian Parliament, 01 May 1958, Available at *House of Representatives, Debates, 1 May 1958: Historic Hansard*, (Accessed November 11, 2020).

14. David Lowe, "Australia at the United Nations in the 1950s: The Paradox of Empire ", *Australian Journal of International Affairs,* Vol. 51, No. 2, 1997.

15. Morrell, WP, *"British Colonial Policy in the Age of Peel and Russel"*, Frank Cass & Co Ltd, 1966, p 89.

16. Australia, House of Representatives, Debates, 13 October 1955, Available at, *https://historichansard.net/hofreps/1901/19010906_reps_1_4/*, (Accessed November 29, 2020).

17. James Stephen July 17, 1841, Quoted in Paul Knaplund, *"The British Empire 1815-1939"*, Harper & Brothers, New York, 1941, p 276.

18. Australia, House of Representatives, Debates, 06 September 1901, Available at, *https://historichansard.net/hofreps/1901/19010906_reps_1_4/*, (Accessed November 29, 2020).

19. Ibid.

20. Debate in Australian Parliament, 09 February 1949, Available at *House of Representatives, Debates, 9 February 1949: Historic Hansard*, (Accessed December 29, 2020).

21. Prof. David Walker (2006) General Cariappa encounters 'White Australia': Australia, India and the Commonwealth in the 1950s, *The Journal of Imperial and Commonwealth History, https://doi.org/10.1080/03086530600826017*, (Accessed January 17, 2021).

22. Ibid.

23. Statement by Australian Prime Minister in the House of Representatives, 11 April 1961. Available at, *Transcript 298 | PM Transcripts (pmc.gov.au)* (Accessed December 21, 2020).

24. Prof. David Walker (2006) General Cariappa encounters 'White Australia': Australia, India and the commonwealth in the 1950s, The Journal of Imperial and Commonwealth History, *https://doi.org/10.1080/03086530600826017*, (Accessed January 17, 2021).

25. Sean Brawley, *The White Peril,* Sydney: University of NSW Press, 1995, 243.

26. Gurry, Meg, *India: Australia's Neglected Neighbour?* 1947–1996, Brisbane: Griffith University Centre for the Study of Australia-Asia Relations, 1996.

27. Speech of Prime Minister Jawaharlal Nehru in the Constituent Assembly, 16 May 1949. Resolution and Re Ratification of Commonwealth Decision, Volume VIII (16th May to 16th June 1949),

28. Miller TB, *Australia in Peace and War: External Relations 1788 -1977*, St Martin's Press, New York, 1978, p. 296.

29. Pearson, M.N. (2003). The Indian Ocean (1st ed.). Routledge. *https://doi. org/10.4324/9780203414132*,

30. Dorothy Norman, (ed.), *"Nehru: The First Sixty Years", Vol.* II, John Lane, The John Day Company, New York, 1965, p 473.

31. India (Commonwealth Relations), Debate in Common Chamber, 28 April 1949, Available at: *House of Commons - Hansard - UK Parliament,* (Accessed July 23, 2020).

32. The Changing Commonwealth ", the first Smuts Memorial Lecture, by R.G. Menzies, delivered at the University of Cambridge, 16 May 1960. Available at *Search | PM Transcripts (pmc.gov.au),* (Accessed December 23, 2020)

33. Prof. David Walker (2006) General Cariappa encounters 'White Australia': Australia, India and the commonwealth in the 1950s, The Journal of Imperial and Commonwealth History, *https://doi.org/10.1080/03086530600826017,* (Accessed January 17, 2021).

34. The Sydney Morning Herald, May 4, 1949, *"Chifley Back: Will report to the Cabinet",* Available at: *https://news.google.com/newspapers?nid=1301&dat=19490504&id=Ox-0QAAAAIBAJ&sjid=IZMDAAAAIBAJ&pg=7470,611771&hl=en,* (Accessed June 21, 2020).

35. Brecher, Michael, *"India and World Politics: Krishna Menon's View of the World",* *Frederick A. Praeger, New York,* 1968, p 30-31.

36. E.S Reddy, Pandit Nehru and South Africa, Hindustan Times, 30 September 2006. Available at *Pandit Nehru and South Africa | Hindustan Times,* (Accessed January 08, 2021).

37. *"Scores die in Sharpeville shoot-out",* BBC on this day, Available at, *http://news. bbc.co.uk/onthisday/hi/dates/stories/march/21/newsid_2653000/2653405.stm,* (Accessed July 29, 2020).

38. Reddy Enuga, *"India and the Struggle against Apartheid",* India and South Africa: A Collection of papers by E.S. REDDY, The University of Durban-Westville, Durban. Occasional Papers Series No. 1, 1991. p 10.

39. "The Changing Commonwealth ", the first Smuts Memorial Lecture, by R.G. Menzies, delivered at the University of Cambridge, 16 May 1960. Available at *Search | PM Transcripts (pmc.gov.au),* (Accessed on 21 December 2020)

40. Ibid.

41. Statement by Australian Prime Minister in the House of Representatives, 11 April 1961. Available at, *Transcript 298 | PM Transcripts (pmc.gov.au)* (Accessed on 21 December 2020).

42. Quoted in Nihal R Henry Kuruppu, An Indian Perspective of the Relationship between India and Australia, 1947 to 1975: Personalities and Policies, Peaks and Troughs, p. 146, Available at Victoria University Research Repository, Available at, *KURUPPU Nihal-thesis_nosignature.pdf (vu.edu.au)*, (Accessed on 23 December 2020).

43. India's Foreign Policy: Selected Speeches, Jawaharlal Nehru, September 1946-April 1961, Ministry of Information & Broadcasting, Government of India, New Delhi, 1961, p 550.

44. Statement by Australian Prime Minister in the House of Representatives, 11 April 1961. Available at, *Transcript 298 | PM Transcripts (pmc.gov.au)* (Accessed December 21, 2020).

45. Debate in Australian Parliament on Immigration Policies, 05 July 1949, Available at, *House of Representatives, Debates, 05 July 1949: Historic Hansard*, (Accessed November 23, 2020).

46. Spender will aim at a new deal for Asians, The Sun Sydney, 03 January 1950, Available at, *03 Jan 1950 - Spender will aim at new deal for Asians - Trove (nla.gov. au)*, (Accessed January 23, 2021).

47. Debate in Australian Parliament on Immigration Policies, 05 July 1949, Available at, *House of Representatives, Debates, 05 July 1949: Historic Hansard,* (Accessed November 23, 2020).

48. Quoted in Nihal R Henry Kuruppu, An Indian Perspective of the Relationship between India and Australia, 1947 to 1975: Personalities and Policies, Peaks and Troughs, p. 284, Available at Victoria University Research Repository, *KURUPPU Nihal-thesis_nosignature.pdf (vu.edu.au)*, (Accessed December 29, 2020).

49. *"1956: Egypt Seizes Suez Canal.* BBC, 26 July 1956. Available at, *http://news.bbc. co.uk/onthisday/hi/dates/stories/july/26/newsid_2701000/2701603.stm,* (Accessed March 12, 2020).

50. Robert Menzies, The Suez Crisis 1956, Originally broadcast on 24th September 2006, Available at, *http://www.abc.net.au/radionational/programs/ backgroundbriefing/the-suez-crisis-1956/3386572,* (Accessed March 16, 2020).

51. Ibid.

52. Quoted in Nihal R Henry Kuruppu, An Indian Perspective of the Relationship between India and Australia, 1947 to 1975: Personalities and Policies, Peaks and Troughs, p. 163, Available at Victoria University Research Repository, *KURUPPU Nihal-thesis_nosignature.pdf (vu.edu.au)*, (Accessed December 26, 2020).

53. Speech of Prime Minister Jawaharlal Nehru, 08 August 1956, Lok Sabha Debates, Volume V 1956, Thirteenth Session 1956,

54. Speech of Prime Minister Jawaharlal Nehru, 08 August 1956, Lok Sabha Debates, Volume V 1956, Thirteenth Session 1956, Lok Sabha Secretariat, New Delhi.

55. Ibid.

56. Nihal R Henry Kuruppu, An Indian Perspective of the Relationship between India and Australia, 1947 to 1975: Personalities and Policies, Peaks and Troughs, p. 165.

57. Ibid.

58. Ibid.

59. Ibid.

60. Ibid.

61. Statement of Anderson Hume in Australian Parliament, 01 May 1958, Available at, *House of Representatives, Debates, 1 May 1958: Historic Hansard*, (Accessed November 11, 2020).

62. *"India's Foreign Policy, Selected Speeches"*, Sept 1946-April 1961, Ministry of Information and Broadcasting, Government of India, New Delhi, 1961, p 488.

63. Nihal R Henry Kuruppu, An Indian Perspective of the Relationship between India and Australia, 1947 to 1975: Personalities and Policies, Peaks and Troughs, p. 262.

64. Lok Sabha Debates – 29 September 1954, Volume IV 1954, Seventh Session 1954, Lok Sabha Secretariat, New Delhi.

65. Ibid.

66. Statement of Prime Minister Menzies in Australian Parliament, 04 April 1957, Available at, *House of Representatives, Debates, 04 April 1957: Historic Hansard*, (Accessed November 11, 2020).

67. *India's Foreign Policy: Selected Speeches September 1946-April 1961*, Ministry of Information and Broadcasting, Government of India, New Delhi, 1961, pp 487-488.

68. Menzies, R.G, *"Afternoon Light: Some Memories of Men and Events"*, Coward McCann, New York, 1967, p 268-269.

69. Statement of Anderson Hume in Australian Parliament, 01 May 1958, Available at, *House of Representatives, Debates, 1 May 1958: Historic Hansard*, (Accessed November 01, 2020).

70. Lok Sabha Debates – 20 March 1956, Volume II 1956, Twelfth Session 1956, Lok Sabha Secretariat, New Delhi.

71. Quoted in Nihal R Henry Kuruppu, An Indian Perspective of the Relationship between India and Australia, 1947 to 1975: Personalities and Policies, Peaks and Troughs, p. 271.

72. "Arms Sale does not Fit Policy", C. M. Bhandari, Deputy High Commissioner, High Commission of India, The Canberra Times (ACT: 1926 - 1995) Mon 14 May 1990, Page 8, Available at: *http://trove.nla.gov.au/newspaper/article/122247080?searchTerm=sale%20of%20mirage%20spares%20to%20pakistan&searchLimits=l-availability=y*, (Accessed on July 23, 2020).

73. Mike Ticher, A Farewell to Arms, May 1991, University of Wollongong, Available at *https://ro.uow.edu.au/cgi/viewcontent.cgi?*, (Accessed January 21, 2021).

74. Daniel Flitton, Jet sales to Pakistan haunt Canberra, 07 November, 2007*Jet sales to Pakistan haunt Canberra (theage.com.au)*, (Accessed January 23, 2021).

75. Michael Clarke, "*Australia, India and the Uranium Question*", Australian Journal of Political Science, 46:3, 489-502, DOI: 10.1080/10361146.2011.595389, 2011.

76. Ibid.

77. Marty Harris, Foreign Affairs, Defence and Security Section, The origins of Australia's uranium export policy, Parliament of Australia, Available at, *https://www.aph.gov.au/About_Parliament/Parliamentary_Departments/Parliamentary_Library/pubs/BN/2011-2012/UraniumPolicy*, (Accessed July 01, 2020)

78. Christine Leah and Rod Lyon, "*Three Visions of the Bomb: Australian thinking about Nuclear Weapons and Strategy*", Australian Journal of International Affairs, Vol. 64, No 4, August 2010.

79. Rekha Chakraborty, "*India and Nuclear Disarmament: Chasing a Dream*", CBRN brief, No 12, March 2009.

80. Press Conference transcript of the Prime Minister, Parliament House, Canberra, 14 May 1998, Available at, *Transcript 10661 | PM Transcripts (pmc.gov.au)*, (Accessed on January 21, 2021).

81. Ibid.

82. Michael Hillman (2000), "*The grand old Duke of York: Indo-Australian Relations Post Test*", South Asia: Journal of South Asian Studies, 23:s1, 151-158, DOI: 10.1080/00856400008723405.

83. Sandy Gordon (2009), "*An Australian Perspective on the Indo-US Nuclear Deal*", South Asian Survey, Vol.16, no.1 pp. 48-49.

84. Crispin Rovere and Kalman A. Robertson, "*Australia's Uranium and India: Linking Exports to CTBT Ratification, Security Challenges*", Vol. 9, No. 1 (2013), p.1, Available at, *SC 9-1 Proof - Inc Authors revisions 130320 (anu.edu.au)*, (Accessed June 23, 2020).

85. *Australia – India Relations: Trade and Security*, Senate standing Committee on Foreign Affairs, Defence and Trade, Australian Government Publishing Service, Canberra July 1990, P 95, Available at, *Australia India Relations - Trade and security*, (Accessed on 23 January 2021).

86. Strong and Secure: A Strategy for Australia's National Security, *Australian Policy Online.*

87. K.M Panikkar, India and the Indian Ocean: An Essay on the Influence of Sea Power on Indian History, (Delhi: George Allen and Unwin, 1946).

88. Ibid.

89. Panikkar, India and the Indian Ocean: An Essay on the Influence of Sea Power on Indian History, 1946.

90. Brewster, The India-Australia Security Engagement: Opportunities and Challenges, 2013.

91. Nirupama Rao, "India as a consensual stakeholder in the Indian Ocean: Policy Contours", *Journal of the Indian Ocean Region*, Volume 7, Issue 1, 2011.

92. Frederic Grare and Amitabh Mattoo, *India and ASEAN: The Politics of India's Look East Policy*, ed. (New Delhi: Manohar Publishers, 2001, 41-46).

93. John Peter Brobst, *The Future of the Great Game: Indian Independence and the Defence of Asia*, (Ohio: University of Ohio Press, 2005).

94. Government of India, Prime Minister Office, Former Prime Minister Manmohan Singh's address to Asia Society Corporate Conference, Mumbai, 18 March 2006, Available at: *http://www.pmindia.nic.in/speeches.html* (Accessed March 21, 2020).

95. Brig Vinod Anand, *"India's "Act East " Policy: A Perspective"*, 27 November, 2014, Available at: *http://blog.vifindia.org/2014/11/indias-act-east-policy-perspective.html* (Accessed June 09, 2020).

96. N.N Vohra, eds. *India and Australasia: History Culture and Society*, (New Delhi: Shipra Publications, 2004, 132).

97. Richardson, Michael, "Australia-Southeast Asia relations and the East Asian Summit ", *Australian Journal of International Affairs*, Vol. 59, no. 3, p.364.

98. Ikins Charles, "What's next in the Indian Ocean ", *Australian Defence Force Journal*, no.186 (2011): 14-15.

99. Nehru, Jawaharlal, *"The Discovery of India: The Centenary Edition* (London: Oxford University Press, 1989), 536.

100. J. Gentilli, "Australia-Indian or Pacific? " *The Australian Quarterly*, Vol. 21, No. 1 (Mar., 1949), pp. 72-76, *http://www.jstor.org/stable/20633131* (Accessed June 25, 2020).

101. Government of Australia, Department of Foreign Affairs & Trade, The Senate Foreign Affairs, Defence and Trade References Committee, *The Importance of the Indian Ocean Rim for Australia's Foreign, Trade And Defence Policy*, 2013, Canberra, Senate Printing Unit, Parliament House.

102. Rory Medcalf, Pivoting the Map: Australia's Indo-Pacific System.

103. Auriol Weigold, **"Looking West Again - To the Indian Ocean and India"**, **February** 16**, 2011,** *Available at: http://asiapacific.anu.edu.au/blogs/*

southasiamasala/2011/02/16/looking-west-again-to-the-indian-ocean-and-india/ (Accessed May 17, 2020).

104. Kevin Andrews, Australian Minister of Defence, "Australia's Defence Policy and Relationship with India", Available at: *http://www.idsa.in/keyspeeches/ AustralianMinisterforDefence2015* (Accessed September 11, 2020).

105. The Strategic Defence Update: 2020, Department of Defence, Government of Australia.

106. Ibid.

107. Smith, Stephen, *"Australia and India: Building the Strategic Partnership,"* Speech at the Asia Society, Mumbai, 09 December 2011.

108. Jha, Pankaj K, *"India and Australia – Building Strategic Convergence",* India and the Oceania: Exploring Vistas for Cooperation, ICWA, New Delhi 2016.

109. Indian Prime Minister's Address to the joint session of the Australian Parliament, 18 November 2014, Strategic Digest, Vol 44, Number 11-12, Nov – Dec 2014, IDSA, New Delhi.

110. Government of India, Prime Minister Office, Former Prime Minister Manmohan Singh's Address to Asia Society.

111. David Brewster, *"Strategic Convergences between India and Australia in Southeast Asia",* Available at: *https://openresearch-repository.anu.edu.au/bitstream/1885/13285/2/ Brewster%20D%20Strategic%20Convergences%20between%20India%20 and%20Australia%20in%20Southeast%20Asia%202014.pdf* (Accessed July 22, 2020).

112. Jacqui Ooi, *"Australia - Asia relations: A 60 - year history of growth and understanding",* Available at: *http://www.australianbusinessasia.org/publication2012/ upfront/40-upfront/253-australia-asia-relations-a-60-year-history-of-growth-and-understanding.html* (Accessed May 29, 2020).

113. Goh Chok Tong, *"Constructing East Asia",* Asia Society, Bangkok, 09 June 2005, Available at: *http://www.asiasociety.org/conference05/goh.html* (Accessed April 23, 2020).

114. The Strategic Defence Update: 2020, Department of Defence, Government of Australia.

115. ASEAN Outlook on the Indo-Pacific, Association of South East Asian Nations, Available at *ASEAN Outlook on the Indo-Pacific - ASEAN | ONE VISION ONE IDENTITY ONE COMMUNITY,* (Accessed on December 22, 2020).

116. Prime Minister's Keynote Address at Shangri La Dialogue, 01 June 2018, Ministry of External Affairs, Government of India.

117. Available at: *http://dfat.gov.au/international* (Accessed September 06, 2020).

118. Michael Richardson, "Some in East Asia fear US", *International Herald Tribune*, February 9, 1993, *http://www.nytimes.com/1993/02/09/news/09iht-asia.html* (accessed September 03, 2020).

119. "Australia not part of Asia: Keating", *The Canberra Times*, 17 Dec 1995, Available at: *http://trove.nla.gov.au/newspaper/article/133920413?searchTerm=australia%20 in%20East%20Asia%20summit&searchLimits* (Accessed October 11, 2020).

120. Australia not part of Asia: Keating, *The Canberra Times.*

121. Muni, East Asia Summit And India.

122. Alexander Downer, address to Federal Parliament, Jun 2005, Available at: *http://www.aph.gov.au/Senators_and_Members/Parliamentarian?MPID=4G4*, (Accessed September 21, 2020).

123. "The East Asia Summit ", *Strategic Comments,* The International Institute For Strategic Studies, London, Vol.11, Issue 10, December 2005. Available at: *http:// www.iiss.org/en/publications/strategic* (Accessed July 13, 2020).

124. India-Australia Joint Statement during the State visit of Prime Minister of Australia to India, 10 April 2017, Media Centre, Ministry of External Affairs, Government of India, Available at: *https://www.mea.gov.in/bilateral,* (Accessed September 24, 2020).

125. Indo-Pacific is a 'bread-and-butter expression' says External Affairs Minister, Sidhant Sibal, 17 Dec 2020, WION News.

126. Ibid.

127. Joachim Krause and Sebastian Bruns, "Routledge Handbook of Naval Strategy and Security", (London: Routledge, December 2015).

128. The Strategic Defence Update: 2020, Department of Defence, Government of Australia.

129. Anit Mukherjee., "India's Strategic Engagement in the Asia Pacific: The Role of the ADMM-Plus", *Policy Report*, (S. Rajaratnam School of International Studies, Nanyang Technological University, Singapore.

130. The Strategic Defence Update: 2020, Department of Defence, Government of Australia.

131. Address of India Defence Minister to ADMM Plus. 10 Dec 2020, Hindustan Times.

132. Ruchita Beri, *"India's Africa Policy in the Post-Cold War Era: An Assessment"*, IDSA, Available at: *http://www.idsa.in/system/files/strategicanalysis_rberi_0603. pdf,* (Accessed September 01, 2020).

133. David Brewster, The India-Australia Security Engagement: Opportunities and Challenges.

134. Ibid.

135. Government of India, Ministry of External Affairs, *"Joint Press Statement on the State Visit of Prime Minister of Australia to India",* 17 October 2012.

136. Joint Statement on a Comprehensive Strategic Partnership between Republic of India and Australia June 04, 2020, Media Centre, Ministry of External Affairs, Government of India, Available at: *https://mea.gov.in/bilateral,* (Accessed September 26 2020).

137. Address of Indian Prime Minister to the first IONS held at New Delhi, 2008, Available at: *http://sainiksamachar.nic.in/englisharchives/2008/mar01-08/h1.html,*(Accessed November 10, 2020).

138. Ravi Vohra, ed., *Contemporary Transnational Challenges: International Maritime Connectivity,* (New Delhi: KW Publishers, 2008).

139. *"14th Meeting of the Council of Ministers of the Indian Ocean Rim Association",* *Perth Communiqué,* 09 October 2014, Available at: *http://www.iora.net/media/151273/communiqu__final.pdf,* (Accessed June 12, 2020).

140. Ashok Sajjanhar, *"Why is NSG Membership important for India?"* June 21, 2016, *Institute for Defence Studies and Analyses,* Available at: *http://www.idsa.in,* (Accessed June 19, 2020).

141. Suhasini Haider, *"India pushes for NSG membership",* *The Hindu,* November 03, 2015.

142. Atul Aneja, *"India's NSG entry bid: China puts the blame on U.S.",* Available at: *http://www.thehindu.com/news/international,* (Accessed August 23, 2020).

143. External Affairs Ministry spokesperson Vikas Swarup, "Malcolm Turnbull assures PM Modi of Australia's support to India's NSG bid", Hangzhou, *Press Trust of India,* September 04, 2016.

144. PTI, Australia expresses 'strong support' for India's NSG membership bid, Economic Times, 04 Jun 2020, Available at: *https://economictimes.indiatimes.com/news/politics-and-nation/australia-expresses-strong-support-for-indias-nsg-membership-bid/articleshow/76197820.cms,* (Accessed September 26, 2020)

145. *Kallol Bhattacherjee,* India admitted to Australia Group, 19 January 2018, The Hindu, Available at: *https://www.thehindu.com/news/national/india-admitted-to-australia-group/article22475433.ece,* (Accessed September 27, 2020).

146. James Kurth, "Confronting a Powerful China with Western Characteristics", *Orbis,* Vol. 56, No. 1, winter 2012, pp. 39-59.

147. Chinese Communist Party, *China's National Defence in 2010,* 31 March 2011, Information Office of the State Council, Available at: *http://www.china.org.cn/government/whitepaper/node_7114675.htm* (Accessed May 23, 2020).

148. Chinese Communist Party, *China's National Defence in 2010.*

149. "China's Strategic Objectives in the Indian Ocean Region", *Future Directions International Workshop* Report 23 May 2011, Future Directions International, Perth, 2011.

150. Dhruva Jaishankar, The Australia–India Strategic Partnership: Accelerating Security Cooperation in the Indo–Pacific, Lowy Institute Analysis, Available

at Available at: *https://www.lowyinstitute.org/publications/australia-india-strategic,* (Accessed October 14, 2020).

151. Indian Navy Chief, "China Shaping the Maritime Battlefield", Available at: *http://chinadigitaltimes.net/2006/12/china-shaping-the-maritime* (Accessed March 21, 2020).

152. Barton Deakin, "*China-Australia Economic Relationship*", Available at: *www.bartondeakin.com*, (Accessed June 21, 2020).

153. Statistics on who invests in Australia, Foreign investment statistics, Department of Foreign Affairs and Trade, Government of Australia, Available at Available at: *https://www.dfat.gov.au/trade/resources,* (Accessed October 14, 2020).

154. TB Miller, *Australia and the Future in Asia*, (London: Hurst & Company, 1978).

155. John Howard's Address on Iraq to the National Press Club, Available at: *http://australianpolitics.com/2003/03/13/john-howard-iraq-speech-npc.html* (Accessed June 13, 2020).

156. Shi Yongming, "Australia tries to redefine its position in the Asia-Pacific region", *International Studies*, No.2, 1997, pp.24-25.

157. "In the National Interest- Australia's Foreign and Trade Policy", *White Paper*, Available at: http://repository.jeffmalone.org/files/foreign/In_the_National_Interest.pdf (Accessed October 09, 2020).

158. Li Xuejiang, "Australia's pragmatic foreign policies", *People's Daily*, 30 August 1997.

159. David Wroe, "China's military might is Australia's new defence reality", *The Sunday Morning Herald*, 15 February 2014.

160. Defence Strategic Update, 2020, Department of Defence, Government of Australia, Available at, *2020 Defence Strategic Update & 2020 Force Structure Plan | About | Strategy & Policy | Department of Defence*, (Accessed January 10, 2021).

161. How China's Intelligence Law of 2017 authorizes global tech giants for espionage, Geeta Mohan, 27 July 2020, India Today

162. Huawei banned from 5G mobile infrastructure rollout in Australia, 23 August 2018, ABC News, Available at *https://www.abc.net.au/news/2018-08-23/huawei-banned-from-providing-5g-mobile-technology,* (Accessed October 13, 2020).

163. James Massdorp, Australia and China's relationship has become tetchy over the past two months. Here's how we got to this point, ABC News, Available at *https://www.abc.net.au/news/2020-06-07/australia-china-racism-coronavirus-how-did-relationship-get-here/12330250*, (Accessed on October 21, 2020).

164. Aashi Sadana, Explained: Why Australia-China ties have gone down under, The Indian Express, 09 October 2020, Available at *https://indianexpress.com/article/explained/explained-why-australia-china-ties-have-gone-down-under-6707112/*, (Accessed October 23, 2020).

165. Dhruva Jaishankar, The Australia–India Strategic Partnership: Accelerating Security Cooperation in the Indo–Pacific, Lowy Institute Analysis, Available at *https://www.lowyinstitute.org/publications/australia-india-strategic,* (Accessed October 24, 2020).

166. Views About China as a Security Threat or an Economic Partner, Adapted from Lowy Polls 2020, Available at *https://www.lowyinstitute.org/publications/australia-india-strategic,* (Accessed October 24, 2020).

167. Rory Medcalf, "Mapping Our Indo–Pacific Future", Address to National Security College, Canberra, 21 May 2018, Available at: *https://nsc.crawford.anu.edu.au/news-events/news/12677/mapping-our-indo-pacific-future-rory-medcalfs-public-lecture,* (Accessed July 23, 2020).

168. John Ravenhill (1998), 'Cycles of middle power activism: Constraint and choice in Australian and Canadian foreign policies', Australian Journal of International Affairs, 52(3): 309-327.

169. Premesha Saha, Ben Bland and Evan A. Laksmana, Anchoring the Indo-Pacific: The Case for Deeper Australia, India, Indonesia Trilateral Cooperation. Lowy Institute, Observer Research Foundation and Centre for Strategic and International Studies. Available at *https://www.orfonline.org/wp-content/uploads/2020/01/Anchoring_the_Indo-Pacific.pdf,* (Accessed on 21 December 2020).

170. Australian High Commission India, Meeting between the Prime Minister of India, Dr Manmohan Singh, and the Prime Minister of Australia, Mr Kevin Rudd - Joint Statement, A. Government, Editor 2009: New Delhi.

171. D Jaishankar, The Australia–India Strategic Partnership: Accelerating Security Cooperation in the Indo–Pacific, Lowy Institute Analysis, September 2020.

172. David Lang, "The not-quite-quadrilateral: Australia, Japan and India", *Strategic Insight*, Australian Strategic Policy Institute, December 2015.

173. Ian Hall (2017), 'The Australia–India–Japan trilateral: converging interests… and converging perceptions?', The Strategist, Available at: *https://www.aspistrategist.org.au/australia%C2%AD%C2%AD-india-japantrilateral-converging-interests-converging-perceptions,* (Accessed September 13, 2020)

174. Ibid.

175. Rajeswari P Gopalan, Rise of the minilaterals: Examining the India-France-Australia trilateral, Observer Reasearch Foundation, 18 September 2020, Available at *Rise of the minilaterals: Examining the India-France-Australia trilateral | ORF (orfonline.org),* (Accessed on January 04, 2021).

176. 1st Senior Officials' India-France-Australia Trilateral Dialogue, September 09, 2020, Media Center, Ministry of External Affairs, Government of India, Available at: *https://mea.gov.in/press-releases.*

htm?dtl/32950/1st+Senior+Officials+IndiaFranceAustralia+Trilateral+Dialogue, (Accessed January 04, 2021).

177. Tanya Spisbah, director of the Australia India Institute, The Economic Times, 28 Aug 2019, India, Australia & France to jointly create inclusive Indo-Pacific, Available at: *https://economictimes.indiatimes.com/news/defence,* (Accessed September 22, 2020).

178. Rajeswari P Gopalan, Rise of the minilaterals: Examining the India-France-Australia trilateral.

179. Dipanjan Roy Chaudhury, India's Indo-Pacific Ocean's initiative aims maritime security pillar for inclusive region, 21 Nov 2019, The Economic Times.

180. Premesha Saha, Ben Bland and Evan A. Laksmana, Anchoring the Indo-Pacific: The Case for Deeper Australia, India, Indonesia Trilateral Cooperation. Lowy Institute, Observer Research Foundation and Centre for Strategic and International Studies. Available at *https://www.orfonline.org/wp-content/uploads/2020/01/Anchoring_the_Indo-Pacific.pdf*, (Accessed on 21 December 2020).

181. Ibid.

182. Ibid.

183. Grossman, Marc. "The Tsunami Core Group: A Step toward a Transformed Diplomacy in Asia and Beyond." *Security Challenges* 1, no. 1 (2005): 11-14. *https://www.jstor.org/stable/26459016.*

184. Ankit Panda, "Shinzo Abe's 'Quadrilateral Initiative': Gone and Forgotten?" Available at: *http://thediplomat.com/2014/05/shinzo-abes-quadrilateral-initiative* (Accessed September 02, 2020).

185. Sudha Ramachandran, *"What are friends for…?" Asia Times Online*, August 25, 2007. Available at: *www.atimes.com*, (Accessed March 23, 2020).

186. Sun Cheng, "A Comparative Analysis of Abe's and Fukada's Asia Diplomacy, " *China International Studies,* Spring 2008, pp.58-72.

187. "Chinese President Hu to sign energy deals on trip to Australia", *China Post*, 28 August 2007 at, *http://www.chinapost.com.tw/headlines/2007/08/28/48639/Chinese-President*, (Accessed July 23, 2020).

188. D.S Rajan, "China: Media Fears over India Becoming Part of Western Alliance," *Chennai Centre for China Studies Paper* No.46, August 29, 2007.

189. Hon Dr Brendan Nelson, MP, Minister for Defence, "Doorstop, Press Conference", New Delhi, 11 July 2007 at Available at: *http://www.minister.defence* (Accessed March 21, 2020).

190. D Jaishankar, The Australia–India Strategic Partnership: Accelerating Security Cooperation in the Indo–Pacific, Lowy Institute Analysis, September 2020.

191. Australia-India-Japan-United States 'Quad' Consultations, 04 November 2019, Department of Foreign Affairs and Trade, Government of Australia, Available

at Available at: *https://www.dfat.gov.au/news/media/Pages/australia-india-japan-united-states-quad,* (Accessed March 21, 2020).

192. Quad ministerial meet held with an eye on China; no announcement on military exercise yet, Geeta Mohan, 06 October 2020, India Today, Available at *https://www.indiatoday.in/world/story/quad,* (Accessed March 21, 2020).

193. Quad ministerial meet held with an eye on China; no announcement on military exercise yet, Geeta Mohan, 06 October 2020, India Today, Available at *https://www.indiatoday.in/world/story/quad,* (Accessed March 21, 2020).

194. Purnendra Jain and Peter Mayer, Beyond Cricket: Australia India Evolving Relations.

195. Kevin Rudd, 'The First National Security Statement to the Parliament', Available at: *http://parlinfo.aph.gov.au/parlInfo/search/display/display.w3p;query=Id%3A%22chamber%2Fhansardr%2F2008-12-04%2F0045%22* (Accessed April 17, 2020).

196. Ibid.

197. Prime Minister's Address to the Joint Session of the Australian Parliament, November 18, 2014, Media Centre, Ministry of External Affairs, Government of India, Available at*https://mea.gov.in/Speeches-Statements.htm?dtl/24269/Prime_Ministers_Address_to_the_Joint_Session_of_the_Australian_Parliament_18_November_2014,* (Accessed September 29, 2020).

198. Adapted from, Anchoring the Indo-Pacific: The Case for Deeper Australia, India, Indonesia Trilateral Cooperation. Lowy Institute, Observer Research Foundation and Centre for Strategic and International Studies. Available at *https://www.orfonline.org/wp-content/uploads/2020/01/Anchoring_the_Indo-Pacific.pdf,* (Accessed on 21 December 2020).

199. Adapted from Bilateral/Multilateral Documents & Indian Treaties Database, Ministry of External Affairs, Government of India, Available at *https://mea.gov.in/bilateral* and *https://mea.gov.in/treaty.htm,* (Accessed September 30, 2020).

200. Anthony. Mely Caballero, *Regional security in Southeast Asia: beyond the ASEAN way,* (Singapore: Institute of Southeast Asian Studies, S Rajaratnam School of International Studies, 2005).

201. William T and Chin Kin Wah, ASEAN -India-Australia: towards Closer Engagement in a New Asia.

202. Kumar.S Utham and Anuradha. C.S, "Indo Australian Strategic Framework: Possibilities for the New Millenium", *Journal of Indian Ocean Studies,* Vol.11, No.1, April 2003, P.24.

203. ADF Defence White Paper, "Defending Australia in the Asia Pacific Century: Force 2013", *http://www.defence* (accessed January 14, 2021).

204. S Utham Kumar Jamadhagni and S.I. Humayun, *Non Traditional Challenges to Indian Ocean Security: Prospects for India-Australia Cooperation* (New Delhi: IDSA, 2008).

205. Zimmerman. Erin, "Security cooperation in the Indo-Pacific: Non-traditional security as a catalyst ", *Journal of the Indian Ocean Region*, 2014; 10(2):150-165.

206. William T and Chin Kin Wah, ASEAN -India-Australia: towards Closer Engagement in a New Asia.

207. Government of India, Ministry of External Affairs, Prime Minister's Address to the Joint Session of the Australian Parliament.

208. Statement of Ms Marise Payne, Minister for Foreign Affairs, Government of Australia, Australia Strengthens Global Discussion on Cyber and Critical Technology, Asia Pacific Defence Reporter, 27 December 2020, Available at *STATEMENT: Foreign Minister on cyber,* (Accessed on 04 January 2021).

209. Dr J Jaishankar, External Affairs Minister, Government of India, Remarks at Global Technology Summit, Available at *EAM's remarks at the Global Technology Summit (mea.gov.in)*, (Accessed on 07 January 2021).

210. Joint Declaration on a Shared Vision for Maritime Cooperation in the Indo-Pacific Between the Republic of India and the Government of Australia, June 04, 2020, Media Centre, Ministry of External Affairs, Government of India, Available at: *https://www.mea.gov.in/bilateral,* (Accessed September 23, 2020).

211. Keith Pitt, Resources Minister, Government of Australia, Australia to Supply Critical Minerals to India, Available at *India, Australia sign MoU on critical,* (Accessed on 05 January 2021).

212. Kevin Rudd, *"From Fitful Engagement to Strategic Partnership,"* Address to the Indian Council of World Affairs in New Delhi, 12 November 2009.

213. Government of India, Ministry of External Affairs, *"India-Australia Joint Declaration on Security Cooperation during visit of Prime Minister Kevin Rudd"*, 12 November 2009.

214. Ibid.

215. "Minister for Defence and India's Minister of Defence, Joint Statement, Visit of Mr A. K. Antony, Defence Minister of India, to Australia 4-5 June 2013", Available at: *http://www.minister.defence,* (Accessed August 23, 2020).

216. Australian Defence Forces, Defence White Paper.

217. Government of India, Ministry of External Affairs, "Framework for Security Cooperation between India and Australia", November 18, 2014.

218. David Brewster, *"The Australia–India Framework for Security Cooperation: another Step towards an Indo-Pacific Security Partnership"*, Available at: *http://www.regionalsecurity.org.au/Resources/Documents/11-1%20-%20Brewster.pdf* (Accessed November 01, 2020).

219. Ibid.

220. Future Directions International, "Strategic Objectives of the United States in the Indian Ocean Region", *Workshop Report*, 29 September 2011, Available at: *http://www.futuredirections.org.au/publication/strategic* (Accessed September 03, 2020).

221. David Brewster, The India-Australia Security Engagement: Opportunities and Challenges.

222. Para 5.70, Defence White Paper; 2016, Government of Australia, Department of Defence, *Defence White Paper,* 2016.

223. Barry O'Farell, How India and Australia have elevated their ties, Hindustan Times, 04 June 2020, Available at: *https://www.hindustantimes.com/analysis/how-india-and-australia-have-elevated-their-ties/story-922R723zL8Dv67fLXqdffI.html,* (Accessed September 23, 2020).

224. Joint Declaration on a Shared Vision for Maritime Cooperation in the Indo-Pacific Between the Republic of India and the Government of Australia, June 04, 2020, Media Centre, Ministry of External Affairs, Government of India, Available at: *https://www.mea.gov.in/bilateral,* (Accessed September 23, 2020).

225. India-Australia Foreign and Defence Secretaries' Dialogue (2+2) December 09, 2019, Media Centre, Ministry of External Affairs, Government of India, Available at: *https://www.mea.gov.in/bilateral,* (Accessed September 23, 2020).

226. Dave Sharma, A diplomatic step-up to match our military step-up, The Interpreter, 13 July 2020, Available at: *https://www.lowyinstitute.org/the-interpreter/diplomatic-step-match-our-military-step*, (Accessed September 23, 2020).

227. Asia Power Index, 2020 Edition, Lowy Institute, Australia, Available at *https://power.lowyinstitute.org/countries/india/*, (Accessed October 19, 2020).

228. Harsh V. Pant and Niranjan C. Oak, Locating the Mutual Logistics Support Agreement in India-Australia Strategic Relations, Observer Research Foundation, Issue No 316, September 2019.

229. Huma Siddiqui, India – Australia: Indo-Pacific maritime powers ink MLSA for access to military bases, Financial Express, June 4, 2020

230. Harsh V. Pant and Niranjan Chandrashekhar Oak, "Locating the Mutual Logistics Support Agreement in India-Australia Strategic Relations", *ORF Issue Brief No. 316*, September 2019, Observer Research Foundation.

231. Ramanand Garge, *"AUSINDEX – Mid-Power Bonhomie in the Indo-Pacific"*, Available at: *http://www.vifindia.org/article/2015/october/09/ausindex-mid-power-bonhomie-in-the-indo-pacific*, (Accessed August 15, 2020).

232. Rear Admiral Jonathan Mead, "AUSINDEX-15: Bilateral maritime exercise between India and Australia begins", *The Economic Times*, September 12, 2015.

233. "'India-Australia bilateral defence exercise will deepen strategic ties'", The Economic Times, March 28, 2019.

234. Australia, India joint defence activities increased four-fold in 6 years, says Envoy O'Farrell, Nayanima Basu, The Print, 04 December 2020, Available at *Australia, India joint defence activities increased four-fold in 6 years, says envoy O'Farrell (theprint.in)*, (Accessed on 201 December 2020).

235. Dhruva Jaishankar, The Australia–India Strategic Partnership: Accelerating Security Cooperation in the Indo–Pacific, September 2020, Lowy Institute, Available at *https://www.lowyinstitute.org/publications/australia-india-strategic,* (Accessed August 15, 2020).

236. Harsh V. Pant and Niranjan Chandrashekhar Oak, "Locating the Mutual Logistics Support Agreement in India-Australia Strategic Relations", *ORF Issue Brief No. 316*, September 2019, Observer Research Foundation.

237. Siddharth Varadarajan, 'Four-power meeting drew Chinese demarche', *The Hindu*, June 14, 2007, at *http://www.thehindu.com/todays-paper/tp-national/ Four-power-meeting-drew-Chinese-d%C3%A9marche/article14777286.ece* (accessed September 24, 2020)

238. Transcript, Joint doorstop, Australian Embassy, Tokyo, Minister for Foreign Affairs, the Hon Julie Bishop MP and Minister for Defence, Senator the Hon Marise Payne, April 20, 2017, Available at: *https://www.foreignminister.gov. au/minister/julie-bishop/transcript-eoe/joint-doorstop-australian-embassy-tokyo,* (Accessed August 15, 2020).

239. Aarti Betigree, India, Australia and containing the China Challenge, The Interpreter, 21 July 2020, Available at: *https://www.lowyinstitute.org/the-interpreter/india-australia-and-containing-china-challenge,* (Accessed September 23, 2020).

240. Australia, India joint defence activities increased four-fold in 6 years, says Envoy O'Farrell, Nayanima Basu, The Print, 04 December 2020, Available at *Australia, India joint defence activities increased four-fold in 6 years, says envoy O'Farrell (theprint.in)*, (Accessed December 15, 2020).

241. Datar Singh, "Trade between India and Australia", *Journal of the Royal Society of Arts*, Vol. 93, No. 4703, 26 October 1945, pp. 624-625, Available at: *http:// www.jstor.org/stable/41362468* (Accessed March 25, 2020).

242. M. Abramowitz (1956) 'Resource and Output Trends in the United States since 1870', *American Economic Review,*46 5–23.

243. Indians most keen to send children overseas for studies: HSBC survey, Mint, 15 July 2015, Available at: *https://www.livemint.com/Politics/3usP0KsZh0o1kShsz4vyYI/ Indians-most-keen-to-send-children-overseas-for-studies-HSB.html,* (Accessed September 27, 2020).

244. Ibid.

245. Public Diplomacy Strategy, Department of Foreign Affairs and Trade, Government of Australia, Available at: *https://www.dfat.gov.au/people-to-people/public-diplomacy,* (Accessed September 10, 2020).

246. Ibid.

247. Statement of the then Australian Prime Minister, Australia in damage control over Indian attacks, 01 June 2009, ABC News, *https://www.abc.net.au/news/2009-06-01/australia-in-damage-control-over-indian-attacks/1699936,* Accessed 13 Sept 2020.

248. Australian Deputy Prime Minister Julia Gillard to visit India, Australian High Commission, New Delhi, *https://india.embassy.gov.au/ndli/visitone.html,* (accessed 13 September 2020).

249. Lowy Institute Polls 2010, Theme: Immigration and Refugees, Lowy Institute, *https://poll.lowyinstitute.org/themes/immigration,* (Accessed 14 September 2020)

250. Ibid.

251. Ibid.

252. Mazzarol, T. (2001) "Push-Pull Factors Influencing International Student Destination Choice", *CEMI Discussion Paper Series*, DP 0105, Centre for Entrepreneurial Management and Innovation, Available at *www.cemi.com.au,* (Accessed September 18, 2020).

253. Ibid.

254. Lawson Christopher, Studying in Australia: views from six key countries, Department of Education Skills and Employment, Government of Australia, Available at: *https://internationaleducation.gov.au/research,* (Accessed September 13, 2020).

255. Ibid.

256. Lawson Christopher, Studying in Australia: Views from Six Key Countries, Department of Education Skills and Employment, Government of Australia, Available at: *https://internationaleducation.gov.au/research,* (Accessed September 13, 2020).

257. The Times Higher Education World University Rankings 2021, World University Rankings 2021, Available at: *https://www.timeshighereducation.com/world-university,* (Accessed September 14, 2020).

258. Eric Meadows, Education in the Bilateral Relationship between India and Australia, Deakin's University Research Depository, 2013, Available at *http://hdl.handle.net/10536/DRO/DU:30051700,* (Accessed September 15, 2020).

259. Ibid.

260. Birrell, B et al. 2006, *Australia's Net Gains from International Skilled Movement - Skilled Movements in 2004–05 and earlier years,* Centre for Population and Urban Research, Monash University.

261. Australia Trade and Investment Commission, Government of Australia, Available at: *https://www.austrade.gov.au/australian/education,* (Accessed September 13, 2020).

262. Erik Jensen, School's in for Stayers, The Sunday Morning Herald, 04 July 2007, Available at: *https://www.smh.com.au/national/schools-in-for-stayers-20070704-gdqjdg.html,* (Accessed September 29, 2020).

263. DIAC, *Annual report 2008–2009*, p. 63.

264. Temporary visas selected categories, 2015-16 to 2018-19, Country Profile: India, Department of Home Affairs, Government of Australia, Available at *Permanent migration,* (Accessed on 25 December 2020).

265. India and Australia map common standards on job roles across the two geographies; further strengthen bilateral cooperation on skill development, "3rd India Australia Skills Conference: Skills for Better Business", Available at: *https://nsdcindia.org/international,* (Accessed September 16, 2020).

266. An India Economic Strategy To 2035, Department of Foreign Affairs and Trade, Government of Australia, Available at: *http://indiaeconomicstrategy.dfat.gov.au/,* (Accessed September 12, 2020).

267. MoU on cooperation in TVET between the National Skill Development Corporation, Republic of India and the Commonwealth of Australia represented by the Department of Industry, 05 September 2014, Indian Treaties Database, Ministry of External Affairs, Government of India, Available at: *https://mea.gov.in/TreatyDetail.htm?2172,* (Accessed September 14, 2020).

268. Status of Skill Engagement MoUs, Ministry of Skill Development and Entrepreneurship, Government of India, Available at: *http://www.skilldevelopment.gov.in/reports-documents/Skill-Engagements/MoU,* (Accessed September 16, 2020).

269. List of project and workshop grant recipients, Government of Australia, Department of Industry, Science, Energy& Resources. Collaborating with India on Science and Research, Available at: *https://www.industry,* (Accessed April 05, 2020).

270. Ibid.

271. Ibid.

272. Australia Economic Strategy Report 2020, Available at *https://aes2020.in/chapters/foreword/,* (Accessed on December 23, 2020).

273. Government of India, Ministry of Human Resource Development, Indian Institute of Technology Kharagpur, SPARCS (Approved Projects Till Date), Available at: *https://sparc.iitkgp.ac.in/apProposal_list.php,* (Accessed April 04, 2020).

274. 2019 Grant Round Outcomes, Australia India Education Council, Department of Foreign Affairs and Trade, Government of Australia, Available at: *https://www.dfat.gov.au/people-to-people/foundations-councils-institutes/australia-india-council/grants/Pages/2019-grant-round-outcomes,* (Accessed April 08, 2020).

275. Harinder Sidhu, Australian High Commissioner to India, Australia India Youth Dialogue (AIYD), Strategy 218-2022, Available at: *https://www.aiyd.org/wp-content/uploads/2018/08/AIYD-Strategy-Document.pdf*, (Accessed April 08, 2020).

276. Australia India Youth Dialogue (AIYD), Strategy 218-2022, Available at: *https://www.aiyd.org/wp-content/uploads/2018/08/AIYD-Strategy-Document.pdf*, (Accessed April 08, 2020).

277. Ibid.

278. Ibid.

279. Australia India Institute (AII), Available at: *https://www.aii.unimelb.edu.au/about/about-us/#*, (Accessed September 20, 2020).

280. Ibid.

281. New Australia/India partnership established to address global issues of food security and climate change, Hawkesbury Institute for the Environment, Western Sydney University, Available at *https://www.westernsydney.edu.au/hie/stories/new_australia_india_partnership_established_to_address_global_issues_of_food_security_and_climate_change*, (Accessed November 01,2020).

282. Vanessa Zhou, AusIMM signs MOU with Indian School of Mines, 03 March 2020, Australian Mining, Available at *https://www.australianmining.com.au/news/ausimm-signs-mou-with-indian-school-of-mines/*, (Accessed November 01,2020).

283. Research Collaboration between Australian and Indian Universities: Potential for Growth, Australia India Institute, July 2016.

284. O.P. Jindal Global University signs agreements with seven top Australian Universities, 06 December 2019, Business Standard, Available at: *https://www.business-standard.com/article/news-ani/o-p-jindal-global-university*, (Accessed September 05, 2020).

285. Ibid.

286. Larissa Mavros, UNSW enters landmark partnership with leading Indian university, 05 Aug 2019, Available at: *https://newsroom.unsw.edu.au/news/general/unsw-enters-landmark-partnership-leading-indian-university*, (Accessed September 19, 2020).

287. University of Wollongong Media Centre.

288. Ibid.

289. Ibid.

290. National Education Policy, Ministry of Human Resource Development. Government of India, Available at *https://ncert.nic.in/pdf/nep//NEP_2020.pdf*, (Accessed October 23, 2020).

291. Indian Tech Education Market Insights: Opportunities for Australia, Australian Trade & Investment Commission (Austrade), Government of

Australia. Available at: *https://www.austrade.gov.au/Australian/Education/News/ Data/report-on-india-edtech-markets-insights-released*, (Accessed September 19, 2020).

292. Education Minister And Australian High Commissioner Discuss Ways To Advance Ties In Education, NDTV Education, 03 September 2020, Available at *https://www.ndtv.com/education,* (Accessed September 19, 2020).

293. Joint Statement during Prime Minister's visit to Australia, 18 November 2014, Strategic Digest, Vol 44, Number 11-12, Nov-Dec 2014.

294. Joint Statement on a Comprehensive Strategic Partnership between Republic of India and Australia, 04 June 2020, Media Centre, Ministry of External Affairs, Government of India, Available at: *https://mea.gov.in/bilateral,* (Accessed September 12, 2020).

295. Government of Australia, Parliamentary Debates, 21 September to 11 November 1954, 12 October 1954, *http://www.aph.gov.au/Parliamentary_Business/Hansard/ Hansreps_2011* (Accessed September 23, 2020).

296. Strahan Lachlan, *Australia's China: Changing Perceptions from the 1930s to the 1990s*, (Cambridge: Cambridge University Press, 1996, 146).

297. Migrant Intake into Australia, Productivity Commission Inquiry Report, 13 April 2016, Available at *https://www.pc.gov.au/search?collection=productivity,* (Accessed October 03, 2020).

298. Ibid.

299. Gardiner-Garden, J. 1993, *The Multiculturalism and Immigration Debate 1973–1993*, Background Paper Number 8, Department of the Parliamentary Library, Canberra Available at: *https://www.aph.gov.au/binaries/library/pubs/ bp/1993/93bp08.pdf,* (Accessed October 03, 2020).

300. Ray, R. 1989, *Minister Ray hails start of new era in immigration*, Media Release, 18 December, Canberra. Available at *https://www.aph.gov.au/Parliamentary_ Business/Committees/Senate/Former_Committees/minmig/report/index,* (Accessed October 23, 2020).

301. Migrant Intake into Australia, *Productivity Commission Inquiry Report*, 13 April 2016, Available at *https://www.pc.gov.au/search?collection=productivity,* (Accessed October 23, 2020).

302. Ibid.

303. *Migration to Australia since Federation: A Guide to the Statistics*, Department of Parliamentary Services, Government of Australia, Available at: *https://www.aph. gov.au/binaries/library/pubs/bn/sp/migrationpopulation.pdf,* (Accessed September 03, 2020).

304. Net Overseas Migration to Australia – 1971-72 to 2018-19, Reference Period: 2019-19, Migration Australia, Australian Bureau of Statistics, Available at:

https://www.abs.gov.au/statistics/people/population, (Accessed September 26, 2020).

305. Robin Jeffrey, *Pillar of Changed Relationship? Australia's New Indian Diaspora*, 05 Jun 2020. Institute of South Asian Studies. ISAS Insights, National University of Singapore, Available at *https://www.isas.nus.edu.sg/papers/pillar-of-changed-relationship-australias-new-indian-diaspora,* (Accessed September 27, 2020).

306. Prepared by Author from *Data of Migration to Australia since Federation: A Guide to the Statistics*, Department of Parliamentary Services, Government of Australia, Available at: *https://www.aph.gov.au/binaries/library/pubs/bn/sp/migrationpopulation.pdf,* (Accessed September 23, 2020).

307. Tumbe Chinmay, *India Moving A History of Migration*, (Gurugram, India: Penguin Random House, 2018).

308. Bilal Rafi, Tala Talgaswatta, *The Characteristics and Performance of 457 Migrant Visa Sponsoring Businesses*, Department of Industry, Innovation and Science, Government of Australia, Available at: *https://www.industry,* (Accessed September 23, 2020).

309. Dustmann C, Okatengo A. Out-migration, wealth constraints and the quality of local amenities. J Dev Econ 2014; 110:52–63, *https://doi.org/10.1016/j.jdeveco.2014.05.008*, (Accessed September 15, 2020).

310. Cummings C, Pacitto J, Lauro D, Foresti M. *Why people move: Understanding the Drivers and Trends of Migration to Europe*. London: Overseas Development Institute (ODI), 2015, Available at: *https://www.odi.org/publications/10217-why-people-move-understanding-drivers-and-trends-migration,* (Accessed September 13, 2020).

311. *Harriet Spinks, Overseas students: Immigration Policy Changes 1997–2015,* Research Paper Series: 2015-2016, Parliament of Australia, Government of Australia, Available at *https://www.aph.gov.au/About_Parliament/Parliamentary_Departments/Parliamentary_Library/pubs/rp/rp1516/OverseasStudents,* (Accessed September12, 2020).

312. Markus et al, *Australia's Immigration Revolution,*(Australia: Allen & Unwin, 2009, p. 11).

313. Harriet Spinks, *Overseas Students: Immigration Policy Changes 1997–2015,* Research Paper Series: 2015-2016, Parliament of Australia, Government of Australia, Available at: *https://www.aph.gov.au/About_Parliament/Parliamentary_Departments/Parliamentary_Library/pubs/rp/rp1516/OverseasStudents,* (Accessed September 13, 2020).

314. Rizvi,F. and Lingard,B. *Globalizing Education Policy*. (Routledge: 2013).

315. *Net Overseas Migration by Country of Birth: Financial Years 2004-05 to 2019-19,* Australian Bureau of Statistics, Census 2016.

316. Liu, X. (2016), *Australia's Chinese and Indian Business Diasporas: Demographic Characteristics and Engagement in Business, Trade and Investment.* Report for Securing Australia's Future project 11 'Australia's Diaspora Advantage: Realizing the potential for building transnational business networks with Asia' on behalf of the Australian Council of Learned Academies, Melbourne Australia, Available at: *www.acola.org.au,* (Accessed September 23, 2020).

317. Surjeet Dogra Dhanji and Haripriya Rangan, *Leveraging Australia's Indian Diaspora for Deeper Bilateral Trade and Investment Relations with India,* January 2018, Australia India Institute, Available at: *https://www.aii.unimelb.edu.au/wp-content/uploads/2019/01/Aii_Diaspora,* (Accessed September 23, 2020).

318. Press Statement by Prime Minister during the State visit of Prime Minister of Australia to India, April 10, 2017, Media Centre, Ministry of External Affairs, Government of India, *Available at: https://www.mea.gov.in/Speeches-Statements.htm?dtl/28364/ Press_Statement_by_Prime_Minister_during_the_State_visit_of_Prime_Minister_of_ Australia_to_India_April_10_2017,* (Accessed October 02, 2020).

319. *Significance of Migration From India,* Australian Bureau of Statistics and Department of Home Affairs, Government of Australia, Available at: *https:// www.homeaffairs.gov.au/research-and-statistics/statistics/country-profiles/profiles/ india,* (Accessed September 14, 2020).

320. Chen,Q.(2014).*Negotiating the Meaning of Citizenship Chinese Academics in the Transnational Space.* In Koyama, J.,& Subramanian, M.(Eds.).(2014).*US Education in a World of Migration: Implications for Policy and Practice.* Routledge

321. Ben-Moshe, Danny, Pyke, Joanne and Baldassar, Loretta 2012, *Diasporas in Australia: Current and Potential Links with the Homeland,* Centre for Citizenship and Globalisation Research Paper Series, vol. 3, no. 4, pp. 1-25.

322. Ibid.

323. Hofstede Insights: India and Australia, Available at: *https://www.hofstede-insights. com/,* (Accessed October 05, 2020).

324. Religious Diversity of Indian Migrants, Census of Population and Housing, Reflecting Australia, Stories from Census 2016, Cultural Diversity, Australian Bureau of Statistics, Census 2016.

325. Main occupations, 2015—16 to 2018—19, Country Profile: India, Department of Home Affairs, Government of Australia, Available at *Permanent migration,* (Accessed on 25 December 2020).

326. India Born Community Information Summary, Department of Home Affairs, Government of Australia, Available at *https://www.homeaffairs.gov.au/mca/ files/2016-cis-india.PDF,* (Accessed October 14, 2020).

327. Tejada,G.,Hercog, M., Kuptsch, C.,& Bolay,J.C. (2014).The Link with a Home Country. *Global Diasporas and Development* (pp. 39--68).Springer India.

328. *Shaping a Nation: Population and Immigration Growth Overtime*, The Treasury and Department of Home Affairs, Government of Australia, Available at *https://research.treasury.gov.au/external-paper/shaping-a-nation/*, (Accessed October 02, 2020).

329. Ibid.

330. Visa Type by Country of Birth: Permanent Migrants: Financial Years 2004-05 to 2019-19, Australian Bureau of Statistics, Census 2016.

331. *Shaping a Nation: Population and Immigration Growth Overtime*, The Treasury and Department of Home Affairs, Government of Australia, Available at *https://research.treasury.gov.au/external-paper/shaping-a-nation/*, (Accessed October 03, 2020).

332. Percentage of Labour Force (Skilled) to Total Population of Skilled: India & China, Australian Bureau of Statistics, Census 2016.

333. *Percentage Proficiency in spoken English/language by country of birth*, Permanent Migrants, India, China and Others, Australian Bureau of Statistics, Census 2016.

334. *Migrant Taxpayers*, Proportion of Income by Top Five Countries of Birth and Type of Income, 2016-17, Australian Bureau of Statistics, Census 2016.

335. *Migrant Taxpayers*, Proportion of Total Income by Visa Stream and Type of Income, 2016-17, Australian Bureau of Statistics, Census 2016.

336. Migration & Remittances Data, The World Bank, Available at *https://www.worldbank.org/en/topic/migrationremittancesdiasporaissues/brief/migration*, (Accessed November 18, 2020).

337. Ibid.

338. Globalising People: India's Inward Remittances, 14 November 2018, Reserve Bank of India, Available at *https://www.rbi.org.in/Scripts/BS_ViewBulletin.aspx?Id=17882*, (Accessed November 19, 2020).

339. Bilateral Remittance Flows, Migration Policy Institute, Available at *https://www.migrationpolicy.org/programs/data-hub/charts/bilateral*, (Accessed November 19, 2020).

340. International Migration Report 2019, Department of Economic and Social Affairs, United Nations. Available at *https://www.un.org/en/development/desa/population*, (Accessed September 23, 2020).

341. The Gyan Network, High Commission of India, Canberra, Australia, Ministry of External Affairs, Government of India, Available at *https://www.hcicanberra.gov.in/page/the-gyan-network/*, (Accessed September 26,2020).

342. Phillips, M. W., & Stahl, C. W. (2001). International Trade in Higher Education Services in the Asia Pacific Region: Trends and Issues. *Asian and Pacific Migration Journal*, 10(2), 273–301. *https://doi.org/10.1177/011719680101000203*.

343. *Australia Global Alumni Engagement Strategy: The Blueprint 2016-2020*, DFAT, Government of Australia, Available at *https://www.dfat.gov.au/about-us/publications/Pages/australia-global-alumni,* (Accessed November 17, 2020).

344. P Ellis, 'Social Ties and Foreign Market Entry', *Journal of International Business Studies*, Vol. 31:3 (Third Quarter 2000), p. 443.

345. Australia India Business Council (AIBC), Available at *https://aibc.org.au/about-australia-india-business-council/,* (Accessed on 10 October 2020).

346. Professor Arun Sharma, National Chairman, Australia India Business Council (AIBC), Committee Hansard, 08 February 2012, p. 2.

347. Indo Australian Chamber of Commerce, Available at *https://indoaustchamber.com/overview-2/,* (Accessed October 17, 2020).

348. *India Economic Strategy to 2035*, Navigating from Potential to Delivery, A report to the Australian Government by Mr Peter N Varghese AO, Available at *https://www.dfat.gov.au/geo/india/ies/pdf/dfat-an-india-economic* (Accessed September 21, 2020).

349. Geeta Mohan, How India Economic Strategy 2035 seeks to bring India, Australia closer, India Today, 09 August 2018, Available at *https://www.indiatoday.in/india/story/how-india-economic,* (Accessed November 02, 2020).

350. Ibid.

351. *Australia Economic Strategy Report 2020*, Available at *https://aes2020.in/chapters/foreword/,* (Accessed on 23 December 2020).

352. Ibid.

353. Market Snapshots: India, Tourism Australia, Available at *https://www.tourism,* (Accessed November 19, 2020).

354. Grant of Tourist Visas to Indians by Department of Home Affairs, Government of Australia, Available at *https://www.homeaffairs.gov.au/research-and-statistics/statistics/country-profiles/profiles/india,* (Accessed November 19,2020).

355. IEA (2015), *Understanding Energy Challenges in India: Policies, Players and Issues,* IEA Partner Country Series, IEA, Paris, *https://doi.org/10.1787/9789264247444-en,* (Accessed November 12, 2020).

356. Ibid.

357. Hazarika, Obja Borah, and Sriparna Pathak. "Energy Security Dynamics in India–Australia Relations." Jadavpur Journal of International Relations 23, no. 1 (June 2019): 26–47. *https://doi.org/10.1177/0973598418803480,* (Accessed November 12, 2020).

358. Ibid.

359. Piyush Goyal offers Australian resources and technology new passage to India, Greg Earl, Australia Financial Review, 13 Feb 2016, Available at *https://www.afr.com/companies/energy,* (Accessed November 18, 2020).

360. Natasha Jha Bhaskar, Why Australia, India should increase business and trade exchange, 04 March 2020, Business Today, Available at *https://www.businesstoday.in/opinion/columns/australia-india-business-and-trade-exchange-import-export-economy-partnership-investment/story/397535.html*, (Accessed November 04, 2020).

361. Australia - India Joint Free Trade Agreement (FTA) Feasibility Study, Department of Commerce, Government of India and Department of Foreign Affairs and Trade, Government of Australia, Available at *Australia-India Joint Free Trade Agreement Feasibility Study (dfat.gov.au)*, (Accessed on 26 December 2020).

362. Ibid.

363. Statement of Australian High Commissioner to India, Deepak Patel, *India-Australia CECA Talks under 'Slow Period' Now*, The Indian Express, 09 August 2018.

364. Nayanima Basu, Will support whatever India decides on RCEP, says Envoy O'Farrell, The Print, 04 December 2020, Available at *Australia, India joint defence,* (Accessed on 201 December 2020).

365. Statement of External Affairs Minister of India, India in talks with Australia for free trade pact: Foreign Minister, Reuters, 09 December 2020.

366. *India Economic Strategy to 2035*, Navigating from Potential to Delivery, A report to the Australian Government by Mr Peter N Varghese AO, Available at *https://www.dfat.gov.au/geo/india/ies/pdf/dfat-an-india-economic* (Accessed December 23, 2020).

367. Ibid.

368. Pattern (2003-2019) of FDI from India to Australia (US $ Billions), FDI Intelligence by the Financial Times (Australia Economic Strategy).

369. Pattern (2003-2019) of FDI from Australia to India (US $ Billions), FDI Intelligence by the Financial Times (Australia Economic Strategy).

370. Prabha Raghavan, Explained: The economic implications of India opting out of RCEP, Indian Express, 26 November 2020.

371. Ibid.

372. Nayanima Basu, Will support whatever India decides on RCEP, says Envoy O'Farrell, The Print, 04 December 2020, Available at *Australia, India joint defence,* (Accessed on 20 December 2020).

373. Ibid.

374. Australia looks to India amid ongoing trade tensions with China, Sky News Australia, December 31, 2020.

375. Transcript of the Prime Minister John Howard joint doorstop interview with the Prime Minister of India Dr Manmohan Singh, New Delhi, 6 March 2006, http://www.pm.gov.au/.news/interviews/Interview1809.html (accessed July 26, 2020).

INDEX

A

abolished, 105, 134

academia, 102, 121, 145, 152, 156

academic, 11-12, 14, 21, 25, 64, 89, 106, 119, 126-127, 145-146, 152, 168-170, 197

academicians, 6, 105, 168

Act East, 11, 56, 181

adaptability - pg 77 and 149

advancements - 125, 145

agreements, 5, 9, 45, 78, 86, 89, 96, 102-103, 106, 108, 116-117, 125-126, 128, 162, 168-169, 171, 194

agriculture, 118, 125, 160, 163

AILD, 11, 124

AISRF, 11, 17, 117-119

AIYD, 11, 17, 122-124, 194

alliances, 24, 45, 51, 58, 64, 72-73, 118

alumni, 8, 25, 103, 123-124, 152-153, 168, 172, 199

ancestry, 132, 140

anchor, 82

antipathy, 32

apartheid, 37-38, 177

apprenticeships, 116

arbitrariness, 7, 78, 159, 163

architecture, 55, 61, 63, 69, 75, 78-79, 86, 104

ASEAN Regional Forum, 11, 63, 90-92

ASEAN Treaty of Amity and Cooperation, 11, 65

ASEAN, 11-12, 24, 60, 62-67, 69, 73, 78, 87, 90-92, 99, 163, 181-182, 188-189

Asiatics, 39

assignments, 128

Australia Group, 71-72, 184

B

Bandung, 42, 65

barriers, 33, 103, 161

belligerent, 5, 44, 96

Belt and Road, 74

biculturalism, 141-143

biculturism, 142

bilateral relations, 5-6, 22, 25, 31, 34, 47-48, 56, 80-81, 84, 91, 102, 106, 113, 116, 119, 124, 153, 169

bilateral relationship, 7-10, 17, 22-25, 28, 30, 34-35, 41, 47, 49-51, 61-64, 67, 69-70, 73, 79, 85-86, 88-90, 95, 97, 99, 102, 104, 106, 112, 116-118, 121-129, 131, 140-141, 143-144, 146-147, 151, 153-162, 164-172, 174, 192

bilateral, 5-11, 17-18, 22-25, 28, 30-31, 34-35, 40-41, 46-51, 56-57, 59-64, 67-74, 79-82, 84-86, 88-92, 94-99, 102, 104, 106, 108, 112-113, 116-129, 131, 140-141, 143-144, 146-147, 151, 153-174, 183-184, 188-193, 195, 197-198

bilateralism, 22, 62, 127

bilinguism, 144

bio geographic, 56

biomedical, 118

Brain Circulation, 7-8, 25, 142, 146, 169, 171

brain circulation, 7-8, 25, 142, 146, 169, 171
Brain Drain, 7, 25, 138, 146
Brain Gain, 7-8, 146, 169
British, 23, 28-33, 35-43, 46, 50-51, 55, 132-134, 136, 176
burgeoning, 128, 145, 166

C
Camel, 31, 135
catalyst, 86, 105, 129, 146, 189
CECA, 12, 161, 200
centrality, 23, 53-54, 57-58, 73, 84-85, 96
challenges, 6, 21, 61, 67-70, 81, 84-85, 87-88, 94, 107, 125, 128, 180-181, 183-184, 187, 189-190, 199
Chemical Weapons Convention, 11, 71
China, 5, 12, 17-18, 24, 48, 57, 59-60, 63, 65, 67-68, 71-78, 80-84, 96, 98-99, 103, 105, 132, 140, 148-151, 156, 159-160, 163-164, 166, 184-188, 191, 195, 198, 200
collaboration, 9, 93, 106, 117-122, 125-126, 128-129, 143, 146, 156, 168-169, 194
Collaborations, 102, 116, 120-121, 126-128, 145-146, 156, 169-170
collaborations, 102, 116, 120-121, 126-128, 145-146, 156, 169-170
collaborative, 118, 121, 124-125, 152
collaborator, 120
Colombo Plan, 13, 39-40, 104-105
Colombo, 13, 39-40, 104-105
colonial, 23, 29-32, 43-44, 104, 132-133, 176
colonialism, 29-30, 43-44
colonization, 28-29
colony, 2, 28-33, 39, 132-133
commercial, 50, 54, 56, 106, 115, 157, 161
Commonwealth Heads of Government Meeting, 105
Commonwealth, 12, 22, 28, 32, 34-43, 105, 132-133, 176-177, 193

commonwealth, 12, 22, 28, 32, 34-43, 105, 132-133, 176-177, 193
communication, 7, 12, 14, 44, 46, 70, 72, 76, 87, 95-96, 118, 143-145
communism, 34, 39-40, 44-45, 133
Communist, 45, 75, 184
communities, 59, 120, 126, 138, 142, 154
community, 43, 49, 58, 96, 99, 131, 134, 141-142, 146, 151-152, 154-155, 182, 197
competitive, 70, 110, 143-144, 172
Comprehensive Security Partnership, 12, 24, 61, 69-71, 84, 95, 125, 169
Comprehensive Strategic Partnership, 5, 7, 24, 94, 167, 184, 195
compulsions, 9, 15, 43, 45, 50, 53, 55, 57, 59, 61, 63, 65, 67, 69, 71, 73, 75, 77, 79, 81, 83, 85, 87, 89, 91, 93, 95, 97, 99, 163, 171
concerns, 24-25, 35, 37, 44-47, 54, 63, 67, 69, 71, 74, 76-77, 80-81, 87-88, 99, 107, 135, 163-164, 170, 174
conferences, 66, 89, 124, 126, 128
configure, 125
congruence, 7-8, 22, 24, 72, 80, 85, 90, 99, 156, 166
connect, 23-24, 28, 89-90, 126, 141, 153
construct, 7-9, 22, 51, 56, 60, 68-69, 73, 82, 86, 99, 165
contemporary, 7-8, 22, 27, 58, 63, 73, 78-79, 89, 101-102, 131, 134-135, 138, 142, 147, 155, 165-168, 184
continental, 54, 73
continuance, 36, 142
conventional, 45, 72
convergence, 21, 46, 57, 66, 82, 87, 89, 120, 159-160, 171-173, 182
convergences, 143, 182
convict, 31
convicts, 29, 132, 135
cooperation, 7, 9, 11-13, 22, 24, 30, 49-50, 56, 60-71, 77-82, 84-95, 97, 99, 104, 106, 108, 113, 116-117, 120, 125-126, 128-129, 153-154, 156, 158-

159, 161-162, 164, 166-169, 171-173, 182, 184, 186-191, 193
Core Interests, 8, 22, 25, 66
corollary, 102, 147, 151
corroborating, 111, 136, 153
counselor, 106
credentials, 103, 129, 153
critical, 5, 7, 25, 38, 83, 88-89, 94, 102-103, 110, 115, 117, 120, 125-126, 129, 134, 145, 154, 156-157, 167-168, 189
Crown, 36-37
cruise, 47
Cultural, 54-56, 83, 106, 117, 123, 127, 131-132, 139, 141-143, 154, 197
cyber, 24, 68, 87-89, 94, 125, 168, 189

D
decoupled, 163
Defence, 1, 5-9, 11-12, 15, 19, 23-25, 37, 39, 44-45, 47, 49-50, 53-63, 65-69, 71, 73, 75, 77, 79, 81, 83-99, 115, 157, 165-168, 180-185, 187-191, 200
defence, 1, 5-9, 11-12, 15, 19, 23-25, 37, 39, 44-45, 47, 49-50, 53-63, 65-69, 71, 73, 75, 77, 79, 81, 83-99, 115, 157, 165-168, 180-185, 187-191, 200
degrees, 103, 121, 142
delegations, 93, 154
demand, 30, 34, 43, 89, 113-114, 116, 128, 132-133, 138, 158-159
Department, 12, 25, 34, 46-47, 59-60, 83, 92, 109, 115-117, 119, 133, 135, 141, 166, 181-183, 185, 187, 190, 192-193, 195-200
destination, 19, 102-103, 108-109, 111, 139, 153, 160, 171-172, 192
developmental, 68, 104, 126, 174
dialogue, 11, 13, 62-68, 70, 80-84, 87, 89-92, 95, 122-125, 182, 186-187, 190, 194
Diaspora, 1, 5-9, 15, 24-25, 31, 34, 74, 112, 116, 129, 131-133, 135, 137-147, 149-155, 157, 159, 161, 163, 165, 169, 172, 196-197

diaspora, 1, 5-9, 15, 24-25, 31, 34, 74, 112, 116, 129, 131-133, 135, 137-147, 149-155, 157, 159, 161, 163, 165, 169, 172, 196-197
Dictation, 133
dictum, 160
differential, 40, 47, 142, 168, 174
diffused, 141
dilemma, 37, 49, 73, 75, 133
Diplomacy, 1, 5-6, 8-9, 22, 24-25, 61, 64, 74, 79, 81, 85, 89, 95-97, 102, 104, 123, 153, 165, 187, 192
diplomacy, 1, 5-6, 8-9, 22, 24-25, 61, 64, 74, 79, 81, 85, 89, 95-97, 102, 104, 123, 153, 165, 187, 192
diplomatic, 5, 7, 9, 15, 24, 44, 53, 55-57, 59, 61, 63, 65, 67, 69, 71, 73-75, 77-79, 81, 83, 85, 87, 89, 91, 93, 95, 97, 99, 102, 104, 119, 153-154, 166, 190
disconnect, 101
Discrimination, 13, 136
discriminatory, 33-34, 48
dispersion, 131
dissonance, 44, 106
dividend, 40, 56, 62, 117, 153, 156
domestic, 12, 34, 38, 49, 86, 148, 158-159
dominions, 23, 36, 43
Dynamic Mix, 121
dynamics, 1, 5, 8-9, 23, 43, 61, 76, 79, 137, 160, 168, 171, 199

E
East Asia Summit, 12, 57, 63-64, 66, 81, 84, 90-93, 183
East Asian Economic Group, 12, 64
East Asian Summit, 57, 181
East Asian, 11-12, 14, 44, 57, 60, 63-64, 87, 106, 175, 181-182
echelons, 157
Economic, 5, 7, 9, 11-13, 17, 21-22, 24-25, 27, 30-33, 39-41, 48, 50-51, 54-64, 66-69, 72, 74-75, 77, 82-85, 89, 92, 97, 101-102, 104, 107, 116, 122, 125, 134-135, 137-139, 141-142,

146-148, 152-167, 169, 171-172, 174, 184-187, 190-191, 193, 198-200
economic, 5, 7, 9, 11-13, 17, 21-22, 24-25, 27, 30-33, 39-41, 48, 50-51, 54-64, 66-69, 72, 74-75, 77, 82-85, 92, 97, 101-102, 104, 107, 116, 122, 125, 134-135, 137-139, 141-142, 146-148, 152-167, 171-172, 174, 184-187, 190-191, 193, 198-200
economics, 89, 101, 125, 153, 155, 169
economies, 24, 39-40, 60, 80, 126, 142, 146-147, 153, 164
economy, 7, 56, 62, 64, 66, 68, 74-76, 89, 101, 103, 125, 133, 146-147, 150, 156, 158, 160, 164, 171, 175
ecosystem, 82, 116, 148
Education agents, 19, 109-110
education, 7-9, 11-15, 19, 101-117, 119-129, 137-139, 141, 153, 156-157, 169-171, 173, 192-198
educational, 106, 113, 120, 127-129, 137-138, 145, 153, 171, 173
emotional, 142
Empire, 28, 35, 176
employment, 31-32, 110, 116, 141, 146, 149, 192
encompassing, 50, 89-90, 129, 131
energy, 13, 25, 48, 70, 118, 158-159, 163, 187, 193, 199
engagement, 8, 25, 51, 55, 60, 66, 79, 85, 88, 92, 95, 98-99, 119, 123, 144, 152-153, 155-157, 159, 162, 164, 168, 171-172, 174, 181, 183, 188-190, 193, 197, 199
engagements, 5, 7, 24, 56, 59, 61, 67-68, 81, 85, 92, 94-96, 102, 119, 157, 166, 193
engine, 101
enormous, 45, 155, 157, 161
enrolled, 112
enrolment, 17, 106-108, 114-115, 138-139
entrepreneurial, 155, 192
Entrepreneurship, 117, 193
ethnic, 152
ethno linguistic, 27

ethnocentric, 133
evolution, 54, 61, 104, 159
exchange agreements, 106
exemplary, 77, 82, 124
expansion, 8, 54, 65, 86, 96, 121, 131, 145
expertise, 126, 145, 152, 159
explicit, 7, 28, 47, 67, 139, 172
exploitation, 29, 106
exponential, 24, 61, 104, 108, 112, 116, 139-140
exponentially, 9, 114
exposure, 164
extended neighborhood, 55

F
faculty, 14, 119-121, 128
feasibility, 31, 80, 161, 200
federation, 29-30, 152, 195-196
fellowships, 118
fluctuations, 151
forecasting, 159
Foreign Ministers' Framework Dialogue, 95
foreign policy, 9, 29, 44, 47, 50-51, 55-56, 58, 62, 65, 75, 77, 79, 85, 92, 95, 124, 178-179, 185-186
Foreign, 9, 12, 19, 29, 39, 43-44, 47, 50-51, 55-56, 58, 61-62, 64-65, 74-75, 77, 79, 83-86, 89, 92, 95, 103, 110, 115, 124, 154-155, 162, 166-167, 170, 173-174, 178-181, 185-187, 189-193, 199-200
framework, 6, 11, 13, 61, 63, 66, 88, 90-95, 97, 109, 114, 125-126, 134, 164, 167, 170-171, 188-189
free fall, 106
Free Trade Agreement, 12, 25, 74, 160-162, 174, 200
FTA, 12, 160-161, 164, 174, 200
functional, 120

G
generation, 13, 32, 122, 124, 131-132, 140, 143, 150, 159
geo political, 7, 51, 57, 66, 69, 85, 99, 159

geographical, 27, 39, 51, 53-54, 67, 72, 109, 139

geopolitical, 5, 25, 54, 58, 68, 81, 156, 165

geopolitics, 54, 57, 125, 163

Ghans, 31

GIAN, 12, 119-120

Gondwana, 27

H

Heterogeneity, 131

High Commission, 106, 180, 186, 192, 198

historical, 6, 8, 24-25, 27-28, 41, 54-55, 65, 90-91, 99, 104, 132, 165

holistic, 89-90, 99, 106, 109-110, 131, 139, 150, 157, 161

homogeneous, 34

homogenous, 131

Huawei, 76, 185

humanitarian, 12, 49, 93, 96, 148, 150

I

identification, 142

ideological, 39-40

illicit, 88, 169

immigrants, 32, 132, 134, 136, 143

immigration, 31-34, 91, 109, 115, 132-136, 138, 147, 150, 178, 192, 195-196, 198

impetus, 22, 56, 85, 95, 162, 171, 174

incentives, 146, 156

increment, 24, 118, 166

indentured, 31-32

independent, 36-37, 39, 44, 50, 54, 58-59, 67, 73, 76, 104, 156

index, 15, 28, 96, 154, 160, 168, 190, 195

Indian Ocean Naval Symposium, 12, 69-70, 92

Indian Ocean Rim Association, 12, 68-69, 92, 184

Indian Ocean, 9, 12, 21, 23, 27, 50-51, 53-55, 57-59, 61, 68-70, 72, 74, 76, 78, 87, 91-93, 177, 181, 184, 188-190

Indian students 8–9, 17, 103, 106–108, 110–116, 120, 139, 157, 168, 172

indigenous - 27, 28, 29

Indo Pacific, 1, 7-9, 12, 15, 17, 21-25, 51, 53, 56-61, 63, 66, 68-70, 73-74, 78-82, 85-87, 89, 94-95, 97, 99, 125, 165

Indo-Pacific, 5, 21, 23, 57, 59-61, 63, 67, 72-73, 77, 79-82, 84-85, 87, 92, 94, 97, 159, 164, 175, 181-184, 186-191

industry, 12, 31, 89, 93, 116, 119, 121, 126-127, 138, 154, 156-157, 163, 172, 193, 196

information, 12, 76, 87, 90, 104, 109-111, 114, 116-118, 144-145, 152, 154, 172, 176, 178-179, 184, 197

infrastructure, 76, 83, 156, 167, 171-172, 185

initiative, 9-10, 12, 14, 22, 24, 28, 37, 39-40, 51, 55-56, 66-70, 74, 78-80, 82-85, 94-95, 104-105, 116, 118-122, 124-128, 136-137, 146, 152, 154, 187

Innovation, 8, 102, 113, 119-120, 148, 153, 156, 192, 196

innovation, 8, 102, 119-120, 148, 153, 156, 192, 196

innovations, 102, 113

innovative, 101, 121-122, 125

insecurity, 45

institution, 23, 40, 61, 77, 79, 85, 90-91, 93-94, 99, 103, 105, 110-111, 120-121, 125-127, 145, 168

institutional, 66, 103-104, 111, 121, 158

integrated, 21, 173

intercultural, 119

interdependence, 27, 165

interlinguism, 144

international degrees, 103

international education, 103, 105, 107-108, 110, 138-139, 141, 153, 173

international students, 5, 17, 25, 102-108, 110-114, 122, 132, 138, 140-141, 169, 173

international university education, 103

international, 5-7, 11, 13, 17, 25, 34, 43, 47-49, 60-61, 67, 69-70, 72, 79, 81, 84, 88-89, 91-92, 97-98, 101-115, 118-120, 122, 124, 126-127, 129, 132, 137-143, 145, 148, 152-154, 159, 169, 171-173, 175-176, 180-188, 190, 192-193, 198-199

internationalization, 104-106

IOR 12, 53–54, 56–59, 68–69, 73

J

jurisprudence, 28

K

Kashmir, 43-44, 46

kinship, 142

knowledge economy, 7, 103, 142

knowledge partnerships 8–9, 15, 101–102, 125, 168–170

knowledge, 7-9, 15, 19, 91, 101-103, 105, 107-109, 111, 113, 115, 117, 119, 121-129, 142, 145-147, 153-155, 168-170

L

landscape, 25, 72, 99, 116, 169

Language, 12, 18, 23, 28, 112, 133, 142-144, 149, 152, 198

lead, 39, 59, 63, 80, 125, 147, 150, 156-157

littoral, 27, 55, 57, 69

Look East, 8, 13, 51, 55-56, 62, 72, 87, 181

Lowy Institute, 47, 76, 84, 96, 107, 184, 186-188, 190-192

M

Malabar, 5, 24, 82, 84, 97-99

Malacca, 73

Manila, 44

maritime, 12, 23, 41, 50, 53-55, 61, 63, 66, 68-70, 72-74, 76, 81-82, 87, 90-91, 93-94, 96-98, 184-185, 187, 189-190

mechanisms, 63, 73, 85, 92, 102-103, 128, 173

median, 149-150

mediator, 43

medieval, 53

Memorandums of Understanding, 9, 108

Memorandums, 9, 108

microliths, 27

migrants, 17-19, 31-32, 131-133, 135, 137-138, 140-141, 143-150, 152, 197-198

migrate, 109, 138

migration, 7, 9, 13, 17, 19, 25, 27, 75, 87, 103, 112, 114-116, 129, 131-132, 134-141, 144-148, 152, 169, 171, 173, 193, 195-198

military training, 91

military, 9, 41-42, 44-47, 50, 58-61, 67, 72-76, 82-83, 86-87, 91, 95-99, 166, 185, 188, 190

minilaterals, 7, 9, 62, 77-78, 186-187

miniscule, 106, 160

Missile Technology Control Regime, 13, 71-72

mobile, 76, 102, 128, 185

mobility, 101, 108, 121, 131, 139, 142, 167, 169

multicultural, 143

multiculturalism, 134, 136, 143, 195

Multilateral Export Control Regime, 13, 72

multilateral, 13, 22, 24, 55, 57, 59-62, 64, 66-69, 72, 77-79, 82-83, 85, 90, 92-93, 98-99, 161, 163, 188

multilaterals, 7, 9, 57, 77-78

multilingual, 143

multilingualism, 143

Mutual Logistics Support Agreement, 24, 190-191

mutual, 7-9, 13, 22, 24-25, 28, 35, 39-40, 45, 49, 51, 56, 60, 63, 67-68, 70, 77-78, 86, 89, 96, 101, 106, 116, 121, 126, 159, 164-166, 170, 174, 190-191

N

National Education Policy, 129, 194

nationalism, 29, 44

nationalization, 41-42

Naturalisation, 133

negativity, 138, 146
negotiations, 42, 48, 160-161, 163, 174
negotiators, 161
New Framework for Security
    Cooperation, 13, 92
niche, 157, 168
Non Alignment, 29, 35, 50, 53, 55
Non Proliferation Treaty, 13, 47, 71
Non Traditional Security, 13, 67, 86
nontraditional, 24, 63, 67, 87-88, 168
nourishing, 153
Nuclear Suppliers Group, 13, 50, 70, 72
nuclear, 13, 47-50, 70-72, 106, 158-
    159, 180

O
objectives, 21, 119, 184, 190
Oceania, 85, 182
optimal, 156, 160, 167, 171
Organization for Economic Co-operation
    and Development, 102
overhang, 142
Overseas Student Charge, 13, 105
overseas, 12-13, 17, 103, 105, 109, 112,
    115, 135-136, 138-140, 147-148, 150-
    151, 191, 195-196
overwhelm, 154

P
Pacific Ocean, 12, 21, 23, 51, 53, 57-58,
    66, 69, 83, 187
Pacific, 1, 5, 7-9, 11-12, 15, 17, 21-25,
    51, 53, 56-61, 63-64, 66-70, 72-87,
    89, 91-95, 97-99, 125, 133, 159, 164-
    165, 175, 181-191, 198
Pakistan, 13, 34, 40, 43-47, 71, 74, 83,
    105, 152, 166-167, 180
pastoral, 31, 135
pedagogies, 128
peers, 111
penal, 28-29
people to people links, 99, 123, 129, 152,
    157, 168-169, 172
people to people relations, 5, 7, 102, 121-
    122, 156

people to people, 5, 7-8, 34-35, 56, 99,
    102, 116-118, 120-123, 126, 128-129,
    146, 152, 156-158, 166-170, 172
people-to-people contacts - 108
permanent, 17-18, 29, 32, 74, 93, 98,
    114, 131-132, 134-136, 138-139, 148-
    149, 193, 197-198
plebiscite, 44
pluralism, 144
plurilateral, 24
population, 17-18, 29, 32-34, 37, 40,
    84, 133, 136, 140-142, 145, 148-150,
    153, 157-158, 172, 192, 196-198
positivity, 119, 146
post-graduate studies, 103
potential, 6-9, 21, 24, 41, 45, 48-49,
    54, 59-61, 66, 69-71, 73, 75, 78, 80,
    82, 89, 93, 102, 106, 116-117, 120,
    124-125, 128, 142-144, 153-160,
    166-168, 170-172, 174, 194, 197,
    199-200
prehistoric, 27, 175
proactive, 47, 71
production, 101, 145, 159, 167
productivity, 148, 155, 195
professional, 91, 126, 128, 145
professionals, 7, 25, 114, 126, 136, 144-
    145, 169
propensity, 162
protectionist, 160
Public Diplomacy, 102, 104, 192
publications, 124, 128, 152, 181, 183,
    185-186, 191, 196, 199
push and pull factors, 103-104
push' factors, 103, 109

Q
quad, 5, 83-84, 99, 187-188
Quadrilateral, 5, 13, 82-84, 96, 98,
    186-187
qualification, 114, 145, 170-171
qualifications, 11, 109-111, 134, 145-
    146, 170-171
qualitative, 113, 143
quasi, 38

R

racial, 13, 29, 32-34, 37-39, 107, 136
RCEP, 13, 160, 162-164, 200
recession, 107
reciprocity, 143
region, 5, 8-10, 12, 21-23, 25, 29, 35, 41-44, 46-47, 49-51, 53-64, 66-70, 72-85, 87-88, 90-96, 99, 129, 137, 152-153, 156, 159, 163, 175, 181, 184-185, 187, 189-190, 198
Regional Comprehensive Economic Partnership, 13, 25, 160, 162-163
reinforcing, 73, 162
religious, 17, 55, 87, 142-144, 197
relocation, 32, 81
Remittances, 18, 151, 198
remittances, 18, 151, 198
remunerations, 146
Republic, 35-37, 39, 74-75, 131, 184, 189-190, 193, 195
research, 6, 9, 11-14, 80-81, 93-94, 99, 101-103, 111, 115-121, 124-129, 141, 145-146, 153-154, 156, 168, 173, 178, 186-188, 190-194, 196-199
researchers, 6, 8, 21, 25, 64, 101-102, 105, 117-118, 126, 145, 169, 172
resources, 25, 32, 66, 73-74, 81-82, 89, 96, 116, 125-126, 137-138, 152, 156, 185, 189, 193, 199
reticence, 164
rivalry, 44, 76, 78, 175
robust, 5, 28, 70, 155

S

safety, 12-13, 45, 49, 66, 75, 126-127
satellite, 28
scholars, 59, 64, 101, 117, 124, 146, 168
scholastic, 101
sectoral, 128
sectors, 17, 80, 112-115, 117, 125-126, 156-157, 162, 172-173
security, 5, 12-14, 17, 21-24, 37, 42-45, 48-51, 54-58, 60-73, 75-77, 79-92, 94-99, 108, 118, 125, 134, 145, 167-169, 175, 180-181, 183-184, 186-191, 194, 199

self interest, 7, 164
seminal, 108
settlement, 29, 31, 43, 131, 138
settlers, 31-32, 132, 134
shift, 51, 56, 59-60, 62, 70, 73, 87
similarity, 7, 27-28, 81, 92, 123, 160
skill sets, 137
Skill, 6, 13-14, 80, 116-117, 126, 136-138, 141, 144, 146, 148, 150, 192-193
societal, 77, 157
South Asian, 50, 180, 196
South China Sea, 57, 60, 67, 76
South-East, 44, 57, 63
Southeast, 55-56, 58-59, 61-63, 65-66, 77, 82, 181-182, 188
sovereign, 35-37, 41
sovereignty, 34-35, 72
SPARC, 14, 119-120, 193
squalor, 43
strategic interests, 8, 23-24, 54, 61, 67-68, 80-81, 92, 94-95, 156, 160
strategic, 5-8, 11, 17, 21-25, 40-41, 43, 45, 49-51, 53-63, 66-68, 72-77, 79-85, 87-90, 92, 94-97, 99, 117-119, 121-122, 156, 158, 160, 163, 166-167, 170, 182-191, 195
strategically, 58-59, 82, 87, 118
strategies, 8, 25, 102, 126, 147, 152, 155-157, 162, 164, 168, 172, 174
strategists, 21, 59, 74
Strategy, 8, 25, 54, 68, 72, 75, 77-78, 81, 102, 104, 116, 125-126, 147, 152-153, 155-157, 160, 162, 164, 167-168, 171-172, 174-175, 180-181, 183, 185, 192-194, 199-200
subcontinent, 31, 54
subjective, 142
subversion, 46, 75
Suez Canal, 41, 178
super power, 44
supplement, 81, 104
Supply Chain Resilience Initiative, 14, 80
symbiotic, 9, 15, 101, 103, 105, 107, 109, 111, 113, 115, 117, 119, 121, 123, 125, 127, 129, 156, 159
synergy, 117, 126, 160

T
tangibles, 143
tariff, 74, 77, 161, 164
Technical Vocational Education and
  Training, 14, 108
technological, 12, 89, 99, 117, 125,
  147, 183
technology, 12-14, 70-72, 89, 93-94, 114,
  118-119, 122, 124-129, 144-145, 153,
  157, 159, 167-168, 185, 189, 193, 199
Temporary, 14, 19, 115, 128, 132, 134,
  137-138, 140-141, 166, 193
territoriality, 139
tourism, 80, 104, 156-157, 160, 172-
  173, 199
trade, 5, 12, 15, 23-25, 28-29, 56, 58-60,
  64, 68-69, 74-75, 77, 81, 83, 88, 92,
  97, 105, 110, 114-115, 123, 125, 128,
  131, 133, 135, 137, 139, 141, 143,
  145, 147, 149, 151, 153-155, 157,
  159-166, 173-174, 180-181, 185, 187,
  191-194, 197-198, 200
transformation, 22, 55, 60, 62, 121
transmission, 143
transnational education, 7-9, 15, 101,
  103, 105-107, 109, 111, 113, 115,
  117, 119, 121, 123-125, 127, 129
transnational flow, 102, 104-108, 145-146
transnational 7–9, 15, 67, 86, 88, 90,
  101–102, 104–108, 113, 117, 124,
  129, 142, 145–146, 184, 197
transported, 132
treaties, 44, 55, 86, 188, 193
tremendous, 24, 30, 63, 102, 157, 167
tribesmen, 31
triggered, 107, 147
trilateral, 22, 78-82, 93, 163, 186-188

tuition, 105, 110
typologies, 141-142

U
underdeveloped, 147
undesirable, 33
unidirectional, 146
United Nations, 14, 33, 37-38, 41, 43,
  69, 92, 152, 176, 198
universities, 9, 25, 103, 105, 110-111,
  118, 120-121, 124-129, 152-153, 168-
  173, 194
university, 13-14, 80, 103, 105, 110-111,
  113-114, 120, 124-125, 127, 142,
  169-171, 176-178, 180-181, 183, 192,
  194-196
uranium, 48, 50, 70, 159, 180

V
VAJRA, 14, 119
visa, 17-19, 105, 110, 114-115, 132, 137,
  140, 148, 150, 158, 166, 173, 193,
  196, 198-199
Vocational Education and Training, 14,
  108, 112

W
weapons, 11, 47-49, 71-72, 180
welfare, 35, 108, 161
White Australia Policy', 33, 133
White Australia Policy, 33-34, 39, 104,
  133-134, 136
White Australia policy, 33-34, 39, 104,
  133-134, 136
White Australia' policy, 39, 134, 136
workshops, 117-118
World Health Organisation, 14, 76